Lecture Notes in Economics and Mathematical Systems

403

Gunnar Brennscheidt

Predictive Behavior

An Experimental Study

Springer-Verlag
Berlin Heidelberg New York
London Paris Tokyo
Hong Kong Barcelona
Budapest

Author

Dr. Gunnar Brennscheidt
Universität Bonn
Institut für Ökonometrie und Operations Research
Adenauerallee 24-42
D-53113 Bonn, FRG

ISBN-13: 978-3-540-57311-1 e-ISBN-13: 978-3-642-95718-5
DOI: 10.1007/978-3-642-95718-5

Typesetting: Camera ready by author

42/3140-543210 - Printed on acid-free paper

Contents

0. Literature Review

0.1. Empirical Studies and Experimental Studies

Generally, studies on expectation formation/predictive behavior have the following pattern: There is a time series describing the development of a certain economic variable (endogenous variable). At the beginning of each period, the forecasters have to predict the next realization of this variable, using some information which includes the past history of the variable. Thus, the subjects already know something about the pattern of the time series when they have to give their first forecast.

The studies can be subdivided into two groups: empirical studies and experimental studies. Empirical studies use survey data whereas experimental studies use data collected in laboratory experiments.

In both groups there are two approaches:[1] the direct and the indirect one. The direct approach asks for forecasts reported by the respondents/subjects. In this case, hypotheses on expectation formation can be tested directly. The indirect approach asks for economic decisions based on expectations (for example, investment decisions), or observes some economic variables related to expectations. Since expectations themselves are not observed, the economist can only test the joint hypothesis that the model relating the expectations to the decisions/observations is true and that expectations reveal a certain behavior.

In what follows a brief description of the two groups of studies, including their advantages and disadvantages, will be given.

Empirical studies

The most commonly known time series of survey data on expectations has been compiled by Joseph A. Livingston who conducted semiannual surveys of economists since 1947. In these surveys, about 30 economists

---

[1] This distinction is due to Aiginger (1981, [1]).

were asked to predict several economic variables, including the consumer price index (CPI).

Another well-known time series has been published by the Michigan Institute for Social Research, based on quarterly surveys of 1,000 randomly selected households since 1948. These surveys are much larger than Livingston's but, unfortunately, up to 1966, the respondents were asked only for qualitative statements.

Since 1952, the Italian journal "Mondo Economico" has surveyed businessmen and experts about their expectations of the percentage change of various economic variables, among them the wholesale price index and the consumer price index. The surveys have been conducted semiannually until 1980 and quarterly since 1981.

These are all time-series of direct observations. As Aiginger[2] points out, reported expectations may not represent respondents' true expectations because they have no incentive to reflect on their expectations.

This is an argument in favor of the indirect approach[3]. Expectations are regarded as unobservable, so there must be a model assumed to be true ("Hypothesis 1") relating expectations to some observable variables. A certain hypothesis on expectation formation ("Hypothesis 2"), can only be tested jointly with Hypothesis 1.

For example, suppose that, according to "Hypothesis 2", inflation expectations are rational, and conform to Fisher's hypothesis that the nominal interest rate is the sum of expected inflation and a constant real rate of return (economic model, "Hypothesis 1"). The joint hypothesis then implies that the difference between nominal interest rate and inflation rate (= constant real rate of return minus forecast error) is not serially correlated.[4]

The indirect approach has the crucial disadvantage that only the joint hypothesis may be tested. A rejection may be due to an incorrect model or a false hypothesis on expectations. Even worse, the joint hypothesis may be accepted because of the combination of an incorrect model and a false hypothesis on expectations.

---

[2] [1], pp. 26-28.

[3] Aiginger [1], p. 26.

[4] Aiginger [1], p. 27.

The consideration of direct and indirect approaches reveals two serious disadvantages of empirical studies:

First, the individuals are not facing well-defined incentives (see the comments on direct observation).

Second, the underlying economic model is not known (see the comments on indirect observation).

In addition, the information used by the respondents is not known to the inquirer.

Experimental studies

Experimental studies generally combine the observation of behavior with a financial reward to the subjects. The distinction between direct and indirect approach also applies to laboratory experiments.

Most studies conducted so far use direct observations. Since the financial reward may be set according to forecast accuracy, the participants have an incentive to reflect on their expectations - in contrast to empirical studies.

Here are some criteria for experimental design:

(1) *Empirical Time Series or Artificial Time Series.* The time series to be predicted may be an empirical one,[5] or, alternatively, may be generated in the laboratory by a model. The alternative most widely chosen is the generation of artificial data.

(2) *Forecast Feedback.* If the time series is generated by a model, this model may allow forecasts to influence future realizations of the variable to be predicted.

(3) *Exogenous variables.* The model generating the time series may include exogenous variables, and the information available to the subjects may consist not only of the past history of the time series to be predicted but also include the history and a scenario of some exogenous variables. Among these there may be some irrelevant variables ("sunspot variables").

---

[5] Schmalensee (1976 [26]) used the time-series of deflated wheat prices in England during the second halfth of the 19th century.

0.2 Hypotheses to Be Tested

This section contains a brief description of the most commonly known hypotheses on expectation formation. In the sequel, let p be the endogenous variable to be predicted, and let ${}_{t-d}f_{t+k}$ denote the prediction of p_{t+k}, made at the beginning of period $(t-d)$, i.e., using some information available at the beginning that period. Sometimes the first subscript is dropped for the case $d=0, k=0$, i.e. $f_t := {}_tf_t$.

Adaptive Expectations (Cagan 1956 [9], Nerlove 1958 [24]). The previous forecast is corrected by a fraction of the forecast error:

$$f_t = f_{t-1} + \lambda(p_{t-1} - f_{t-1}) \ , \tag{0.1}$$

where λ is the error adjustment coefficient. The case $\lambda = 1$ represents the naive forecasting rule $f_t = p_{t-1}$. The model may include an intercept to allow for trend predictions:

$$f_t = \alpha + f_{t-1} + \lambda(p_{t-1} - f_{t-1}). \tag{0.2}$$

Extrapolative Expectations. (Metzler 1941 [21]) The forecasters simply extrapolate the last change of p:

$$f_t = p_{t-1} + \lambda(p_{t-1} - p_{t-2}) \ . \tag{0.3}$$

Rational Expectations (Muth 1961 [23]). In its original version, the Rational Expectations Hypothesis (REH) states that the forecast is the conditional expectation, given the information I available forecasting time, where the information consists of the underlying model describing the development of the endogenous variables, and of the history of all relevant variables:

$${}_{t-d}f_{t+k} = E\left[p_{t+k} \mid I_{t-d}\right] \ . \tag{0.4}$$

There are several relaxations of the Rational Expectations Hypothesis in the literature. The first one is technical in nature: since the true conditional expectation is hard to calculate, one can use the conditional linear expectation instead, i.e.

$$_{t-d}f_{t+k} = EL\left[p_{t+k} \mid p_{t-d-1}, p_{t-d-2}, \ldots, x_{t-d}, x_{t-d-1}, \ldots\right] \tag{0.5}$$

where x denotes the vector of relevant exogenous variables.

Second, one may alter the conditioning $\sigma-$algebra saying that f is *rational with respect to the stochastic process* $\{z_t\}$ if

$$_{t-d}f_{t+k} = EL\left[y_{t+k} \mid z_{t-d}, z_{t-d-1}, \ldots\right] \tag{0.6}$$

holds. The conditioning variables may represent a subset of the set of relevant variables, but may as well contain other variables.

Implicit Expectations. (Mills 1957 [22]) In contrast to the implication $p_t = f_t + u_t$ of the REH (with the u_t's serially uncorrelated and uncorrelated with f_t), the implicit expectations hypothesis states

$$f_t = p_t + v_t \ , \tag{0.7}$$

where v_t and p_t are uncorrelated. This means that the actual realization is a proxy for the unobserved expectation.

Ferber's Law. This rule has been stated by Robert Ferber (1953, [14]) in analyzing the railroad shippers' anticipations data. Ferber found that the firms allow for seasonal movements which results in the following formula, based on quarterly data:

$$f_t = \alpha + p_{t-4}\left(\beta + \gamma\,\frac{p_{t-1} - p_{t-5}}{p_{t-5}}\right) + u_t \ . \tag{0.8}$$

Least-Squares Learning. The forecasters are assumed to adopt the auxiliary model

$$p_t = z'_{t-k}\gamma + v_t \tag{0.9}$$

where z represents an $n-$dimensional vector of predetermined variables which need not necessarily coincide with the variables relevant for the underlying model. Using this (possibly misspecified) auxiliary model, the forecasters calculate the OLS estimate of the parameter vector γ, at the beginning of each period:

$$\hat{\gamma}_t = \left(\sum_{\tau=t_0}^{t-1} z_{\tau-k} z'_{\tau-k} \right)^{-1} \sum_{\tau=t_0}^{t-1} z_{\tau-k} p_\tau \qquad (0.10)$$

where $t_0 \geq k+1$ and $t \geq t_0 + n$ has to be assumed. Then the forecast is simply obtained by applying the usual OLS prediction estimator in the auxiliary model:

$$_t f_{t+k} = z'_t \hat{\gamma}_t \qquad (0.11)$$

Note that forecasters are assumed to stick to the auxiliary variables once chosen, they do not replace irrelevant variables variables during their learning procedure. This is a very restrictive assumption: In general, a misspecified model will soon lead to large mispredictions. The normal reaction would be a respecification of the model, e.g. by altering the set of exogenous variables. But so far, the theory of least-squares learning does not allow the agents to do this. Therefore, least-squares learning makes sense only if the agents start with a correctly specified model. This requires not only the correct set of exogenous variables but also linearity of the underlying model.

Moreover, if some relevant exogenous variables have *contemporary* influence, the agents need the values of the exogenous variables for the prediction period *(scenario)* in order to apply the prediction estimator.

Bayesian learning[6] This learning procedure resembles least-squares learning. The individuals adopt the auxiliary model

$$p_t = z'_{t-1}\gamma + v_t \qquad (0.12)$$

where γ has the prior distribution $\gamma \sim N(\gamma_0, \sigma^2 V_0^{-1})$. The parameter vector γ is reestimated every period by the recursive equations of the Kalman filter:

$$\hat{\gamma}_t = \hat{\gamma}_{t-1} + k_t(p_t - z'_{t-1}\hat{\gamma}_{t-1})$$

---

[6] See Caskey (1985 [11].

$$\hat{V}_t^{-1} = \hat{V}_{t-1}^{-1} - k_t z'_{t-1} \hat{V}_{t-1}^{-1} \tag{0.13}$$

$$k_t = \hat{V}_{t-1}^{-1} z_{t-1} \left(z'_{t-1} \hat{V}_{t-1}^{-1} z_{t-1} + 1 \right)^{-1} .$$

Then the forecast is

$${}_t f_{t+1} = z'_t \hat{\gamma}_t . \tag{0.14}$$

0.3 Description of Selected Empirical Studies

Six empirical studies will be described here:

1. Pesando (1976)
2. Aiginger (1981)
3. Gramlich (1983)
4. Visco (1984)
5. Caskey (1985)

The description will focus on the hypotheses tested since this may be of importance also for experimental studies.

1. Pesando (1976)

Pesando presented two rationality criteria applicable to autoregressive processes. The first one, called "efficiency", requires that "one-period forecasts and realizations share a common autoregressive pattern", and the second criterion, called "consistency", means that "multispan forecasts are obtained recursively, with the rational forecasts being substituted for the as yet unobserved realizations of the series".[7]

The full rationality requirement implicitly assumes that information is costless. Dropping this assumption, Pesando stated the "extended rational expectations hypothesis" which allows forecasts to fail to meet those criteria which could only be achieved by high costs. Considering the two criteria stated above for autoregressive processes, Pesando

[7] Pesando (1976, [25]), p. 37.

supposed that forecasts are consistent but not efficient because efficiency is "expensive" to achieve.

The criteria were tested empirically, using the quarterly cash flow surveys conducted by the LIAA since 1957. In these surveys, life insurance companies were asked to predict several components of cash flow for each of the succeeding two quarters. Based on the data from the 1958-72 period, Pesando estimated the regression equations:[8]

$$p_t = b_1 p_{t-1} + b_2 p_{t-2} + \ldots + b_n p_{t-n} + u_{1,t} \tag{0.15}$$

$$_t f_t = b'_1 p_{t-1} + b'_2 p_{t-2} + \ldots b'_n p_{t-n} + u_{2,t} \tag{0.16}$$

$$_{t-1} f_t = b''_1 \, _{t-1} f_{t-1} + b''_2 p_{t-2} + \ldots + b''_n p_{t-n} \ , \tag{0.17}$$

(where f denotes average forecasts) for six time series of exogenous cash-flow components. Then the null hypotheses

$$b_i = b'_i = b''_i \ \forall n \qquad \text{(Full Rationality)}$$

$$b_i = b'_i \ \forall n \qquad \text{(Efficiency)}$$

$$b'_i = b''_i \ \forall n \qquad \text{(Consistency)}$$

were tested using the Chow statistic.[9]

The results are quite clear: Full rationality was rejected at the one-percent level for four out of six time series. For exactly the same four time series, efficiency was rejected at the 1% level, too, whereas consistency was in no case rejected at the 5% level. These results are in favor of Pesando's extended rationality hypothesis.

---

[8] The time series to be predicted is denoted by p as above.

[9] Chow (1960 [12]).

2. Aiginger (1981)

Aiginger's study presented the most detailed analysis of conditions following from the Rational Expectations Hypothesis. He quoted five criteria necessary for rationality of expectations (again, the time series to be predicted is denoted by p)

1. "Identity of Means": $H_0 : E[f_t] = E[p_t] \; \forall t$, to be tested by t statistic.

2. "Unbiasedness": $H_0 : (\alpha, \beta) = (0, 1)$ in $p_t = \alpha + \beta f_t + u_t$, to be tested by F statistic.

3. "Sufficiency":
   $H_0^1 : cov[u_t, u_{t-1}] = 0 \;\; \forall t$ in $p_t = \alpha + \beta f_t + u_t$,
   to be tested by the Durbin-Watson statistic.
   $H_0^2 : \gamma = \delta = 0$ in $p_t = \alpha + \beta f_t + \gamma z_{t-1} + \delta z_{t-2} + u_t$,
   to be tested by F statistic, z represents an arbitrary variable.

4. "Efficiency" (see Pesando)
   $H_0^1 : (\alpha, \beta_1, \beta_2) = (\alpha', \beta_1', \beta_2')$
   in: $p_t = \alpha + \beta_1 p_{t-1} + \beta_2 p_{t-2} + u_t$, $f_t = \alpha' + \beta_1' p_{t-1} + \beta_2' p_{t-2} + v_t$
   to be tested by F statistic.
   $H_0^2 : R^2(\text{coefficient of determination}) = 0$
   in: $p_t - f_t = \alpha + \beta_1 p_{t-1} + \beta_2 p_{t-2} + u_t$
   to be tested by F statistic.

5. "Consistency" (see Pesando)
   $H_0^1 : (\alpha', \beta_1', \beta_2') = (\alpha", \beta_1", \beta_2")$
   in: ${}_{t-1}f_{t+1} = \alpha" + \beta_1" {}_{t-1}f_t + \beta_2" p_{t-1} + w_t$
   to be tested by F statistic,
   with $(\alpha', \beta_1', \beta_2')$ as above in hypothesis (4)
   $H_0^2 : (\alpha, \beta) = (0, 1)$ in: ${}_t f_{t+1} = \alpha + \beta_{t-1} f_{t+1} + u_t$
   to be tested by F statistic.

Aiginger evaluated a wide variety of time series of directly observed expectations (among others price expectations data from consumer surveys, investment and sales anticipations data from business surveys, real GNP forecasts from experts)[10] for these criteria. The results were summarized in a table for each time series and each criterion. Here is only a table showing the proportion of rejections for each criterion:

---

[10] For details see Aiginger [1], S. 32-38.

Table 0.1: Proportion of rejections for each criterion in Aiginger's study

Criterion	No. of Rejections (5% level)	(1% level)	Total number
Identity of Means	15	13	39
Unbiasedness	21	16	39
Sufficiency 1	23	19	39
Sufficiency 2*	7	6	37
Efficiency 1	29	23	39
Efficiency 2	15	13	39
Consistency 1	11	9	26
Consistency 2	11	9	26

* The variable P chosen is "manufacturing production".

Aiginger also evaluated the data for business forecasts, consumer surveys, and experts' forecasts separately.[11] Generally, business forecasts showed the highest proportion of rejections, and experts' forecasts the lowest one.[12] The only case where none of the eight criteria was rejected are experts' consumer price forecasts in Austria for the period from 1964 until 1984.

The criteria were only tested separately, not taking into account that

1. some criteria imply others
   (for example, unbiasedness implies identity of means)
2. the fact that rationality implies all criteria to hold jointly.

To summarize, Aiginger found little evidence in favor of rational expectations. Especially the hypotheses "Unbiasedness", "Sufficiency 1", and "Efficiency 1" were rejected for the majority of forecast time series.

3. Gramlich (1983)

Gramlich (1983 [16]) compared household, economist, and business forecasts. The household data were taken from the surveys of Michigan's Institute for Social Research (for the time-span 1956-1980), the

---

11 [1], p. 44/45.

12 Note, however, that the variables to be predicted are not the same throughout the three groups.

economists' forecasts were taken from the Livingston series (for 1956-1980); and the business expectations from the Bureau of Economic Analysis (BEA) which had surveyed businesses on their estimates of rates of price change for goods and services sold and capital goods purchased (for 1970-1980).

Rationality was tested by estimating the equation

$$p_t = \alpha + \beta f_t + u_t \tag{0.18}$$

and then testing the joint hypothesis $(\alpha, \beta) = (0, 1)$ by the usual F-statistic. This criterion was called "unbiasedness" as in Aiginger's study. In addition, Gramlich calculated the Durbin-Watson statistics. For the household and economist data, these calculations were made for 1956-1969 and 1970-1980 separately, in order to get results comparable to the business data.

Unbiasedness was rejected for all three groups at the one percent level except households' forecasts for the period 1970-80, in the latter case the significance level was only slightly above 1%. The Durbin-Watson statistics showed very small values, indicating positive autocorrelation of the residuals.

Bryan and Gavin (1986 [7]) found a specification error in Gramlich's calculations due to the difference between sampling frequency (quarterly for the Michigan survey and semiannually for the Livingston survey) and the forecast horizon (annual in all surveys). As a consequence, the residuals could not be expected to be uncorrelated, and OLS estimation of equation (0.18) was not efficient.

Bryan and Gavin presented two solutions to this problem. One way is to use only annual observations from similar months. But by this, the number of periods and, therefore, the power of the test is reduced. The other way is to estimate the variance-covariance matrix of the vector of disturbances.

For both approaches, the hypothesis $(\alpha, \beta) = (0, 1)$ could no longer been rejected at the 5% level for household forecasts, but again for economist forecasts (Livingston data).[13] As a result, households seem to predict more rationally than economists, in contrast to Aiginger's study.

---

[13] Bryan and Gavin did not evaluate the business forecasts.

However, since unbiasedness is a necessary but not sufficient condition for rationality, the results do not really support the REH.

4. Visco (1984)

Visco (1984, [28]) analyzed inflation expectations data (wholesale prices and consumer prices) from the Mondo Economico surveys. Unfortunately, the respondents were not asked for precise forecasts but rather to select one out of several intervals for every economic variable. The answers available were:

"up a lot" (5% or more),
"up a little" (between 2% and 4%),
"no change" (between −1% and 1%),
"down a little" (between −4% and −2%),
"down a lot" (−5% or less),
"don't know".

After 1977, two more intervals were added according to the higher level of inflation in the 1970's.

In order to obtain mean and standard deviation of expected inflation rates over the respondents, Visco excluded the "don't know" answers from consideration and assumed a piecewise uniform distribution of inflation expectations, with the intervals[14]

[−7.5,−4.5] ("down a lot"),
]−4.5,−1.5] ("down a little"),
]−1.5, 1.5] ("no change"),
] 1.5, 4.5] ("up a little"),
] 4.5, 7.5] ("up a lot"),

(two more intervals were added after 1977, see above). Under this assumption of a piecewise uniform distribution, Visco calculated the average expected consumer price inflation rate, and the average expected wholesale price inflation rate for every half year. Only these time series of average predictions were studied.

These data were now analyzed. In chapter 5 of his book, Visco tested the following three implications of rational expectations (let p and f denote actual and expected inflation rate, respectively):

---

[14] For extensive considerations of the measurement problem see Visco, pp. 21-62.

– No serial correlation of forecast errors, to be tested using the Box-Pierce statistics.

– Unbiasedness, i.e. $\alpha = 0$ and $\beta = 1$ (and the joint hypothesis $(\alpha, \beta) = (0, 1)$) in:

$$p = \alpha + f + u$$

– Orthogonality, i.e. $\gamma = 0$ in the regression

$$p - f = X_{-1}\gamma + u$$

where X_{-1} is a matrix with rows $x(t-1)$ which represent some information available to the participants when predicting p_t, and γ is a vector of appropriate dimension.

None of these three hypotheses could be rejected at the 5% level for the 1952-1973 period, but all of them were rejected even at the 1% level if the periods 1974-1980 are included. This means that rationality was rejected when periods of high and volatile inflation were included.

In the last chapter of his book, Visco presented his own model of inflation expectations. Using linear regression, Visco found the following variables to have significant influence on inflation expectations:

variable	sign
p_{t-1}: inflation rate of the preceding period	+
$p_{t-1} - p_{t-1}^{NP}$: difference between inflation rate and some "normal" level of inflation*	–
$f_{t-1} - p_{t-1}, f_{t-2} - p_{t-2}$: (lagged forecast errors)	+
UTC_{t-1}: index of capacity utilization	+
$UTC1_{t-1} = UTC_{t-1}(p_{t-1} - p_{t-1}^{NP})$	+
$UNC1_{t-1} = (\sigma_{t-1} - \sigma_{t-1}^{NS})(f_{t-1} - p_{t-1})$ where $(\sigma - \sigma^{NS})$ denotes the difference between the standard deviation of individual expectations and some "normal level"	+

The "normal level" was calculated as a moving average of previous inflation rates, or standard deviations, respectively.

Some dummy variables for periods with political or economic shocks were added.

To sum up, Visco's model of inflation expectations relies substantially on past values of inflation rates. It contains error-learning and autoregresive elements but no extrapolative elements.

5. Caskey (1985)

The last empirical study to be described is the article of Caskey (1985 [11]) who specified a Bayesian learning model as sketched above in Section 0.2. The auxiliary variables chosen were

- the past ten months' annual inflation rate,
- the annual rate of change in the past six-month money stock,
- the past quarter's federal budget surplus as a percentage of GNP.

The forecasts generated by the learning model were compared to the Livingston data and the comparable consumer price index inflation predictions of Data Resources, Incorporated (DRI) from 1973 to April, 1982. As a result, Caskey found a remarkably good explanation. Thus, Caskey's study seems quite encouraging for further analysis of learning models as an explanation of expectation formation.

0.4 Description of Selected Experimental Studies

The following experimental studies will be described in this section:

1. Becker (1967)
2. Carlson (1967)
3. Schmalensee (1976)
4. Garner (1982)
5. Bergmann (1988)
6. Mason(1988)
7. Williams (1987)
8. Daniels/Plott (1988)

1. Becker (1967)

One of the first experiments on expectation formation was that of Otwin Becker, conducted in 1964.[15] The time series to be predicted was a second-order autoregressive process with stochastic disturbance. The only information available to the 26 participants was the past history of the time series, depicted in a graph. At the beginning of each "period", subjects had to predict the next value of the series, and, after that, depict the realization in the graph.

Becker stated a "stimulus-sampling"[16] hypothesis for the time-series of average forecasts. This hypothesis may be verbally described as follows: The participants recognize that the time series has a cyclical pattern with upswings and downswings. Considering the past history of the time series *except the last value*, the subjects define

- the "central region" which is the interval between the last local minimum and the last local maximum.

- the "stationary region" which is the interval between the absolute minimum and the absolute maximum of all values.

Obviously, the stationary region contains the the central region. Then the forecasts are formed by considering the position of the last value relative to these regions (which are formed without the last value). The rule is described by the following table:[17]

---

[15] Becker (1991, [2]).

[16] "Gestaltpsychologische Hypothese", [2], p. 240.

[17] See Becker [2], p. 242.

Table 0.2: Becker's hypothesis

Observation	Prediction
Last value in the central region or in a trend towards the central region	The trend will continue
Last value outside the central region and in a trend away from the central region, but in the stationary region	Stagnation
Last value outside the stationary region and in a trend away from the central region	The trend will reverse

Becker transformed this hypothesis into a mathematical program which he improved once again in 1991 [3], calculated the forecasts according to this program, and compared them to the average observed forecasts of the participants. The hypothesis proved as a very good description of average forecasts. The reason why it has not been taken up by the literature is presumably that it cannot easily be generalized (to situations with non-cyclical pattern or exogenous variables, for example).

2. Carlson (1967)

The next study to be described, Carlson's experiment, did not focus on expectations only but rather on cobweb phenomena.

The experiment was designed to imitate a market with the demand being a function of the actual price and the supply being a function of the expected price. This model is known as the Cobweb model. In the experiment, the subjects represented the suppliers who had to determine their quantity to be supplied, based on their price expectations. They were given a quadratic cost function, unchanged over all periods, of the form

$$c(x) = k_1 x + k_2 x^2 \quad , \tag{0.19}$$

with x denoting the quantity. Thus, individual i's profit for period t was

$$\pi_t = p_t x_t^i - k_1 x_t^i - k_2 (x_t^i)^2 \ , i = 1, \ldots, 25, t = 1, \ldots, 9 \ . \tag{0.20}$$

For convenience, subjects were given a profit table showing the profit for each price-quantity combination (within a reasonable range of prices and quantities), so they could easily determine the profit-maximizing quantity, given their price expectations.

Given the individual quantities $x_t^1, \ldots, x_t^n$, the period t price, p_t, was calculated as the market-clearing price, i.e.

$$x_t^1 + \ldots + x_t^n = a - bp_t \ , \tag{0.21}$$

where $a - bp$ was the aggregate demand function, not known to the participants except for one point, and unchanged over all periods. At the end of the experiment, each subject was paid his/her accumulated profit.

Four experiments were run. In his article, Carlson evaluated only the second pair of experiments in detail. For each pair, in the first experiment the market was "stable", i.e. the demand function was "flatter"[18] than the supply function (the supply function was obtained by summing up the individual theoretical supply functions, the latter being calculated from the cost function). In the second experiment the converse held, i.e. the market was potentially "unstable".

The participants were also asked to state their price expectations but without financial reward. In addition to the stated expectations, Carlson calculated the "implicit" expectations: Let x_i^t denote subject i's quantity for period t. Then i's implicit expectation, $\tilde{f}_t^i$, was calculated according to

$$\tilde{f}_t^i - k_1 - 2k_2 x_t^i = 0 \ , \tag{0.22}$$

which is the profit-maximizing condition. That is, $\tilde{f}$ was calculated as the price under which the chosen quantity would be the profit-maximizing one. Carlson argued that "there is reason to doubt the validity of the stated expectations" and that his "procedure will be to assume

[18] Here the functions are drawn in a diagram with the price on the vertical axis and the quantity on the horizontal axis.

that the subjects acted as maximizers of expected profit".[19] Indeed, the quantity chosen was not always the profit-maximizing one, given the stated price expectation. For further analysis, Carlson used only the implicit expectations, that is, he adopted an indirect approach to measure expectations, with the economic model as given above, assuming the subjects to be risk neutral (i.e they maximize expected profit).

Carlson analyzed the following hypotheses on expectation formation:

1. Adaptive Expectations:

$$f_t - f_{t-1} = \alpha + \beta(p_{t-1} - f_{t-1}) \tag{0.23}$$

2. Extrapolative Expectations:

$$f_t - f_{t-1} = \alpha + \rho(p_{t-1} - p_{t-2}) \tag{0.24}$$

These equations were estimated using OLS regression, for each individual separately as well as for the group average.

In addition to estimating the parameters in Eq. (0.23) and (0.24), Carlson calculated the sum of squared residuals and the "residual reduction ratio", the latter developed as follows:

The estimation of (1) (adaptive model) including intercept is the same as estimating

$$f_t = \alpha + \beta_1 p_{t-1} + \beta_2 f_{t-1} \tag{0.25}$$

under the restriction $\beta_1 + \beta_2 = 1$. Carlson reestimated (0.25), dropping the restriction, and then calculated the "residual reduction ratio" as the reduction in sum of squared residuals, divided by the unrestricted mean squared error.

Comparing the adaptive to the extrapolative model, in the adaptive model the sum of squared residuals (in the restricted estimation) was generally slightly smaller than in the extrapolative model, and the residual reduction ratio was considerably smaller, even negligible in the adaptive model. This indicates that the adaptive model was less

---

19 [10], p.315.

restrictive than the extrapolative. For the extrapolative model, Carlson tested H_0: $\rho_1 + \rho_2 = 1$ by the usual t statistic

$$t = \frac{\hat{\rho}_1 + \hat{\rho}_2 - 1}{s_q} \tag{0.26}$$

(where s_q is the estimated standard deviation of the residuals) and obtained no rejection at the 5% level for the "stable" as well as for the "unstable" market. Since the adaptive model is "less restrictive", the analogous statistic for this model was not calculated.

The experiment resulted in a stable behavior even in the case of a potentially unstable market. This may be due to "induced caution":[20] In the first two periods, greater price fluctuations occured in the potentially unstable market. Observing this, the participants changed their quantities more moderately.

As far as the adaptive model is concerned, this gives rise to the hypothesis that the error adjustment coefficient "will always adapt sufficiently to assure stability".[21] This may be due to the fact that "the greater the fluctuations in prices are, the smaller will be the coefficient of adaptive expectations".[22] Indeed, the estimate $\hat{\beta}$ of the error adjustment coefficient was considerably smaller for the potentially unstable market and was in the stable region for both markets.[23] An analogous result for the extrapolative model is not stated.

To sum up, Carlson's data support the adaptive model, with the error adjustment coefficient becoming smaller when heavy fluctuations occur. Carlson did not claim his results to hold in more general predictive situations.

Indeed, this cannot be expected: If, for example, the time series to be predicted has a cyclical pattern or exogenous variables are present, the forecasters are unlikely to neglect this. The adaptive model can only be regarded as acceptable for situations without those phenomena.

---

[20] Carlson [10], p. 313/314.

[21] [10], p. 317.

[22] [10], p. 317.

[23] The stability condition is $\beta < \frac{2}{d/b+1}$.

An obvious weakness of Carlson's study is the indirect approach. The assumption of risk neutrality - which has to be treated as a part of the underlying economic model - was not tested in the study, so there is no reason to believe that "implicit" forecasts are more reliable than reported ones.

3. Schmalensee (1976)

This is the only experiment described here which used an empirical time series: the deflated wheat prices in England from 1857 until 1913. The participants were told that "the series gave actual wheat prices, corrected for cost of living changes, for a country with free trade in wheat and large imports, over a period with no major political changes."[24] For each period t, before the actual price was made known, the participants had to give a prediction, call it F_t, of the average price in the next five years, i.e. the periods $t, t+1, \ldots, t+4$. In addition "they were asked to bracket their forecast by writing down a second number, call it B_t, such that they felt it likely that the true average for this period, $\bar{A}_t$, would lie between $(F_t - B_t)$ and $(F_t + B_t)$."[25]

At the end of the experiment, the "prediction costs" were calculated for every participant as the sum of prediction costs over all periods, where the period t prediction costs were calculated according to

$$C = |\bar{A}_t - F_t| + 2B_t + 10((F_t - B_t - \bar{A}_t)^+ + (\bar{A}_t - (F_t + B_t))^+) \ . \quad (0.27)$$

The first term refers to the prediction F_t, and is simply the absolute forecast error. The two other terms refer to the interval $[F_t - B_t, F_t + B_t]$, the second term being the length of this interval, and the third term being ten times the distance between the interval and the true average. The participant(s) with the lowest cost was (were) awarded a prize.

Using a simple t test, Schmalensee found a significant upward bias of forecasts: The hypothesis that F (forecast) and $\bar{A}$ (realization) have the same mean was rejected at the 0.0001 per cent level. Further, Schmalensee compared the adaptive model

---

24 Schmalensee (1976 [26]), p. 19.

25 Schmalensee ([26]), p. 19).

$$F_t - F_{t-1} = \alpha + \gamma\,(\beta \bar{A}_{t-1} - F_{t-1}) + \varepsilon_t \tag{0.28}$$

and the extrapolative model

$$F_t = \alpha + \bar{A}_{t-1}\left(\beta + \gamma\frac{\bar{A}_{t-1} - \bar{A}_{t-2}}{\bar{A}_{t-2}}\right) + \varepsilon_t \tag{0.29}$$

for fit by using linear regression. The standard error was lower in the case of the adaptive model for more than twenty out of twenty-three subjects.

Schmalensee's results may be summarized as follows:

(1) The forecasts were significantly biased upwards.

(2) The observed forecasts were best described by the adaptive model with the coefficient of adaptation, γ, falling in turning point periods.

As far as the confidence intervals are concerned, no conclusive results were obtained.[26]

Schmalensee quoted risk-loving behavior and "overestimation of own abilities" as possible reasons for the bias.[27]

But this reasoning seems not very plausible since there may be an effect of the downward trend of the whole time series (which is obvious from viewing the graph of the series)[28]: The subjects possibly did not recognize this trend and, therefore, repeatedly overpredicted the realization.

Another point to be criticized is the lack of appropriate incentive for accurate prediction. Since only the "best" participant was rewarded, there may well be some participants who stopped any mental effort when they had already given some bad forecasts and therefore presumed that there was little chance to be the "winner".

The good performance of the adaptive model is not surprising in this case, as explained in the discussion of Carlson's results.

---

26 [26], p. 30.

27 [26], S. 29.

28 For the graph see [26], p. 20.

4. Garner (1982)

Garner's experiment[29] incorporated exogenous variables into the model. The endogenous variable was the price P of a fictitious agricultural commodity, determined by an autoregressive model with three exogenous variables, among them the prices of two other commodities.[30]

At the beginning of each period t, the participants had to predict P_t and P_{t+1} (one- and two-span forecasts). The information available consisted of the history of the exogenous variables including period t (i.e. a scenario for the prediction period was given), and of the past history of P. At the end of the experiments, the participants received a benefit for participating and a reward according to their individual forecasting accuracy.

Garner tested the observed forecasts for rationality. The first criterion to be tested is well known from other studies: The regression equations

$$P_t = \alpha + \beta \, {}_t f_t + v_t \ , \ t = 1, \dots, T \tag{0.30}$$

$$P_t = \alpha + \beta \, {}_{t-1} f_t + v_t \ , \ t = 2, \dots, T \tag{0.31}$$

where

P_t = price,
${}_t f_t$ = one-span forecast, ${}_{t-1} f_t$ = two-span forecast,
T = number of periods.

were estimated for each subject. The same was done using the arithmetic mean of the individual one-span and two-span forecasts, resp. (average forecasts). Then the hypotheses $\alpha = 0$, $\beta = 1$, and the joint hypothesis $(\alpha, \beta) = (0, 1)$ were tested. For the one-span forecasts, the first two hypotheses were in most cases not rejected at the 5 percent level. This held true in particular for average forecasts. But the joint hypothesis was rejected for most individuals (8 out of 12), and also for the average forecasts.[31] For the two-span forecasts, Garner obtained more rejections,

---

[29] Garner (1982 [15]).

[30] Garner (1982 [15]), p. 116.

[31] See [15], p. 118/119.

the joint hypothesis was rejected for all individuals and for average forecasts.

Garner tested two "strong versions of rationality"[32]. For this purpose, consider the following three equations:

$$P = Xc + w_1 \quad \text{(true model)} \tag{0.32}$$

$$f = Xc' + w_2 \quad \text{(subject's predicion rule)} \tag{0.33}$$

$$P = Xc'' + w_3 \quad \text{(sample estimate)} \tag{0.34}$$

where X denoted the matrix of the explanatory variables. In these equations, the parameter vector c was known from the model, whereas the vector c' is the OLS estimate obtained by regressing observed forecasts on X, and c'' represents the OLS estimate of the true parameter vector c (obtained from regressing the realizations P on X).

Then the first strong rationality hypothesis states that the coefficients of the prediction rule equal the true parameter c: $H_{N1} : c = c'$. The second strong rationality hypothesis states that the coefficients of the prediction rule equal the sample estimate: $H_{N2} : c' = c''$. Both hypotheses were rejected for most participants and for the average forecasts, even at the one-percent level.

Garner then analyzed a weaker version of rationality: He tested the two Pesando [25] rationality criteria for autoregressive processes (see above), i.e. he focused only on the coefficients of the lagged endogenous variables. Consider the equations where the exogenous variables have been dropped:

$$P_t = a_1 P_{t-1} + a_2 P_{t-2} + a_3 P_{t-3} + z_{1t} \tag{0.35}$$

$$_t f_t = a'_1 P_{t-1} + a'_2 P_{t-2} + a'_3 P_{t-3} + z_{2t} \tag{0.36}$$

$$_t f_{t+1} = a''_1 f_{t,1} + a''_2 P_{t-1} + a''_3 P_{t-2} + z_{3t} \tag{0.37}$$

---

32 [15], pp. 118,121.

respectively. Then "efficiency" means $a_i = a'_i, i = 1, 2, 3$, and $a'_i = a''_i, i = 1, 2, 3$, is called "consistency". The tests rejected consistency only for three out of twelve participants, and efficiency was never rejected. These results are in contrast to Pesando who observed more "consistent" than "efficient" behavior. For the average forecasts, neither efficiency nor consistency were rejected.

Finally, Garner calculated the least-squares-learning forecasts for each period and then regressed them on individual forecasts and on average forecasts:

$$f_{LSL,t} = \alpha + \beta f_t + v_t \tag{0.38}$$

where $f_{LSL,t}$ denotes the least-squares-learning forecast for period t. The hypotheses ($\alpha = 0$) and ($\beta = 1$) and the joint hypothesis $(\alpha, \beta) = (0, 1)$ were never rejected at the 5-percent level. Furthermore, no significant serial correlation was indicated by the Durbin-Watson statistics. With these tests, Garner was the first to analyze least-squares learning as a hypothesis on expectation formation.

5. Bergmann (1988)

Barbara R. Bergmann[33] adopted a merely qualitative approach. Each participant was given a package of 18 charts, each chart showing graphically a time-series with cyclical pattern and stochastic disturbance. The subjects only had to give a trend prediction for the next five periods, one for each chart. Available answers were (A): "strongly upwards", (B): "moderately upwards", (C): "constant", (D): "moderately downwards", (E): "strongly downwards". The best forecaster[34] was awarded a prize of $25.

Analyzing the answers, Bergmann found that in cases when the direction of the last segment was upward, 56% of the subjects predicted "upward" (A or B), 10% predicted "constant" (C), and 33% predicted "downward" (D or E). In contrast, when the last segment pointed downward, only 45% predicted "downward", and 42% "upward". This suggests an upward bias of expectations which is confirmed by a chi-square test.

---

[33] 1988 [4].

[34] The criterion is not specified in the article.

More specifically, three characteristics of the series were found to influence significantly the proportion of correct answers: the direction of the last segment, the variance of the disturbance, and the distance from the previous turning point. The predictions were better when the last segment pointed upward, when the variance was small, and when the distance from the last turning point was small.

Bergmann concluded that the forecasting abilities of the subjects are very limited, and that, possibly, expectations do not play that role in economic life that they are often presumed to do.

It has already been stated at the end of the description of Schmalensee's experiment that rewarding only the "best" participant provides inappropriate incentive to the subjects. This may be the reason why the predictions were so poor.

6. Mason (1988)

The time series to be predicted was a pure random walk called "price process" in the experiment. The financial reward consisted of a participation fee and cumulated earnings according to the forecast accuracy.

Since the endogenous variable (P) was a random walk, the rational prediction rule is the naive rule: $f_t = P_{t-1}$ (with f denoting the forecast, and P the realization). With this simple series, Mason found that in absence of (apparent) inflationary or deflationary trends, the implications "unbiasedness" and "efficiency" of the REH cannot be rejected for most participants, where "unbiasedness" meant, as above, $(\alpha^i, \beta^i) = (0, 1)$ in

$$P_t = \alpha_i + \beta_i f_{t,i} + u_{t,i} \ , \tag{0.39}$$

and "efficiency" meant $\beta^i = 0$ in

$$f_{t,i} - P_t = \alpha_i + \beta_i(f_{t-1,i} - P_{t-1}) + v_t \ . \tag{0.40}$$

In these equations, the subscript i denotes the individual ($i = 1, \ldots, n$). However, when the time series seemed to have a trend, the predictions failed to meet these criteria. But, as far as unbiasedness is concerned, this does not mean that the individuals did not behave rationally since, during an inflationary [deflationary] period, the rational prediction rule $f_t = P_{t-1}$ automatically gives downward [upward] biased forecasts. This shows an obvious weakness of this rationality test. Mason provided another rationality test: He estimated the adaptive model

$$f_{t,i} - f_{t-1,i} = \alpha_i + \beta_i(P_{t-1} - f_{t-1,i}) + u_{t,i} \ . \tag{0.41}$$

and tested the hypothesis $(\alpha_i, \beta_i) = (0, 1)$ which, in this case, implies rational expectations. This hypothesis was rejected at the 5% level for more than 66% of the subjects.

In addition, Mason tested the adaptive model, the extrapolative model, and the implicit expectations hypothesis. For the adaptive model, the parameter estimates from the regression (0.41) were used, and the hypotheses $\alpha_i = 0$ and $0 < \beta_i \leq 1$ were tested.[35] The hypotheses were not rejected for 51.7% of the individuals. For these individuals, the coefficient of determination was between 0.444 and 0.98. Furthermore, the data suggested that the average error adjustment coefficient, β, across subjects was greater for the experiments with greater variance of the disturbance term.[36] But Mason did not provide a statistic for testing this hypothesis. He only tested the adaptive parameter for homogeneity across subjects, using the statistic

$$F = \frac{(SSE_p - \sum_i SSE_i)/(2n-2)}{\sum_i SSE_i(N-2n)} \tag{0.42}$$

where n denotes the number of individuals, N the total number of observations (number of individuals multiplied by the number of periods), SSE_i denotes the sum of squared residuals for the regressions based on individual i's data, and SSE_p denotes the sum of squared residuals for the pooled regression which is appropriate in case of homogeneity. Under the null hypothesis of homogeneity, F is asymptotically distributed as $F(2n-2, N-2n)$. The hypothesis of homogeneity was rejected at the 5% level.

For testing the extrapolative model, the regression equation

$$f_{t,i} - P_{t-1} = \alpha_i + \beta_i(P_{t-1} - P_{t-2}) + u_{t,i} \tag{0.43}$$

---

[35] Mason did not tell which statistic was used.

[36] Note that this is in contrast to Carlson's result.

was estimated, and the hypotheses $\alpha_i = 0$ and $\beta_i \geq 0$ were tested. These hypotheses were jointly accepted for only 11% of the participants, with the coefficient of determination ranging from 0.187 to 0.582 in these cases.

The last hypothesis tested was the implicit expectations hypothesis. As the description in Section 0.2 above indicates, this hypothesis seems to be appropriate if the forecast variance is greater than the variance of the realizations. This was the case for 33 out of 89 participants (but in no case significant at the 5% level). For these participants, Mason tested "unbiasedness" and "efficiency", the latter being tested as above, and "unbiasendness" by estimating the parameters in

$$f_{t,i} = \alpha_i + \beta_i P_t + u_{t,i} \tag{0.44}$$

and testing the joint hypothesis $(\alpha_i, \beta_i) = (0, 1)$. The percentage of rejections was more than 50%.

Mason's results may be summarized as follows:

1. The rationality criteria "unbiasedness" and "efficiency" were mostly accepted, except for inflationary or deflationary periods. However, the hypothesis that the error adjustment coefficent in the adaptive model equals one (which would imply rationality in this case) was mostly rejected.

2. The adaptive expectations hypothesis was accepted for slightly more than 50% of the participants. The hypothesis of homogeneity of the error adjustment coefficient across the individuals was rejected.

3. The extrapolative expectations hypothesis was rejected in most cases, and the fitting in the remaining cases was not good.

4. The implicit expectations hypothesis was inappropriate for most individuals.

All in all, Mason's results are not very conclusive, and even if they were, this could be due to the special nature of the process to be predicted: No exogenous variables were present, so that, for example, the relatively good performance of the adaptive hypothesis is not surprising.

7. Williams (1987)

The last two studies described here were auction market experiments, consisting of a series of experimental markets which, in turn, were subdivided into several periods. In every experimental market there was a number of sellers and buyers, characterized by their limit price schemes:

At the beginning of each period, each seller [buyer] was given a limit price table showing the minimal [maximal] price which he/she should require [be willing to pay] for selling [purchasing] the first, the second, ... unit of the good. That is, he/she was given an individual supply curve [demand curve].

The participants' task was to bid and ask, and to trade if an agreement was found (oral double auction). At the end of the experiment, each participant was paid his/her accumulated profit which was the sum of the profits from all transactions. The profit from a transaction was given by

contract price minus limit price (for the seller),

or

limit price minus contract price (for the buyer),

respectively.

In addition, at the beginning of each period, each participant had to predict the average contract price for that period.

Specifically, Williams set up 12 experimental markets, running over 4 or 5 periods, each period lasting 12 minutes, with 6 sellers and 6 buyers. For prediction of the average contract price, the participants already knew their limit price scheme for that period. The scheme was varied every period by adding an arbitrary constant to all limit prices. The participant with the lowest sum of absolute prediction errors was paid a reward of $1 at the end of the experiment.

The market efficiency, defined as the ratio of actual total earnings of subjects to the maximum possible (i.e. the theoretical competitive equilibrium) earnings, was more than 90% on average.

With the data from these experiments, Williams tested several hypotheses on expectation formation:

Rational Expectations: The criteria tested are unbiasedness and efficiency, already known from above. Williams did not test separately for each individual but estimated the pooled time-series-cross-section equations

$$P_t^j = \alpha + \beta f_{t,i}^j + u_{t,i}^j \tag{0.45}$$

and

$$f_{t,i}^j - P_t^j = \alpha + \beta(f_{t-1,j}^j - P_{t-1}^j) + u_{t,i}^j \tag{0.46}$$

(where the index i refers to the individual, and j refers to the market, and, for all markets, period 1 was not included). and tested the hypotheses $\alpha = 0$, $\beta = 1$, $(\alpha, \beta) = (0, 1)$ (for unbiasedness) and $\beta = 0$ (for efficiency). All these hypotheses except ($\alpha = 0$) were rejected even at the 1% level. Estimating only the regression based on data from the 3rd through 5th period, or for each period separately, did not yield "better" results.

Adaptive Expectations: The regression

$$(f_{t,i}^j - f_{t-1,i}^j = \alpha + \beta(P_{t-1}^j - f_{t-1,i}^j) + u_{t,i}^j \tag{0.47}$$

was estimated where periods 1 and 2 are not included. The estimate $\hat{\alpha}$ was negative, and the hypothesis $\alpha = 0$ was rejected at the 1% level. $\hat{\beta}$ was between 0 and 1, and the hypotheses $\beta = 0$ and $\beta = 1$ were rejected at the 1% level. Considering periods 3 through 5 separately yielded similar results. The coefficient of determination ranged from 0.49 to 0.78. Thus, Williams' forecast data were "fairly consistent with the adaptive expectations model".[37]

Extrapolative Expectations: The regression

$$f_{t,i}^j - P_{t-1}^j = \alpha + \beta(P_{t-1}^j - P_{t-2}^j) + u_{t,i}^j \tag{0.48}$$

was estimated, again omitting periods 1 and 2. The hypothesis $\alpha = 0$ could not be rejected at the 5% level, but $\beta = 0$ could not be rejected, too, and the estimate $\hat{\beta}$ was only slightly greater than zero. This means that the data do not support the extrapolative model.

---

37 [29], p. 15.

For each hypothesis, Williams tested the data for significant differences between experienced and inexperienced participants, but such differences were generally not found.

As stated in earlier discussion, the consistency of the data with the adaptive hypothesis may be due to the absence of exogenous variables.

8. Daniels/Plott (1988)

The last experiment described here was another auction market experiment. It consisted of nine 15-period experimental markets (each period lasting 5 minutes), each experimental market with 4 sellers and 4 buyers who were given individual limit price schemes.

As in Williams' experiment, the participants' task was

(1) to predict, at the beginning of each period but - in contrast to Williams' experiment - *before* knowing the limit price scheme, the average contract price for that period.

(2) to "ask" and "bid" in the auction market and to trade if an agreement was found.

At the end of the experiment, each participant was paid his/her accumulated profit. In each period the participant with the lowest absolute forecast error earned an additional reward.

The prediction was complicated by two features of the experiment:

(1) The individual reservation price schemes were rotated each period among participants.

(2) There were inflationary periods in which all reservation prices were risen.

More precisely, seven out of nine experimental markets were "inflationary" ones, with 15% inflation per period except the last three periods in which inflation was zero, and the remaining two markets (control markets) were stationary for the first twelve periods, followed by three periods of inflation.

The experiments resulted in a market efficiency of more than 90% on average, and efficiency slightly higher for the stationary markets.[38]

---

[38] Daniels/Plott [13], p. 204, Table 6.

As a further result, the difference between average contract prices and theoretical equilibrium price converged towards zero over time, but this was significant only for the stationary markets, and for the latter, the dispersion of contract prices around the mean price decreased significantly.[39]

Concerning the properties of aggregate (average) forecasts, Daniels and Plott found no confirmation for the hypothesis that the forecasts of buyers are lower than those of sellers. Further, they estimated the parameters in

$$\bar{P}_t = \alpha + \beta \bar{f}_t + u_t \ , \tag{0.49}$$

with $\bar{P}_t$ denoting the mean contract price in period t, and $\bar{f}_t$ denoting the average forecasts of the individuals. α was not found significantly different from zero, and $\hat{\beta}$ was very close to one.[40] The Durbin-Watson statistic did not indicate a significant autocorrelation of residuals. So far, the forecasts seem to be unbiased and efficient. Further, Daniels/Plott found that the variance in forecasts (among individuals) was positively related to the last period's average forecast error.[41]

Concerning individual forecasts, Daniels/Plott presented results from both "stationary" markets but from only four out of seven "inflationary" markets. They estimated the parameters in

$$f_t^i = \lambda_1^i \bar{P}_{t-1} + \lambda_2^i (f_{t-1}^i - \bar{P}_{t-1}) + \varepsilon_t^i \tag{0.50}$$

(where f_t^i denotes individual i's forecast for period t), and tested the joint hypothesis $H_0^1 : \lambda_1^i = 1, \quad 0 \leq \lambda_2^i < 1$ for the adaptive model, and the hypotheses $(\lambda_1^i, \lambda_2^i) = (1.15, 0)$ (for participants in inflationary markets), and $(\lambda_1^i, \lambda_2^i) = (1, 0)$ (for participants in stationary markets) respectively, for rationality. The adaptive hypothesis was rejected for most individuals, especially for the participants in inflationary markets, whereas the rationality hypothesis was rejected for only 8 out of 32

---

39 Daniels/Plott [13], p. 209, Table 7.

40 However, no test results for $H_0 : \beta = 1$ or the joint hypothesis $(\alpha, \beta) = (0, 1)$ were given, see [13], pp. 211/212.

41 [13], p. 212.

participants in inflationary markets, and for only 1 out of 16 participants in stationary markets.

In addition, Daniels and Plott estimated

$$\bar{P}_t = \alpha^i + \beta^i f_t^i + u_t \ . \tag{0.51}$$

The hypothesis $(\alpha^i, \beta^i) = (0, 1)$ was rejected only once for the inflationary markets, and the coefficient of determination was quite high, in contrast to the participants in stationary markets. In the latter case, the regression results were rather inconclusive, possibly due to the small variance of both average prices and forecasts. Restricting the further analysis to the inflationary markets, Daniels and Plott found that $R < \hat{\beta}_1$ in 21 out 32 cases, indicating[42] that the Muth model

$$\bar{P}_t = f_t^i + \varepsilon_t^i \tag{0.52}$$

was more appropriate than Mills' implicit expectations model

$$f_t^i = \bar{P}_t + \varepsilon_t^i \ . \tag{0.53}$$

As a third rationality criterion, Daniels and Plott estimated

$$\bar{P}_t - (\hat{\alpha}^i - \hat{\beta}^i f_t^i) = \gamma_i \bar{P}_{t-1} + \eta_t^i \tag{0.54}$$

(i.e. they regressed the "rational expectations errors upon the last period's mean contract price"), and tested $H_0 : \gamma_i = 0$. In no case this hypothesis could be rejected.

Summing up, Daniels and Plott found the price forecasts to be captured much better by the rational expectations hypothesis than by the adaptive expectations hypothesis.

---

42 [13], p. 214, see also Michael C. Lovell (1986), Tests of the Rational Expectations Hypothesis, American Economic Review 76, pp. 110-124. R is the square root of the coefficient of determination, R^2.

0.5 Concluding Comments on the Literature

In this section, some comments will be made concerning the following points:

1. Results on Various Hypotheses on Expectation Formation
2. Direct versus indirect approach
3. The reward structure
4. Exogenous variables
5. Model or No Model?
6. Forecast Feedback or Not?
7. Story or No Story?

1. Results on Various Hypotheses on Expectation Formation

Rationality of Expectations was tested in most empirical and experimental studies. Muth's statement

$$\text{"forecast} = \text{conditional expectation"} \qquad (0.55)$$

could only be tested directly if a complete model was available which generated the time series to be predicted. This was not the case if the time series was empirical (i.e. in empirical studies and in Schmalensee's study), or if the subjects' decisions had an influence on the realizations of the variable to be predicted (Carlson, Williams, and Daniels/Plott). In these cases, only some implications of the Rational Expectations Hypothesis could be tested. This was also the approach adopted in those experimental studies where Muth's statement could be tested directly (e.g. Garner, Mason).

The implications most commonly tested are unbiasedness and efficiency. Some other implications were tested by Aiginger (Sufficiency, Consistency), Visco (Orthogonality), and Garner (equality of parameters, and restriction of this equality to the autoregressive components).

The implications were mostly rejected, with the exception of Daniels/ Plott (unbiasedness was not rejected) and Garner (equality of autoregressive parameters was not rejected).

Thus, full rationality was rejected in most studies.

The *adaptive* and the *extrapolative* expectations models were tested by some authors of experimental studies (Carlson, Schmalensee, Mason, Williams). They all accepted the adaptive model as a good explanation, whereas the extrapolative model was rejected.[43] But these results may be due to the absence of exogenous variables.

Least-squares learning and *Bayesian learning* were tested by Garner and Caskey, respectively, and proved as a fairly good description of predictive behavior in presence of exogenous variables.

Some more hypotheses set up by the authors themselves as a satisfactory explanation of their data have to be mentioned:

Becker's stimulus-sampling hypothesis,
Visco's econometric model.

These hypotheses have the obvious disadvantage that they are not general.

So far, most experiments were focused on forecasting situations without exogenous variables. For these situations, Becker's hypothesis or even the adaptive model may be good descriptions of predictive behavior. But this will surely not hold for time series influenced by exogenous variables. In this case, rational expectations and least-squares learning should be tested.

The approach commonly chosen[44] for this purpose is testing ($\alpha = 0$, $\beta = 1$) in the regression

$$\text{hypothetic prediction} = \alpha + \beta \cdot \text{observed prediction} + u \ , \qquad (0.56)$$

This approach, however, is inappropriate: Consider the following simple example:

---

[43] It has to be noted once more that Carlson's study did not focus mainly on expectations, and that his results on expectations were not claimed to be general.

[44] E.g. by Garner, Mason, and Schmalensee, for rational expectations the hypothetic prediction is replaced by the true realizations.

Period	hypothetic forecast	actual forecast
1	−10	−5
2	0	−5
3	10	5
4	0	5

Now apply the above regression. The result is $\hat{\alpha} = 0$ and $\hat{\beta} = 1$. Thus, the hypothesis is not rejected. But the deviations are considerable, and it would obviously be unreasonable to accept the hypothesis. In case of testing unbiasedness as an implication of rationality one should really note that unbiased forecasts may be far from being rational.

More realistic results could be obtained by comparing hypothetic to observed predicted *changes*. In the preceding example, the actual predicted change is always half of the hypothetic predicted change which clearly contradicts the hypothesis.

Moreover, one should remember the simple criteria of mean and mean absolute deviations which allow comparison of various hypotheses according to their deviations from observed forecasts.

It remains to be noted that most experimenters[45] focused on individual predictions only and did not study average predictions. The latter concept may reveal much more regularity and deserves deeper consideration.

2. Direct Versus Indirect Approach

All authors except Carlson adopted a direct approach. There is good reason to doubt the validity of indirectly observed expectations since in this case only a joint hypothesis can be tested (see discussion above).

3. The Reward Structure

Some experimenters rewarded only the best forecaster. As stated above, there may be a "giving-up effect", once a subject thinks that there is no chance to be the winner. Thus, there is a lack of incentive to predict accurately. This suspicion may be enforced by the fact that those studies

---

[45] Except e.g. Becker [1964], Garner [1982].

where only the winner was rewarded (Schmalensee, Bergmann, see also Bolle (1988 [5])) obtained very poor forecasting behavior. Therefore, it seems advisable to reward each participant according to his/her forecasting accuracy.

4. Exogenous Variables

So far, only one experimental study (Garner) and two empirical studies (Visco, Caskey) analyzed the effects of exogenous variables on expectations, i.e. allowed the forecasters to utilize the information contained in the exogenous variables.

5. Model or No Model?

This question arises when experiments are conducted. Schmalensee is the only author who used an empirical time series to be predicted. This has two disadvantages: Firstly, no model generating the series is available, implying that, for example, the time series of rational predictions is not known to the experimenter. Secondly, exogenous variables cannot be included since the experimenter would have to select some variables out of the huge set of possibly relevant variables. This selection will always be arbitrary and will influence the obtained results on expectation formation.

6. Forecast Feedback?

In some market experiments, agents' behavior (which is influenced by their expectations) had an effect on future realizations of the time series to be predicted (generally the price).[46] For the purpose of studying expectations, this forecast feedback unnecessarily complicates the situation and (since the number of participants is relatively small) possibly introduces game-theoretic elements into the experiment.

Moreover, there is an important statistical argument: Without forecast feedback, individuals are independent of one another, i.e., from each experiment, the experimenter obtains as many independent series as there are participants. In presence of a forecast feedback, individual predictions are independent only in the first period, and only one independent series results from each experiment.

---

[46] Carlson [10], Williams [29], and Daniels/Plott [13].

7. Story or No Story?

An experimenter may name the variables involved, i.e., "tell the participants an economic story", or, alternatively, use abstract variables. The alternative most widely chosen is "telling a story". This bears the following problem: The individuals may use their economic knowledge or their experience instead of only viewing the data.[47]

As an example, take Garner's experiment who named the endogenous variable "price of an agricultural good" and one of the exogenous variables "price of a substitute". As every economist knows, the price of a substitute often has a positive effect on the demand for the good in question and, therefore, a positive effect on the price of that good. Thus, the participants already knew the direction of the influence, and their only task was recognizing the strength of that influence. In this case, learning was made "too easy" for the participants. But it is as well possible that the sign of influence in the experimenter's model is different from the sign of influence expected by the participant from his/her experience. In this case, the participant is mislead by own knowledge.

Summing up, if the involved variables are named, the participants are likely to "set up their own model", and do not learn from the data as they would do if the variables were completely abstract.

Therefore, it seems to me more appropriate to use abstract variables.

---

[47] I am grateful to Professor Selten for these considerations.

1. Rationality in Presence of Exogenous Variables

1.1. Fully Rational and Least-Squares-Learning Predictions

Consider linear models of the form

$$p_t = \alpha_0 + r(t)'\alpha + u_t \ , \quad t = 1, \ldots, T \tag{1.1}$$

or

$$p_t = \alpha_0 + r(t-1)'\alpha + u_t \ , \quad t = 1, \ldots, T \tag{1.2}$$

where p is the endogenous variable, $r(t)$ is a vector of exogenous variables, α is a parameter vector of appropriate dimension, and u is stochastically independent white noise. Next, consider information structures of the form

$I_t^1 := \{p_1, r(1), p_2, r(2), \ldots, p_{t-1}, r(t-1)\} \qquad (t = 2, \ldots, T)$

$I_t^2 := I_t^1 \cup \{r(t)\} \qquad (t = 2, \ldots, T)$

In Model (1), the exogenous variables have *contemporary* influence whereas in Model (2) they have *lagged* influence. Information Structure I^1 contains the entire history of p and of the exogenous variables up to the previous period, Information Structure I^2 additionally contains the exogenous variables for the actual period.

Combining a model with an information structure gives four possible situations:

Situation 1: Model (1), Information Structure I^1,

Situation 2: Model (1), Information Structure I^2,

Situation 3: Model (2), Information Structure I^1,

Situation 4: Model (2), Information Structure I^2,

Now, imagine someone who has to forecast p_t based on one of these four situations.

In Situations 2-4, the values of the exogenous variables relevant for the forecast period are assumed to be available which will be called *full information (on exogenous variables)*. In the sequel, rational and least-squares-learning (LSL) predictions are derived for each one of these four situations.

Situation 1: The fully rational prediction (i.e. with knowledge of the true model) is

$$\begin{aligned} f_t^R &= \mathrm{E}[p_t \mid I_t^1] \\ &= \mathrm{E}[\alpha_0 + r(t)'\alpha + u_t \mid I_t^1] \\ &= \alpha_0 + \mathrm{E}[r(t)' \mid I_t^1]\,\alpha \end{aligned} \tag{1.3}$$

In order to forecast p, a rational subject first has to forecast $r(t)$. This is a complicated situation, in general. Some restrictive assumptions (e.g. mutual independence of the exogenous variables, simple stochastic laws governing them, for example random walks, trends) have to be made in order to simplify this task.

An LSL prediction based on a correctly specified model (see Chapter 0) is not possible in this situation since no information on exogenous variables for the forecast period is available and, therefore, the prediction estimator is not applicable.

Situation 2: Now, full information on the exogenous variables is available. The rational prediction is

$$\begin{aligned} f_t^R &= \mathrm{E}[p_t \mid I_t^2] \\ &= \alpha_0 + r(t)'\alpha \end{aligned} \tag{1.4}$$

Assuming t sufficiently large,[1] and denoting the parameter estimates from OLS regression based on the first $(t-1)$ observations by a_0^t, a^t, the least-squares-learning (LSL) prediction is

$$f_t^{LSL} = a_0^t + r(t)'a^t \ . \tag{1.5}$$

[1] $\geq$ number of exogenous variables $+2$.

It remains to be noted that in absence of a disturbance it is possible to forecast perfectly. The rational prediction equals the true value in that case. This holds even if some nonlinearity (e.g. rounding) is introduced. If the model is linear, the equality

$$\text{LSL prediction} \;=\; \text{fully rational prediction} \;=\; \text{true value} \qquad (1.6)$$

holds (in absence of disturbance).

Situation 3: Although the values of the exogenous variables for the forecast period are not given, there is full information on exogenous variables since they have lagged influence. The fully rational prediction is

$$f_t^R = \alpha_0 + r(t-1)'\alpha \qquad (1.7)$$

Provided t is sufficiently large,[2] let a_0^t, a^t denote the OLS estimates from regressing $p_2, \ldots, p_{t-1}$ on the exogenous variables from periods $1, \ldots, t-2$. Then

$$f_t^{LSL} = a_0^t + r(t-1)'a^t \qquad (1.8)$$

is the least-squares-learning prediction. In a deterministic linear model, Eq. (1.6) again holds.

Situation 4: The additional information available on the exogenous variables for the forecast period is not needed because of the lagged influence. Rational and LSL predictions are the same as in Situation 3.

To summarize, Situations 2 and 3 (full information on exogenous variables) provide an optimal background for least-squares learning and rational expectations. Therefore, these situations were investigated in the first nine experiments. Situation 1 is more difficult but also more realistic and was implemented in Exp. 10-14. Situation 4 will no longer be discussed since it is captured by Situation 3.

---

[2] $\geq$ number of exogenous variables $+3$.

1.2 Predictions Based on Misspecified Models

So far, rational and LSL predictions have been expressed in terms of *levels*. If subjects focus on *changes* rather than on levels, they may set up the model

$$p_t - p_{t-1} = (r(t) - r(t-1))'\alpha + \varepsilon_t \tag{1.9}$$

instead of Model (1) in Section 1.1 (contemporary influence), or

$$p_t - p_{t-1} = (r(t-1) - r(t-2))'\alpha + \varepsilon_t \tag{1.10}$$

instead of Model (2) (lagged influence), respectively, and consider ε as white noise. These "Delta Models"[3] are *misspecified*: A model derived from the true model by taking first differences would have a moving-average disturbance. One may now ask: What is the best a forecaster can do who uses this (misspecified) Delta model?

For notational convenience, let, from now on, E denote the conditional expectation, calculated from the *true* model and the information available (i.e. the conditioning will not be made explicit), and E^D denote the conditional expectation, calculated under the (wrong) assumption that the "Delta Model" holds. Furthermore, let $\Delta p_t = p_t - p_{t-1}$, $\Delta r(t) = r(t) - r(t-1)$, and $\Delta u_t = u_t - u_{t-1}$.

Remember that fully rational predictions are[4]

$$f_t^R = Ep_t = p_{-1} + E\Delta p_t$$

$$= p_{-1} + E\Delta r(t)'\alpha + E\Delta u_t \tag{1.11}$$

$$= p_{-1} + E\Delta r(t)'\alpha - u_{-1}$$

---

[3] The relevance of such auxiliary models is discussed below in Chapter 3.

[4] For Model 1 (contemporary influence). In case of lagged influence replace $\Delta r(t)$ by $\Delta r(t-1)$.

In contrast, the best possible prediction based on the delta model ("delta prediction") is

$$
\begin{aligned}
f_t^D &= p_{t-1} + E^D \Delta p_t \\
&= p_{t-1} + E^D \Delta r(t)'\alpha + E^D \varepsilon_t \qquad (1.12)\\
&= p_{t-1} + E^D \Delta r(t)'\alpha
\end{aligned}
$$

Assuming $E\Delta r(t) = E^D \Delta r(t)$[5], the crucial difference is due to the disturbances. For the fully rational forecaster (who knows the true model), u_{t-1} is observable, thus $E\Delta u_t$ is not zero in general. The Delta model, however, neglects this, $E^D \varepsilon_t$ is zero since ε is regarded as independent white noise.

Thus, rational predictions and delta predictions coincide only if the model is not disturbed.

The misspecification may be extended to the exogenous variables: Let $\tilde{r}$ denote a set of exogenous variables different from r (a subset, for example). Based on the misspecified model[6]

$$\Delta p_t = \Delta \tilde{r}(t)\tilde{\alpha} + \varepsilon_t \qquad (1.13)$$

the "misspecified prediction" is[7]

$$f_t^M = p_{-1} + E\Delta \tilde{r}(t)\tilde{\alpha}. \qquad (1.14)$$

The relevance of these "misspecified predictions" is studied below in Chapter 3.

Finally, delta predictions may be modified by introducing a constant c, $0 < c < 1$:

---

[5] This is questionable only for Situation 1 (contemporary influence, incomplete information on exogenous variables). For Situations 2 and 3 (for Situation 3, replace $r(t)$ by $r(t-1)$), the realizations of the exogenous variables are known. Thus, no expectations over $\Delta r(t)$ (or $\Delta r(t-1)$, resp.) have to be taken.

[6] The same considerations as above apply to the case of lagged influence.

[7] Assume $E^M \Delta \tilde{r}(t) = E\Delta \tilde{r}(t)$. See Footnote 5 for the case of full information on exogenous variables.

$$f_t^U = p_{-1} + c\,E^D \Delta p_t \tag{1.15}$$
$$= p_{-1} + c\,E \Delta r(t)'\alpha$$

These predictions are called "underestimating predictions" from now on. $E\Delta r(t)'\alpha$ may be replaced by $E\Delta\tilde{r}(t)'\tilde{\alpha}$ which gives "misspecified underestimating" predictions.

2. Experimental Design and Notation

2.1 Experimental Design

The experiments took place at the computer terminals of the laboratory for experimental economics at the University of Bonn. 14 experiments were run, each experiment with about 12 subjects. In total, there were 167 subjects. The subjects were not allowed to participate in more than one experiment, and they were independent of one another.

Over a number of periods (80 or 100 periods, depending on the experiment), each subject successively had to forecast the next value of a certain time series which contained only integer numbers. The subject had the opportunity to correct an entered forecast (in case of a typing error, for example) before confirming it definitively. After confirmation, the true value was displayed on the screen, and the subject could go on to the next period.

In each period, the subject was given some information on the screen. This information at least consisted of the past development of the time series to be forecasted (time series of the "endogenous variable") and two or three exogenous variables possibly influencing the endogenous variable. This "history" was presented in tabulated form (over the last 15 periods)[1] and in graphical form (over the last 30 periods). Thus, for giving this information already in the starting period ($t = 1$), all involved time series' must start in $t = -29$.

Before starting the experiment, a preliminary discussion took place in order to explain technical details and the general setting (for example: that the variable to be forecasted (p) is influenced by the other variables). Subjects were told that the underlying model did not change in the experiment and, in addition, were given some hints on the model (see below). Subjects were shown (by means of a slide projector) how the tables, the graphics, and the display of the results on the computer screen look like.

---

[1] See Figure 2.1 below.

In order to provide appropriate incentives, each subject was paid out a reward at the end of the experiment. This reward was a constant of DM 5.00 plus an amount proportional to the subject's *final score*. The score was calculated as follows: The initial score was zero, and, after each period,

$$max\{-20, 30 - \text{squared forecast error}\} \tag{2.1}$$

was added. The lower limit at -20 was introduced in order to avoid high losses as a consequence of typing errors.[2] If the resulting score was negative, it was set to zero. Thus, the score was calculated iteratively according to

$$\text{Score}_t = max\{0\ ,\quad \text{Score}_{t-1} + max\{-20, 30 - \text{squ. error in } t\}\}\ . \tag{2.2}$$

The final score is the score after the last period.

Given this general design, each experiment is characterized by
1. the *model* generating the time series to be forecasted,
2. the *information* given for forecasting.

The basic *model* used in all experiments is a linear econometric model involving two or three exogenous variables.

The *information* given varies

1. in the number of exogenous variables displayed. All relevant exogenous variables were displayed but one of the displayed variables could be irrelevant ("sunspot variable").

2. in the inclusion or non-inclusion of the values of the exogenous variables relevent for the forecast period (see the different information structures in Section 1.1).

According to the criteria *model* and *information*, the 11 experiments run so far may be subdivided into three groups:

Group 1 (Exp. 1-6): These are the "simplest" experiments: Four variants of the simple linear model are used, involving the exogenous variables x, y, and z.

---

2 For example, a forecast error of 100 would otherwise lead to a subtraction of 9970.

(a) $p_t = \alpha_0 + \alpha_x x_t + \alpha_y y_t + \alpha_z z_t$
(contemporary influence, no disturbance: Exp. 1-2)

(b) $p_t = \alpha_0 + \alpha_x x_{t-1} + \alpha_y y_{t-1} + \alpha_z z_{t-1}$
(lagged influence, no disturbance: Exp. 3)

(c) $p_t = \alpha_0 + \alpha_x x_t + \alpha_y y_t + \alpha_z z_t + u_t$
(contemporary influence, disturbance): Exp. 4-5)

(d) $p_t = \alpha_0 + \alpha_x x_{t-1} + \alpha_y y_{t-1} + \alpha_z z_{t-1} + u_t$
(lagged influence, disturbance): Exp. 6

(where p denotes the endogenous, x, y, z the exogenous variables, and u is the disturbance term). In Exp. 2 and 4, the parameter α_y was not integer. To avoid non-integer values of p, a slight nonlinearity was introduced by rounding.[3]

The information provided for forecasting consisted of the history of x, y, z, and p. In case of contemporary influence of the exogenous variables, the values of x, y, and z for the forecast period were included (see "Situation 2" in Chapter 1). This was not necessary when the influence was lagged (See "Situation 3" in Ch. 1), but, in this case, subjects were informed about the lagged influence. In either case, full information on exogenous variables is given as explaind above in Chapter 1. The tables showing the "history" looked like this (for Period 1 (starting period), the numbers are only illustrative):

---

[3] See below, Table 2.1.

Figure 2.1: Tabulated information on "history"

Period	X	Y	Z	P
−14	156	119	105	30
−13	155	122	101	35
−12	156	122	97	40
−11	155	125	98	39
−10	158	125	102	38
−9	157	127	101	39
−8	160	131	99	46
−7	159	132	98	47
−6	162	133	104	44
−5	161	136	104	45
−4	167	139	104	52
−3	167	140	103	54
−2	163	141	99	54
−1	164	142	105	50
0	163	143	107	47
1	159	142	106	?

For Period 2, the tabulated history covered Periods $-13, \ldots, 1$, and so forth.

The values of the exogenous variables for the forecast period (Period 1) were included in order to give full information. For experiments with lagged influence of x, y, and z (Exp. 3 and 6), this was not done since it was not necessary (See discussion on "Situation 3" in Section 1.1).

In the deterministic experiments (1-3), the rational prediction equals the true value, and it is possible to forecast perfectly. Indeed, some participants in these experiments eventually grasped the underlying model and forecasted perfectly.

In the preliminary discussion, subjects were informed about the presence of a stochastic disturbance and about its range (for Exp. 4-6 where a disturbance occurred). In case of a lagged influence (Exp. 3 and 6), subjects were informed that the exogenous variables' influence was lagged by one period. For the remaining experiments, the contemporary influence was not explicitly announced but sufficiently suggested by the information on x, y, and z for the forecast period. Indeed, it turned out that no subject erroneously presumed a lagged influence. In no case subjects were told that the model was linear. Concerning the relevance of x, y, and z, subjects were told that at least one of them was relevant and that all relevant variables were displayed (no hidden variables).

Group 2 (Exp. 7-9): After studying the simple models in Exp. 1-6, a seasonal (Exp. 7 and 8) or an autoregressive (Exp. 9) component, resp., was added to the linear model. For simplicity, the disturbance was dropped, only contemporary influence of exogenous variables occurred, and full information on exogenous variables was included as in Exp. 1-6.

Since neither disturbance nor lagged influence was present, there was no need to mention these features in the preliminary discussion. Concerning the relevance of the displayed exogenous variables, the same information was given as in Exp. 1-6. In case of a seasonal component (Exp. 7 and 8), subjects were told that "there may be a seasonal influence". In case of the autoregressive component (Exp. 9), subjects were told that "there is some additional, different influence". As in Exp. 1-6, subjects were not told that the model is linear.

Since all underlying models are deterministic, rational predictions again equal true realizations, and it is possible to forecast perfectly (but no subject in these experiments succeeded in comprehending the model).

Group 3 (Exp. 10-14) This group turned back to simple linear models with partly contemporary influence of exogenous variables but full information on exogenous variables was no longer given. This is a more realistic situation than that studied in the first two groups.

In this situation - incomplete information on exogenous variables - a subject possibly tries to forecast the exogenous variables as a first step to forecast p (see discussion of rational predictions in "Situation 1", Section 1.1). In order to enable the subject to do this, only two exogenous variables following simple stochastic processes were employed: The variable v follows a random walk, and the variable w has an alternating trend: The movement changes direction every 10 periods. More specifically, v was generated as

$$v_1 = 100 \quad , \qquad v_t = v_{t-1} + \varepsilon_t \ , t \geq 2 \ , \tag{2.3}$$

where ε was independent white noise, distributed uniformly on $\{-3, -2, \ldots, 2, 3\}$; and w was generated as

$$w_1 = 150 \quad , \qquad w_t = w_{t-1} + c_t + \eta_t \ , t \geq 2 \ , \tag{2.4}$$

$$c_t = \begin{cases} -2 & t = 1, \ldots, 10, 21, \ldots, 30, \ldots \\ 2 & t = 11, \ldots, 20, 31, \ldots, 40, \ldots \end{cases}$$

where η_t was independent white noise, distributed uniformly on $\{-2, -1, 0, 1, 2\}$.

Eq. (2.3) and (2.4) imply $E\Delta v_t = 0$ for all t, and

$$E\Delta w_t = \begin{cases} -2 & t = 1, \ldots, 10, 21, \ldots, 30, \ldots \\ 2 & t = 11, \ldots, 20, 31, \ldots, 40, \ldots \end{cases} \tag{2.5}$$

The tabulated history looks similar to Fig. 2.1, with the following modifications:

1. The exogenous variables were v and w.
2. The values of v and w for the forecast period (last row in Fig. 2.1) are not given.

Perfect forecasting is not possible - even if the underlying model is not disturbed - since full information on exogenous variables is not available.

For those experiments where partly lagged influence occurred (Exp. 11 and 12), subjects were told that "one of the variables v and w may have lagged influence". In case of a stochastic disturbance (Exp. 13 and 14), subjects were informed about the disturbance and about its range. For all experiments of this group, subjects were told that "v has no systematic trend" and "w has an alternating trend". This was done in order to point out that v and w are simple stochastic processes which can easily be forecasted. Again, subjects were not told that the model is linear.

The exact model specifications and the information given for each experiment are summarized in the following table:

Table 2.1: Characteristics of each experiment

Exp. No.	Model	Information
1	$p = 120 + y - 2z$	History of x, y, z, and p; x, y, and z for actual period.
2	$p = -80 + x + [\frac{1}{2}y] - z$	see Exp. 1
3	$p = 85 - x_{-1} + y_{-1}$	History of x, y, z, and p (full information due to lagged influence); "lagged influence of exogenous variables"
4	$p = -80 + x + [\frac{1}{2}y] - z + u$	see Exp. 1
5	$p = 20 + y - z + u$	see Exp. 1
6	$p = 85 - x_{-1} + y_{-1} + u$	see Exp. 3
7	$p = 12 + y - z + 5(t \textit{ modulo } 4)$	see Exp. 1; "and possibly seasonal influence"
8	$p = 10 + y - z + 5(t \textit{ modulo } 5)$	History of y, z, and p; y and z for actual period; "and possibly seasonal influence"
9	$p = -7 + y - z + [\frac{1}{2}p_{-1}]$	see Exp. 1; "and some additional influence"
10	$p = 100 + v - w$	History of v, w, and p; "v has no systematic trend"; "w has an alternating trend".
11	$p = 100 + v_{-1} - w$	see Exp. 10; "and possibly lagged influence"
12	$p = 100 + v - w_{-1}$	see Exp. 11
13	$p = 200 - w + u$	see Exp. 10
14	$p = 150 - v + u$	see Exp. 10

Notes on the table:

1. The time index t has been dropped for simplicity.
2. $[a]$ denotes the integer part of a.
3. $1 \textit{ modulo } 4 = 1$, $2 \textit{ modulo } 4 = 2$,
   $3 \textit{ modulo } 4 = 3$, $4 \textit{ modulo } 4 = 0$,
   $5 \textit{ modulo } 4 = 1$, $\ldots$, $7 \textit{ modulo } 4 = 3$, $8 \textit{ modulo } 4 = 0$,
   and so forth
4. The disturbance u is independent white noise, uniformly distributed on $\{-2, -1, 0, 1, 2\}$

After the 20th, 40th, 60th, ... period, each subject was asked to fill out a questionnaire on his/her opinion about the relations between the exogenous variables and the endogenous variable.

On the following four pages, the plots of p and of the involved exogenous are given for Exp. 5 (Group 1: Simple linear models), Exp. 7 and 9 (Group 2: Additional influences - seasonality for Exp. 7 and auto-regressive component for Exp. 9), and Exp. 12 (Group 3: Incomplete information, special exogenous variables).

Figure 2.2 Plot of Exp. 5

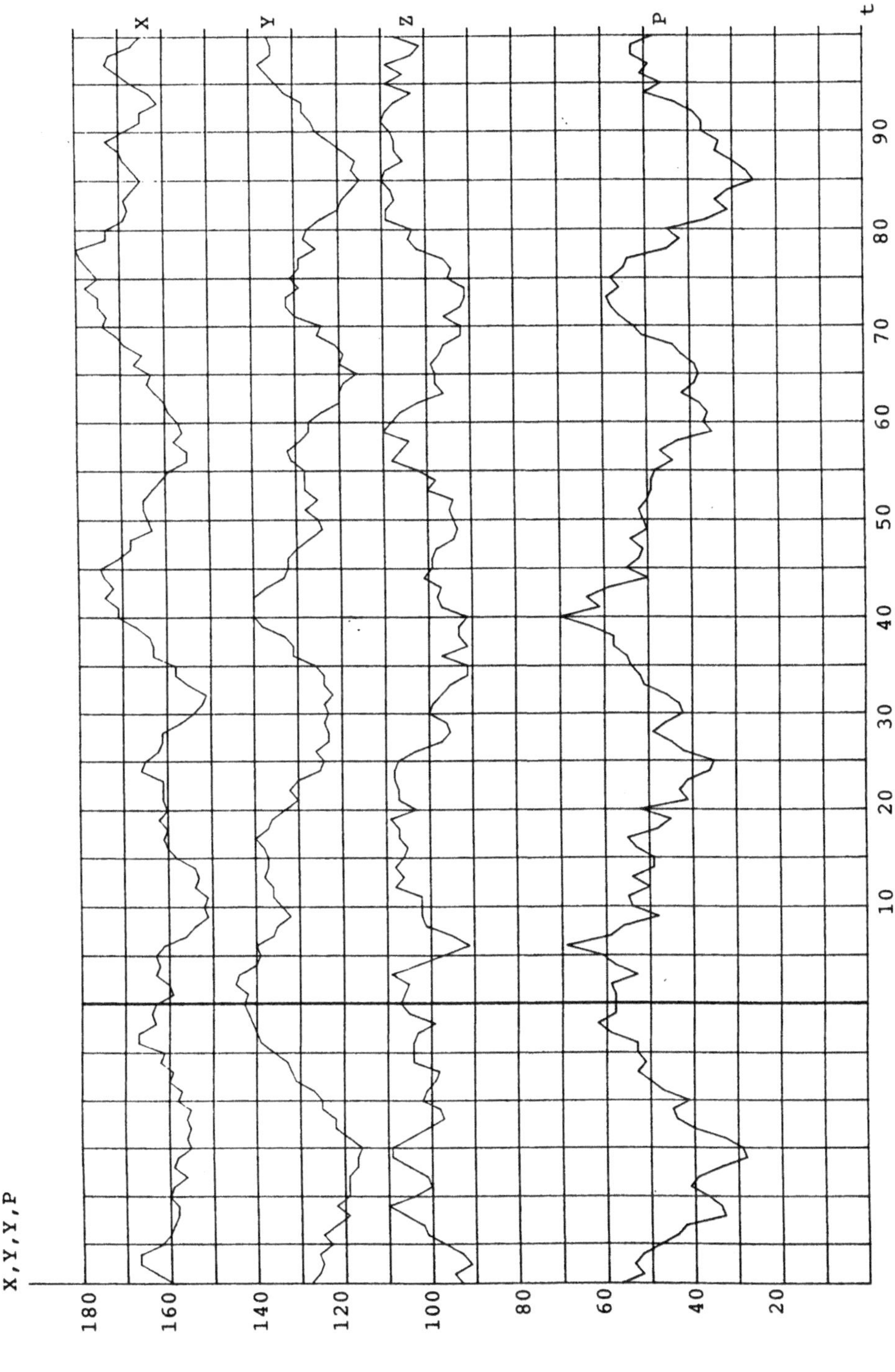

Figure 2.3 Plot of Exp. 7

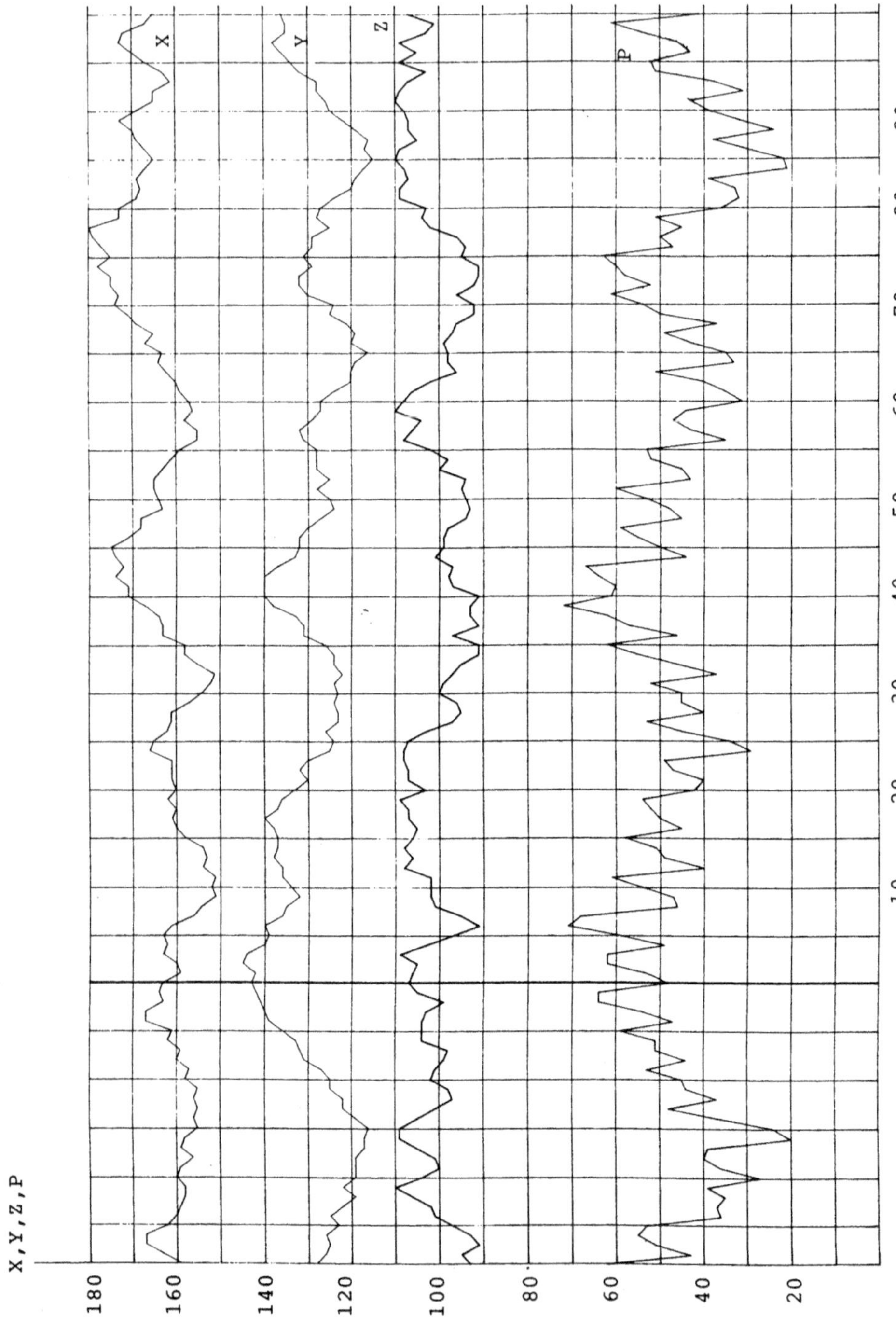

Figure 2.4 Plot of Exp. 9

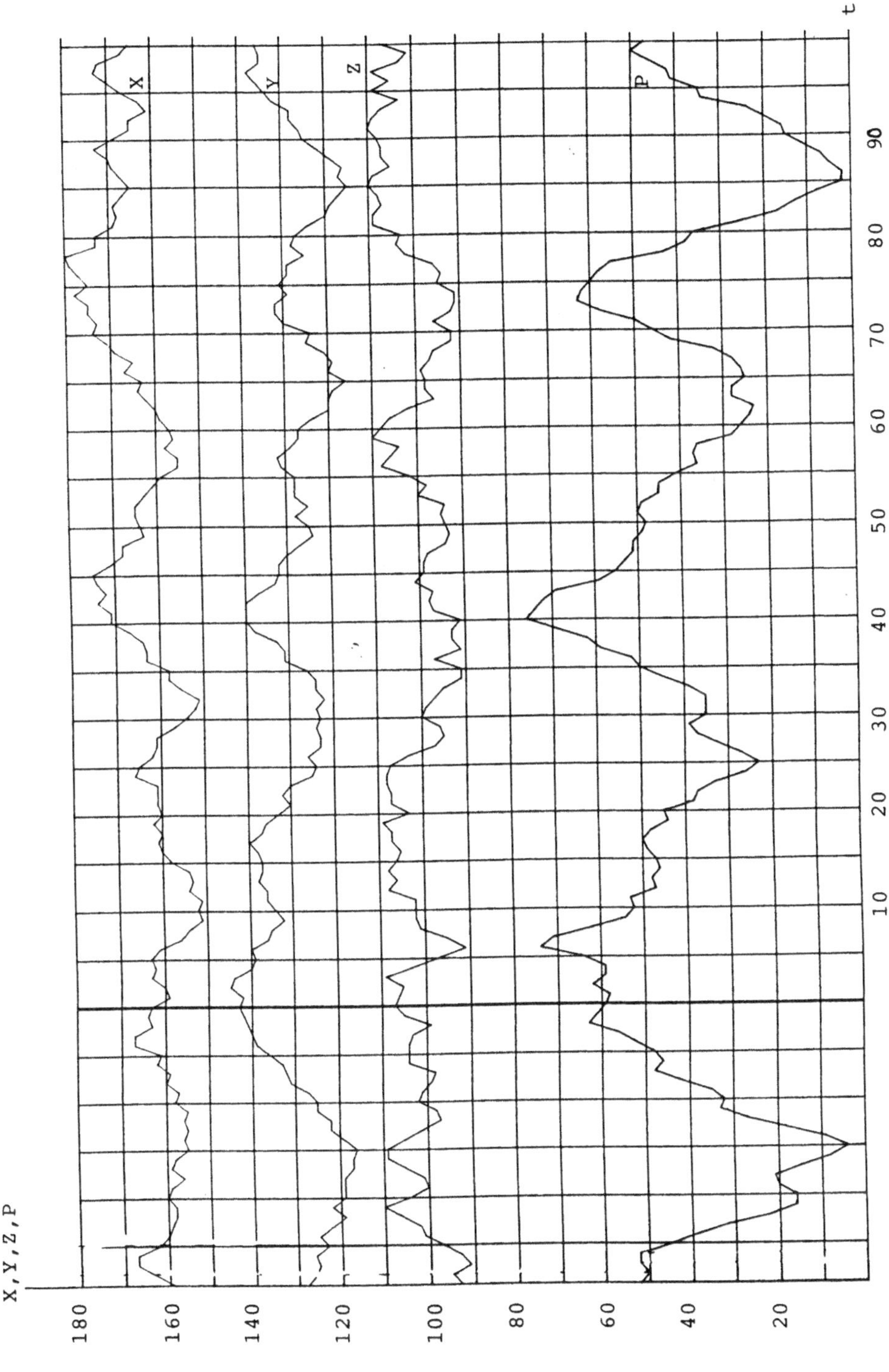

Figure 2.5 Plot of Exp. 12

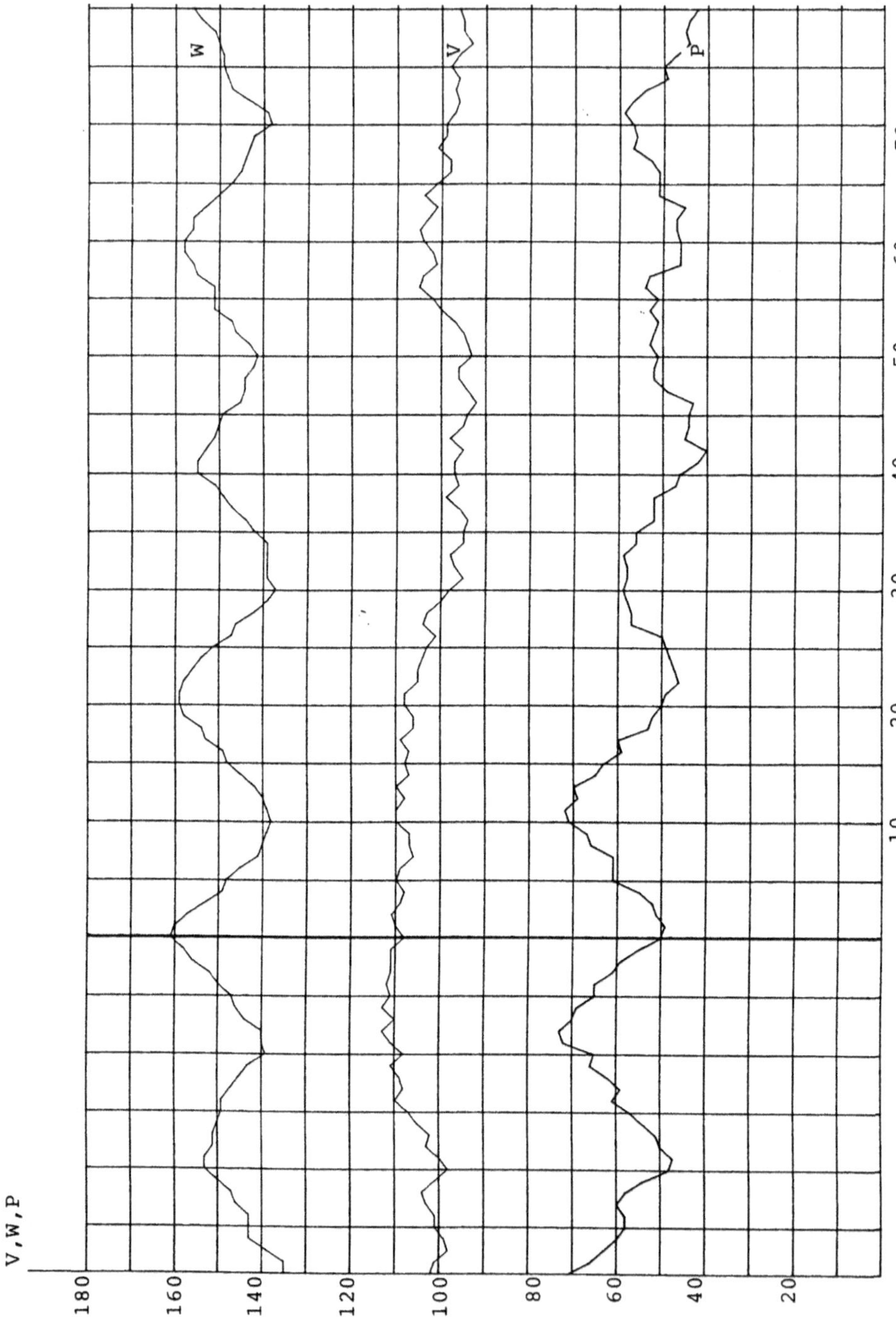

2.2 Notation

To avoid overly long verbal expressions, some notation and abbreviations have to be introduced.

First, the concepts of *prediction*, *forecast*, and *expectations* once again have to be clarified: In the experiments, individual *forecasts* were observed, and aggregate (average and median) *forecasts* were derived from them. In contrast, *predictions* always refer to some theoretical concept (e.g. rational, LSL, or delta predictions). Observed forecasts may be compared to theoretical predictions according to a certain concept. In contrast to this, the notion *expectations* is always referred to statistical expectations. Thus, "expected change" always means statistical expected change, calculated from a (true or misspecified) model, in contrast to *forecasted* changes observed in the experiments.

The time series to be forecasted is denoted by p, and x, y, z, v, w are exogenous variables. Observed forecasts are denoted by f, and predictions according to a certain prediction concept are marked by a superscript; for example, f^{LSL} denotes least-squares learning predictions.

To avoid excessive notation, an index for the experiment number is never included. It will always be obvious from the context which experiment is referred to.

Notation:

N = number of participants in the experiment,
T = number of periods in the experiment.

Forecasts/Predictions:

$f_{t,i}$ = individual i's forecast in period t ($i = 1, \ldots, N$).

$f_{t,A} = (1/N) \sum_{i=1}^{N} f_{t,i}$ = average forecast in period t.

$f_{t,M}$ = Median$[f_{t,1}, \ldots, f_{t,N}]$ = median forecast in period t.

f_t^R = rational prediction for period t (see Section 1.1).

f_t^{LSL} = least-squares-learning prediction for period t (see Section 1.1).

f_t^D = delta prediction for t (see Section 1.2).

f_t^M = misspecified prediction for t (see Section 1.2, to be specified in the context).

f_t^U = underestimating prediction for t (see Section 1.2, to be specified in the context).

Statistics calculated from forecasts/predictions:

$ME_i = (1/T)\sum_{t=1}^{T}(f_{t,i} - p_t)$ = mean forecast error of individual i.

$MAE_i = (1/T)\sum_{t=1}^{T}|f_{t,i} - p_t|$ = i's mean absolute forecast error.

$MD_i^{xx} = (1/T)\sum_{t=1}^{T}(f_{t,i} - f_t^{xx})$ mean deviation of i's forecasts from predictions according to concept xx. For example,

$MD_i^{LSL} = (1/T)\sum_{t=1}^{T}(f_{t,i} - f_t^{LSL})$ = mean deviation from least-squares-learning predictions).

$MAD_i^{xx} = (1/T)\sum_{t=1}^{T}|f_{t,i} - f_t^{xx}|$ = mean absolute deviation of i's forecasts from predictions according to xx.

For average and median predictions, the individual index i is replaced by A and M, respectively. If obvious from the context, sub- or superscripts sometimes are omitted for simplicity.

Expected values:

As already stated in Section 1.2, the notation for conditioning is simplified since all expected values studied are conditional ones.

$E\Delta p_t = \mathrm{E}[p_t - p_{t-1} \mid \text{History, true model}]$ = (rationally) "expected change".

$E^D\Delta p_t = \mathrm{E}[p_t - p_{t-1} \mid \text{History, delta model}]$ = "delta-expected change".

$E^M\Delta p_t = \mathrm{E}[p_t - p_{t-1} \mid \text{History, misspecified model}]$ = "misspecified expected change".

Since, in our setting, conditional expected changes of *exogenous* variables do not differ with respect to the conditioning model, the superscript may be dropped in this case, for example

$$E\Delta w = E^D\Delta w = E^M\Delta w \ .$$

3. Aggregate Forecasts

There are two concepts of aggregating individual forecasts: taking *averages* and *medians*. For each experiment, the time series of *average forecasts*, f_A, consists of the arithmetic means from individual forecasts[1] for each period:

$$f_{t,A} = \frac{1}{N} \sum_{i=1}^{N} f_{t,i} \quad , \qquad t = 1, \ldots, T \tag{3.1}$$

Analogously, the time series f_M of *median forecasts* is obtained as

$$f_{t,M} = \text{Median}[f_{t,1}, \ldots, f_{t,N}] \quad , \qquad t = 1, \ldots, T \tag{3.2}$$

For each experiment, one time series of average forecasts and one series of median forecasts result, i.e. 28 series from all 14 experiments. These series are analyzed in this chapter.

From now on, the first 20 forecasts are always dropped. The results are very similar to those obtained by processing all forecasts (and all results obtained hold for the total, too) which is a consequence of the fact that the initial phase of 20 forecasts is short in relation to the whole experiment which consists of 80 or 100 forecasts, resp. However, as will be shown in Section 3.5, learning behavior occurs within the first 20 periods but generally not after Period 20. In addition, from the questionnaires it is seen that only a minority of subjects changed their opinion on the model after Period 20. This suggests that forecasting behavior is in some sense stable after period 20 but not at the beginning of the experiment. Therefore, the analysis is restricted to the "stable" phase after period 20. As far as the "unstable" phase at the beginning of the experiment is concerned, there are too few observations for serious analysis.

The first natural question is: Do average and median forecasts noticeably differ from one another? The following table shows mean and mean

[1] An extra index for the experiment number is dropped for simplicity, see Section 2.2.

absolute differences between average and median forecasts, calculated as follows:

$$MDif = \frac{1}{T-20}\sum_{t=21}^{T}(f_{t,A} - f_{t,M})$$

$$MADif = \frac{1}{T-20}\sum_{t=21}^{T}|f_{t,A} - f_{t,M}| \qquad (3.3)$$

Note that the first 20 observations have been dropped - as explained above.

For comparison, the *mean absolute forecasted change*

$$MAFC = \frac{1}{T-20}\sum_{t=21}^{T}|f_t - p_{t-1}| \qquad (3.4)$$

is included for both average and median forecasts.

Table 3.1: Mean and Mean Absolute Differences between Average and Median Forecasts (Periods 21-end)

Exp. No.	*MDif*	*MADif*	*MAFC* for average f.	*MAFC* for median f.
1	−0.080	0.771	4.466	4.850
2	0.080	0.695	2.932	3.431
3	0.076	0.605	2.007	2.475
4	0.110	0.427	2.740	2.844
5	0.106	0.425	1.754	1.856
6	−0.007	0.480	1.270	1.367
7	−0.684	1.341	3.358	3.888
8	0.432	1.400	5.847	6.738
9	0.102	0.457	1.995	2.263

(continued)

Table 3.1 (continued)

Exp. No.	*MDif*	*MADif*	*MAFC* for average f.	*MAFC* for median f.
10	0.079	0.376	0.945	0.942
11	−0.004	0.339	1.223	1.283
12	0.049	0.303	1.184	1.300
13	−0.009	0.348	1.124	1.308
14	−0.101	0.346	0.845	0.691

For the simple differences, both signs occur about equally often. The mean absolute differences are generally less than half of the mean absolute forecasted change. Note that for 12 out of 14 experiments (exceptions are Exp. 10 and 14), the mean absolute forecasted change of medians exceeds that of averages. This is the only systematic difference found between average and median forecasts.

3.1 Forecast Error and Deviations from Rational Predictions

The simplest feature of forecasts to be analyzed is the error, i.e. the deviation from realizations of p. For full information[2] experiments with deterministic model (Exp. 1-3, 7-9), the forecast error equals the deviation from expected p, the *rational* prediction. For the remaining experiments - full-information experiments with disturbed model (Exp. 4-6) and incomplete-information experiments (Exp. 10-14), it is natural to compare the forecast error to the deviations from rational predictions.

The following table (split up into two parts) presents the results. The table gives mean and mean absolute errors and deviations from rational predictions (ME, MAE, MD^R, MAD^R, see Section 2.2 on Notation) for average (first part of the table) and median (second part of the table) forecasts. The first 20 periods are dropped as explained above.

---

[2] (on exogenous variables)

Table 3.2: Errors and Deviations from Rational Predictions
Part 1: Average forecasts (Periods 21-end)

Exp. No.	ME_A	MD_A^R	MAE_A	MAD_A^R
1	0.120	1	1.264	1
2	0.086	1	0.921	1
3	0.101	1	0.630	1
4	0.138	−0.058	1.990	1.785
5	0.375	0.038	2.223	1.889
6	0.043	−0.141	2.415	2.031
7	2.066	1	5.711	1
8	0.282	1	3.598	1
9	0.415	1	2.295	1
10	0.087	0.120	2.254	1.192
11	0.130	0.063	2.009	1.863
12	0.249	0.049	1.834	0.836
13	−0.034	0.232	2.071	1.804
14	−0.693	−0.276	2.307	0.905

Part 2: Median forecasts (Periods 21-end)

Exp. No.	ME_M	MD_M^R	MAE_M	MAD_M^R
1	0.200	1	0.538	1
2	0.006	1	0.281	1
3	0.025	1	0.025	1
4	0.169	−0.169	1.894	1.731
5	0.269	−0.069	2.156	1.869
6	0.050	−0.133	2.517	2.133
7	2.750	1	6.175	1
8	−0.150	1	2.638	1
9	0.313	1	2.213	1
10	0.008	0.042	2.342	1.158
11	0.133	0.067	1.933	1.800
12	0.200	0.000	1.800	0.700
13	−0.025	0.242	1.958	1.792
14	−0.592	−0.175	2.292	0.792

Note on the table: [1] means: error = deviation from rational prediction.

Looking at the results column by column, one obtains:

Columns 1 and 2: Mean errors and mean deviations from rational predictions are mainly positive: For example, mean deviations from rational predictions are positive for 9 (median forecasts) or 11 (average forecasts) out of 14 experiments. This indicates an upward bias which will be studied in more detail in Section 3.3.

Columns 3 and 4: For all experiments where rational prediction and true realization differ (Exp. 4-6, 10-14), the MAD from rational predictions is *smaller* than the MAE: Observed aggregate forecasts are more close to rational predictions than to true realizations.

The smallest mean absolute errors occur in the simple deterministic model experiments 1-3, the highest occur in the seasonality experiments (7 and 8). For the latter, the mean absolute change $(1/T)\sum_{t=1}^{T}|p_t - p_{t-1}|$ is about 8 (whereas it ranges from 3 to 5 for the other experiments). This may be the reason for the high errors in the seasonality experiments.

Note that errors of *median* forecasts in the simple deterministic model experiments 1-3 are very small. This is due to the fact that in many periods a majority of subjects forecasted correctly which implies that the median equals the realization (= rational prediction in these experiments). In Exp. 3, after period 40 all median forecasts are correct.

Except for Exp. 1-3, mean absolute deviations from rational predictions are about halfth of the mean absolute change. This is too high for accepting rationality as a good explanation of observed forecasting behavior.

Summing up, the following three statements can be made:

1. Forecasts reveal a slight *upward bias*.
2. Forecasts are more close to rational predictions than to realizations.
3. Compared to the mean absolute change of the variable to be forecasted, the deviations are too high as to accept rationality as an explanation of forecasting behavior.

The "lack of rationality" is also easily verified by estimating the regression

$$f_t - p_{t-1} = \beta_0 + \beta\, E\Delta p + u \tag{3.5}$$

which yields estimated slope coefficients significantly less than one and, therefore, contradicts rationality. The results of these regressions are presented in context with the observed "underestimation of changes" in Section 3.3.

Since this is the first place where tests based on regression results are mentioned, it seems advisable to notify that the application of these tests requires normality of the forecasted changes which is not fulfilled, in general. However, average forecasted changes are nearly normally distributed which can be seen from the following figure (as an example):

Figure 3.1
Frequency distribution of average forecasted changes from Exp. 12

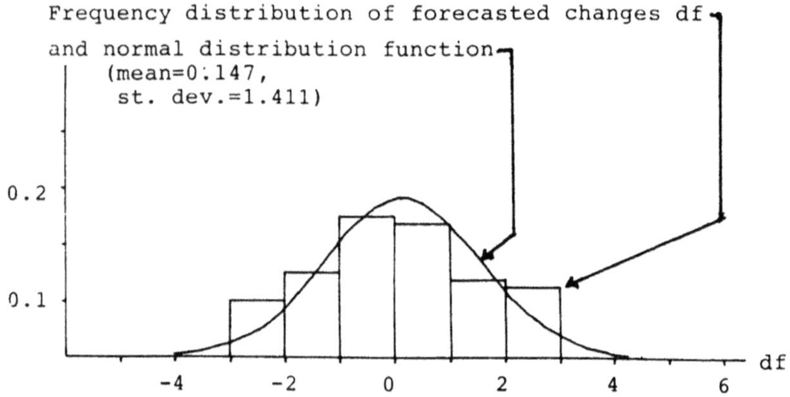

For median forecasts and even for individual forecasts, a similar symmetric distribution is found. However, for individual forecasts only integer numbers occur, and, therefore, for median forecasts, the support is $\{0, \pm\frac{1}{2}, \pm 1, \pm\frac{3}{2}, \ldots\}$ (if the number of subjects is even) and $\{0, \pm 1, \pm 2, \ldots\}$ (if the number of subjects is odd), resp. Thus, some care has to be taken in particular when median and individual forecasts are concerned. This has to be kept in mind throughout this and all following chapters.

3.2 Least-Squares Learning

After studying the deviations from rational predictions which are striking enough to reject rationality, the concept of least-squares learning (LSL) is investigated, without expecting it to reveal better results since the concept closely approximates rational predictions due to the consistency of the OLS estimator.

As explained in previous chapters, LSL is investigated only in context with a correctly specified auxiliary model, thus, the set of variables used for the auxiliary model is fixed. But some freedom remains to choose the set of observations processed in the regression. As stated above in the description of experimental design, in every period, the last 15 observations of all relevant variables are displayed in *tabulated* form, i.e. in ($t = 1$) the observations from periods -14 to 0 in ($t = 2$) the observations from periods -13 to 1 (so the observation from period -14 is no longer displayed); and so forth. A hypothetical subject who implements LSL has at least the following two alternatives:

Implementation 1: Use *all* past observations for regression (in period t: the observations from periods $-14, -13, \ldots, t-1$). The number of observations processed rises each period. Therefore, the resulting estimates should converge to the true model parameters.

Implementation 2: Use only the observations currently displayed on the screen (in period t: the observations from periods $t - 15$, $t - 14$, ..., $t - 1$. The number of observations processed is constant throughout the experiment. Therefore, no consistency results apply.

Many other implementations are imaginable. For both implementations, the following particularities have to be noted:

1. Remember that correctly specified LSL is not possible if information on exogenous variables is incomplete (Exp. 10-14).

2. For full information experiments with linear deterministic model, (Exp. 1, 3, 7, 8), both implementations of LSL give predictions equal to rational predictions and realizations.

3. The latter experiments include the two seasonality experiments (7, 8). For these experiments, a correctly specified OLS regression must include seasonal dummy variables.

4. For the autoregressive model (Exp. 9), the lagged value of p must be included as predetermined variable for correct specification.

Now the time series of LSL predictions can be calculated for each of the first nine experiments and for both implementations. As explained above, LSL predictions differ from rational ones only for Exp. 2, 4-6, and 9.

Mean and mean absolute deviations of average and median forecasts from LSL predictions (*MD*, *MAD*) are summarized in the following two tables (the first for average and the second for median forecasts).

Table 3.3: Deviations from rational and LSL predictions
Average Forecasts, Periods 21-end

	Mean Deviations from ...			Mean Abs. Dev. from ...		
Exp. No.	Rat. Pred.	LSL(1)	LSL(2)	Rat. Pred.	LSL(1)	LSL(2)
2	0.086	0.135	0.122	0.921	0.936	0.928
4	−0.058	0.656	0.345	1.785	1.727	1.598
5	0.038	0.703	0.405	1.889	1.895	1.876
6	−0.141	0.005	0.113	2.031	1.974	1.577
9	0.415	0.425	0.400	2.295	2.281	2.264

Table 3.4: Deviations from rational and LSL predictions
Median Forecasts, Periods 21-end

	Mean Deviations from ...			Mean Abs. Dev. from ...		
Exp. No.	Rat. Pred.	LSL(1)	LSL(2)	Rat. Pred.	LSL(1)	LSL(2)
2	0.006	0.055	0.042	0.281	0.425	0.404
4	−0.169	0.546	0.234	1.731	1.649	1.532
5	−0.069	0.597	0.298	1.869	1.874	1.851
6	−0.133	0.012	0.120	2.133	2.133	1.715
9	0.313	0.323	0.298	2.213	2.220	2.203

In all cases, mean deviations from LSL predictions are positive which confirms the observed upward bias.

Turning to mean absolute deviations, the following is observed:

1. The mean absolute deviations from rational predictions and from LSL (Implementation 1) hardly differ from one another.

2. Comparing the implementations of LSL to each other, the MAD from LSL(2) (only last 15 observations processed) is less than the MAD from LSL(1) (all past observations processed) without exception.

The first observation is easily explained by the fact that LSL closely approximates rational predictions (in particular LSL(1)). Thus, as was expected, least-squares-learning cannot be regarded as a satisfactory explanation of observed forecasting behavior.

The following section discusses some phenomena closely related to this "lack of rationality". After that, a prediction rule is presented which captures observed aggregate forecasts much better.

3.3 Some Non-Rational Features of Forecasts

In this section the following phenomena, closely related to the observed "lack of rationality", are studied:
- Upward Bias
- Concentration on "changes" rather than on "levels"
- Misspecified auxiliary models
- Underestimation of changes
- Adaptive and extrapolative behavior

Upward Bias

No matter what observed aggregate forecasts are compared to - true values, rational predictions, LSL predictions - the mean deviations are positive for at least 9 out of 14 experiments. But some care has to be taken with this result:

First, the positive deviation is not significant (at the 5% level) for any single experiment - except Exp. 7 (based on a Wilcoxon rank sum test of the hypothesis that the mean deviation is zero).

Second, the greatest (positive) mean deviations from rational predictions occur in the seasonality experiment 7. In this experiment repeatedly a moderate growth over 3 or 4 periods was followed by a sharp "crash". Therefore, the bias may be due to the fact that most participants well captured the moderate growth but often failed to forecast the crashes. This asymmetry - high number of (moderate) positive changes and low number of (sharp) negative changes - is obvious in the two seasonality experiments but is also - slightly - present in other experiments since unfortunately the experiments were not designed to test for bias. The time series was only inspected graphically and analytically for the fact that no overall trend occurred (which would mislead the participants).

The following table summarizes the number of negative, null and positive expected changes of p (calculated from the true model), and, reproduced from Table 3.2 above, the mean deviations from rational predictions (for average forecasts, Periods 21-end).

Table 3.5: Summarized results on Bias (Periods 21-end)

Exp. No.	No. of observations	No. of neg. ch.	No. of null ch.	No. of pos. ch.	Mean dev. from rat. pred.
1	80	36	3	41	0.120
2	80	32	10	38	0.086
3	60	27	11	22	0.101
4	80	28	6	46	−0.058
5	80	31	3	46	0.038
6	60	27	8	25	−0.141
7	80	25	1	54	2.066
8	80	22	3	55	0.282
9	80	38	6	36	0.415
10	60	30	–	30	0.120
11	60	24	13	23	0.063
12	60	23	11	26	0.049
13	60	29	7	24	0.232
14	60	23	16	21	−0.276

Viewing the number of negative and positive changes, one sees that Exp. 7-8 are heavily and Exp. 4-5 slightly unbalanced. Exp. 7-8 should definitively be excluded from consideration. For the remaining experiments, the mean deviation is not greater in the "unbalanced" experiments (4-5) than in the "balanced" ones. The hypothesis that positive and negative mean deviations occur with equal frequency, cannot be rejected at the 5% level: three out of twelve (after exclusion of Exp. 7 and 8) experiments have negative mean deviation. For median forecasts, there are even four "exceptions" (Exp. 4-6 and 14, see Table 3.2, Part 2). If, however, all periods are considered, only one exception (Exp. 14) remains for average and two for median forecasts (Exp. 4 and 14) which is significant at the 5% level (one-sided binomial test of H_0: *"equal frequencies"*).

Summing up, upward bias is apparent but not significant. More conclusive results will be obtained by summing over individual forecasts (see Chapter 4).

Concentration on "Changes" rather than on "Levels"

A view over the answers given in the questionnaires showed that those subjects who gave quantitative statements on the model generally did not express their guesses about the model in terms of "levels" (like "$p = 60 + 3x - y$") but rather in terms of "changes" (like "$\Delta p = 3\,\Delta x - \Delta y$"). In particular, no subject (except those who already comprehended the true model) ever worried about the intercept.

In more theoretical terms, subjects seem to set up an auxiliary model ("Delta Model", see Chapter 1)

$$\Delta p = r(t)'\beta + \varepsilon \tag{3.6}$$

and treat the disturbance ε as white noise - a fact that is crucial since it implies that the "Delta Model" is misspecified and predictions based on it differ from rational ones (see Chapter 1). Recall that the delta prediction is

$$f_t^D = p_{t-1} + E\Delta r(t)'\beta \tag{3.7}$$

whereas the rational prediction is

$$f_t^R = p_{t-1} + E\Delta r(t)'\beta + E\Delta u_t \ , \tag{3.8}$$

where $E\Delta u_t$ is not zero in general.[3] Remember that this results from the fact that, based on knowledge of the true model, all past disturbances are observable since they are the difference between actual and expected p's in the past. The "delta model" neglects this which corresponds to the observation that most subjects do not care for "levels".

If the underlying model is not disturbed, delta predictions and fully rational predictions coincide. Therefore, the two concepts may be compared only on the basis of five experiments (Exp. 4-6, 13, 14). Exp. 4-6 are full information experiments, thus, $\Delta r(t)$ is already known when p_t has to be forecasted, and the expectation operator in Eq. (3.7) may be dropped. Exp. 13 and 14, however, do not provide full information on exogenous variables. For Exp. 13 (model $p = 200 - w + u$), the delta prediction is[4]

$$f^D = p_{-1} - E\Delta w \ , \tag{3.9}$$

$$E\Delta w_t = \begin{cases} -2 & t = 1, \ldots, 10, 21, \ldots, 30, \ldots \\ 2 & t = 11, \ldots, 20, 31, \ldots, 40, \ldots \end{cases} \tag{3.10}$$

For Exp. 14 (model $p = 150 - w + u$), the delta prediction is[5]

$$f^D = p_{-1} - E\Delta v = p_{-1} \ . \tag{3.11}$$

The following table gives mean and mean absolute deviations from rational and delta predictions for those experiments:

---

[3] The conditioning is not made explicit, see Section 2.2 on Notation.

[4] See Chapter 2, Eq. (2.3) and (2.5).

[5] See Chapter 2, Eq. (2.4).

Table 3.6: Deviations from Delta and Rational Predictions
(Exp. 4-6, 13, and 14, Periods 21-end)
Average Forecasts

Exp. No.	*MD* Rat.	from Delta	*MAD* Rat.	from Delta
4	−0.058	0.242	1.785	1.329
5	0.038	0.338	1.889	1.591
6	−0.141	0.026	2.031	1.614
13	0.232	0.049	1.804	1.095
14	−0.276	−0.460	0.905	0.845

Table 3.6 (continued)
Median Forecasts

Exp. No.	*MD* Rat.	from Delta	*MAD* Rat.	from Delta
4	−0.169	0.131	1.731	1.244
5	−0.069	0.295	1.869	1.519
6	−0.133	0.033	2.133	1.667
13	0.242	0.058	1.792	0.958
14	−0.175	−0.358	0.792	0.692

Without any exception, mean absolute deviations from delta predictions are less than those from rational predictions. The results will be strengthened below in Chapter 4 by studying individual forecasts.

"Delta predictions" by no means provide a satisfactory explanation of observed aggregate behavior. Nevertheless, the fact that subjects seem to concentrate on expected *changes* rather than on expected *levels* is the key to a better explanation of their behavior.

Misspecified Auxiliary Models

The observed concentration on changes rather than on levels gives rise to the question whether subjects use a misspecified model in the sense that they use an incorrect set of predetermined variables for forecasting.[6]

[6] Strictly speaking, the "delta model" cited above is already misspecified because of the disturbance.

Determining the expected *level* based on such a misspecified model would lead to large forecast errors but this is not the case if expected *changes* are derived from a misspecified model.

For some experiments, a misspecification concerning the exogenous variables seems likely from viewing the questionnaires: In Exp. 7 (first seasonality experiment), most subjects did not recognize the seasonal pattern and, therefore, repeatedly failed to forecast the "crashes". In Exp. 9, no subject noticed the autoregressive component, and a look over the questionnaires shows that about halfth of the subjects erroneously assumed a positive influence of the irrelevant variable x. In Exp. 11, many subjects did not recognize that v has a lagged, but w a contemporary influence. Instead, some subjects thought that both v and w had lagged influence, some others only recognized the influcnce of w. The ideas may be formalized by the misspecified delta models

$$\Delta p_t = \Delta y_t - \Delta z_t + \Delta \tilde{s}_t + \varepsilon_t \ ,$$

$$\Delta \tilde{s}_t = 5\,\mathrm{sign}(t \ modulo\ 4) = \begin{cases} 0 & \text{for } t = 4, 8, 12, \ldots \\ 5 & \text{else} \end{cases} \qquad \text{for Exp. 7,} \tag{3.12}$$

$$\Delta p_t = \frac{1}{2}\Delta x_t + \Delta y_t - \Delta z_t + \varepsilon_t \qquad \text{for Exp. 9,} \tag{3.13}$$

$$\text{and} \qquad \Delta p_t = -\Delta w_t + \varepsilon_t \qquad \text{in Exp. 11} \tag{3.14}$$

replacing the "correct" (in terms of the exogenous variables) delta models[7]

$$\Delta p_t = \Delta y_t - \Delta z_t + \Delta s_t \ ,$$

$$\Delta s_t = \begin{cases} -15 & t = 4, 8, 12, \ldots \\ 5 & \text{else} \end{cases} \qquad \text{for Exp. 7,} \tag{3.15}$$

$$\Delta p_t = \Delta y_t - \Delta z_t + \left[\frac{1}{2}p_{t-1}\right] - \left[\frac{1}{2}p_{t-2}\right] \qquad \text{for Exp. 9,} \tag{3.16}$$

[7] For Eq. (3.16): $[a]$ denotes the integer part of a.

$$\Delta p_t = \Delta v_{t-1} - \Delta w_t \qquad \text{for Exp. 11.} \tag{3.17}$$

(note that the models in Exp. 7, 9, and 11 do not include a disturbance). Misspecified delta models lead to the "misspecified predictions"[8]

$$f_t^M = p_{t-1} + \Delta y_t - \Delta z_t + \Delta \tilde{s}_t \ ,$$

$$\Delta \tilde{s}_t = 5\text{sign}(t \ modulo \ 4) = \begin{cases} 0 & \text{for } t = 4, 8, 12, \ldots \\ 5 & \text{else} \end{cases} \qquad \text{for Exp. 7,} \tag{3.18}$$

$$f_t^M = p_{t-1} + \frac{1}{2}\Delta x_t + \Delta y_t - \Delta z_t \qquad \text{for Exp. 9,} \tag{3.19}$$

and

$$f^M = p_{t-1} - E\Delta w_t \qquad \text{for Exp. 11.} \tag{3.20}$$

The following table compares *MAD*'s from misspecified predictions to *MAD*'s from rational predictions[9]

Table 3.7: *MAD* from "misspecified" predictions, Exp. 7, 9, and 11 (Periods 21-end)
Part 1: Average Forecasts

Exp. No.	*MD* Rat.	from Missp.	*MAD* Rat.	from Missp.
7	2.066	−1.684	5.711	2.939
9	0.415	0.421	2.295	1.609
11	0.063	0.146	1.863	1.108

---

[8] Note that full information on exogenous variables is given in Exp. 7 and 9, but not in Exp. 11.

[9] = delta predictions since no disturbance is present in those experiments.

Table 3.7 (continued)
Part 2: Median Forecasts

Exp. No.	MD from Rat.	MD from Missp.	MAD from Rat.	MAD from Missp.
7	2.750	−1.000	6.175	3.000
9	0.313	0.319	2.213	1.444
11	0.067	0.150	1.800	1.150

The tables show that mean absolute deviations are considerably reduced when passing from rational to misspecified predictions.

At this stage, no general rule may be postulated according to which subjects choose their auxiliary delta model.

Underestimation of Changes

Underestimation of changes basicly means that the *forecasted* change $(f_t - p_{t-1})$ has the same sign but is absolutely less than the *actual* change $(p_t - p_{t-1})$. For experiments where subjects cannot be expected to forecast the *actual* change correctly (i.e. incomplete-information[10] or disturbed-model experiments), observed *forecasted* changes should rather be compared to *conditional expected* changes $E\Delta p$ (rationally expected change) and $E^D\Delta p$ (delta-expected changes).[11]

In Figure 3.2, average forecasted changes are plotted over rationally expected changes for Exp. 5. The figures indicate that most observations fall between the horizontal axis and the 45° line which corresponds to underestimation of changes. Similar pictures are obtained by plotting over delta-expected changes.

---

10 (on exogenous variables)

11 As stated earlier, the two concepts coincide if the model is not disturbed. If, moreover, full information on exogenous variables is given, they are equal to the actual change.

Figure 3.2:
Average Forecasted Changes plotted over Rationally Expected Changes

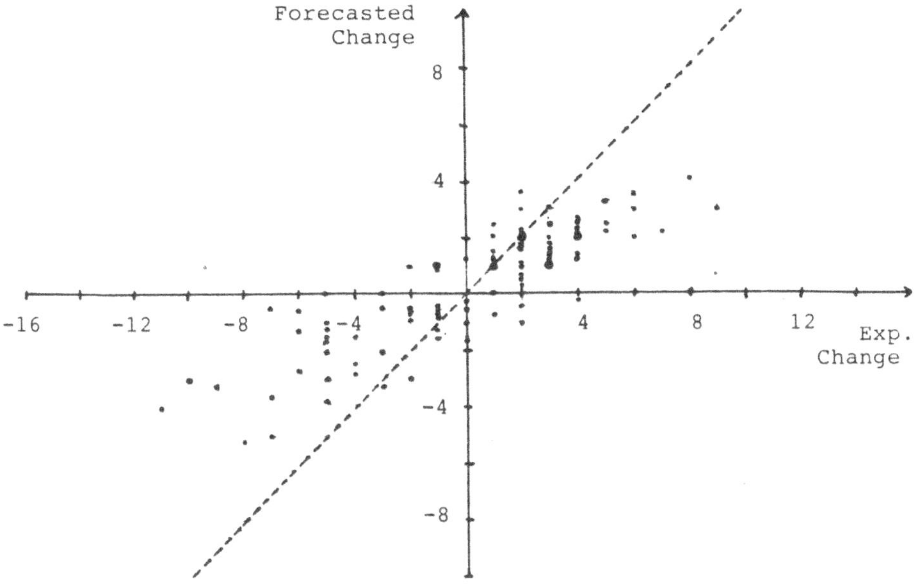

For the subsequent analysis, the following definitions are needed:

Definition Let $\Delta f_t := f_t - p_{t-1}$ (forecasted change). Then we define

Underestimation of change

if $\quad \text{sign}(\Delta f) \cdot \text{sign}(E\Delta p) = 1$ and $|\Delta f| < |E\Delta p|$

Overestimation of change

if $\quad \text{sign}(\Delta f) \cdot \text{sign}(E\Delta p) = 1$ and $|\Delta f| > |E\Delta p|$

Misforecast of change

if $\quad \text{sign}(\Delta f) \cdot \text{sign}(E\Delta p) = -1$

An observation falls in none of these categories if $E\Delta p = 0$ or $\Delta f = 0$ or $\Delta f = E\Delta p$. With respect to delta-expected changes $E^D\Delta p$, the terms may be defined analogously. The following table summarizes (for average forecasts; median forecasts yield similar results) the number of underestimations, overestimations, and misforecasts of change (*UEC*, *OEC*, *MFC*, resp.) for each experiment. The upper part gives the comparisons to rationally expected changes $E\Delta p$. The comparisons for "delta-expected changes" $E^D\Delta p$ (for Exp. 4-6, 13 and 14) and for "misspecified expected changes" $E^M\Delta p$ (for Exp. 7, 9, and 11)[12] are given in the second part of the table and marked by (*).

Table 3.8: Counting results on underestimation of change with respect to $E\Delta p$ ($*$: to $E^D\Delta p$ and $E^M\Delta p$) (Average Forecasts, Periods 21-end)

Exp. No.	No. of *UEC*	No. of *OEC*	No. of *MFC*
1	51	20	3
2	56	11	2
3	39	5	2
4	55	13	4
5	55	15	7
6	33	1	13
7	49	13	17
8	60	8	7
9	49	8	13
10	51	–	9
11	32	4	9
12	40	6	0
13	30	11	9
14	27	5	8
* 4	54	12	2
* 5	58	8	6
* 6	33	4	8
*13	42	4	9
* 7	43	21	13
* 9	52	10	7
*11	41	9	8

Note on the table: For Exp. 14, delta-expected changes are always zero.

---

[12] See "Misspecified Auxiliary Models",
$E^M\Delta p = \Delta y - \Delta z + 5 \cdot sign(t\ modulo\ 4)$ for Exp. 7,
$E^M\Delta p = \frac{1}{2}\Delta x + \Delta y - \Delta z$ for Exp. 9,
$E^M\Delta p = -E\Delta w$ for Exp. 11.

According to a one-sided binomial test of the hypothesis that under- and overestimations of change occur with equal frequency, the number of underestimations significantly (at the 1% level) exceeds the number of overestimations for all 14 experiments. The same holds for the comparison of underestimations to misforecasts.

Note that the number of misforecasts is reduced by comparing to delta-expected changes or misspecified expected changes rather than to rationally expected changes.

Underestimation of changes may also be verified by estimating the regression

$$\Delta f = \beta_0 + \beta_1 E\Delta p + \varepsilon \tag{3.21}$$

(where Δf denotes the forecasted change) and testing the hypotheses $\beta_1 = 1$ and $\beta_1 = 0$ by a simple t test. The estimates and the t statistics (including, for completeness, the t statistic for $H_0 : \beta_0 = 0$), are presented in the following table (for average forecasts). Once again, the upper part summarizes results from regressing on rationally expected changes $E\Delta p$, followed by results from replacing $E\Delta p$ by delta-expected changes $E^D\Delta p$ (for Exp. 4-6 and 13)[13] and by misspecified expected changes $E^M\Delta p$ (for Exp. 7, 9, and 11), resp.

---

[13] Note that for Exp. 14 $E^D\Delta p \equiv 0$, thus, regression on $E^D\Delta p$ is not possible.

Table 3.9: Results of Regression $\Delta f = \beta_0 + \beta_1 E\Delta p + \varepsilon$, t statistics
(∗) $E\Delta p$ replaced by $E^D\Delta p$ (for Exp. 4-6 and 13),
and by $E^M\Delta p = \Delta y - \Delta z + 5\text{sign}(t \textit{ modulo } 4)$ (for Exp. 7),
$E^M\Delta p = \frac{1}{2}\Delta x + \Delta y - \Delta z$ (for Exp. 9),
and $E^M\Delta p = -E\Delta w$ (for Exp. 11).
(Average Forecasts, Periods (21-end))

Exp. No	$\hat{\beta}_0$	$\hat{\beta}_1$	t for H_0 : $\beta_1 = 0$	t for H_0 : $\beta_1 = 1$	t for H_0 : $\beta_0 = 0$
1	0.109	0.828	44.48	−9.27	0.89
2	0.094	0.795	45.08	−11.64	1.17
3	0.072	0.783	40.22	−11.13	1.09
4	0.071	0.616	20.03	−12.49	0.48
5	0.197	0.445	15.87	−19.80	1.75
6	−0.119	0.365	9.77	−16.97	−0.86
7	2.057	0.248	7.71	−23.38	6.72
8	0.295	0.644	29.27	−16.18	1.20
9	0.428	0.474	14.92	−16.57	2.91
10	0.120	0.404	9.03	−13.31	1.34
11	0.118	0.342	8.04	−15.49	0.93
12	0.076	0.594	13.20	−12.95	1.02
13	0.098	0.268	4.78	−13.07	0.68
14	−0.376	0.455	6.46	−7.73	−3.89
* 4	0.253	0.691	31.69	−14.17	2.56
* 5	0.331	0.489	18.12	−19.96	3.43
* 6	−0.048	0.443	14.01	−17.60	−0.45
*13	0.049	0.462	7.78	−9.07	0.41
* 7	0.099	0.523	7.35	−6.71	0.24
* 9	0.429	0.566	24.10	−18.52	4.32
*11	0.146	0.509	7.98	−7.69	1.15

Note that for most experiments the intercept estimate is positive which seems to confirm the upward bias. The results for median forecasts do not differ substantially from those for average forecasts.

The number of degrees of freedom for the t tests is 58 or 78, (depending on the number of periods). Thus, the 1% significance bound is below 2.5 for one-sided tests of the H_0: "*parameter* $= a$" against H_1: "*parameter* $> a$" and above -2.5 for one-sided tests of inversed form. The t statistics for the slope parameter are beyond these bounds for all experiments, implying that the estimated slope is significantly greater than zero and significantly less than one. The latter observation also rejects an implication of rationality.

Note that regressing on delta- or misspecified expected changes always reveals higher slope estimates $\hat{\beta}_1$ than regression on rationally expected changes. Correspondingly, there is a better explanation (greater coefficient of determination, smaller mean squared regression error, these figures are not given in the table). But the estimated slope remains significantly less than one.

Finally, the estimated slope coefficient $\hat{\beta}_1$ tends to be smaller (which corresponds to a stronger underestimation) in the more difficult experiments (seasonality and incomplete-information experiments).

To summarize, throughout all experiments, a highly significant underestimation of changes is observed: Subjects generally forecast the *direction* of change correctly, but they tend to underestimate the *amount* of change. This result will be confirmed by the analysis of individual forecasts in Chapter 4 below.

Adaptive and Extrapolative Behavior

If the simple adaptive model

$$f = f_{-1} + \lambda(f_{-1} - p_{-1}) \tag{3.22}$$

is considered as a special case for the situation of zero expected change, it can be generalized by accounting for the expected change:

$$\begin{aligned} & f = p_{-1} + \beta_1 E\Delta p + \lambda(f_{-1} - p_{-1}) \\ \Longleftrightarrow\ & f - p_{-1} = \beta_1 E\Delta p + \lambda(f_{-1} - p_{-1})\ . \end{aligned} \tag{3.23}$$

The simple extrapolative model

$$f = p_{-1} + \gamma\Delta p_{-1} \tag{3.24}$$

can be generalized analogously:

$$f = p_{-1} + \beta_1 E\Delta p + \gamma \Delta p_{-1}$$

$$\Longleftrightarrow \; f - p_{-1} = \beta_1 E\Delta p + \gamma \Delta p_{-1} \; . \tag{3.25}$$

For aggregate forecasts from each experiment, the relevance of adaptive and extrapolative behavior can be tested by estimating the regression equations (3.23) and (3.25) (with an intercept included). The next table gives the results: the estimates $\hat{\lambda}$ and $\hat{\gamma}$, the improvement in determination,[14] and the significance level of λ and γ, resp.[15] The intercept and the slope estimates for $E\Delta p$ are not included in the table since they do not deviate noticeably from the simple regressions in Table 3.9. For Exp. 4-6 and 13, delta-expected changes have been replaced for rationally expected changes (and the improvement of R^2 compared to the simple regression on $E^D\Delta p$ is given), for Exp. 7, 9, and 11, misspecified expected changes have been used (and R^2 is compared to the determination in the simple regression on $E^M\Delta p$). For the misspecified expected changes used see Table 3.9. The table only presents results for average forecasts, the results for median forecasts are similar.

---

[14] R^2 from the regression including the adaptive/extrapolative component, resp., minus R^2 from the regression without that component.

[15] = Probability of a greater absolute t value under H_0: "parameter = 0".

Table 3.10: Significance of adaptive/extrapolative behavior (Average Forecasts, Periods 21-end)

Exp. No.	$\hat{\lambda}$	Sign. level	Improv. of R^2	$\hat{\gamma}$	Sign. level	Improv. of R^2
	Adaptive Behavior (Eq. 3.23)			Extrapolative Behavior (Eq. 3.25)		
1	0.175	0.02	0.0023	−0.009	0.64	0.0006
2	0.011	0.88	<0.0001	0.007	0.69	0.0001
3	−0.096	0.21	0.0009	0.018	0.40	0.0004
4	0.053	0.16	0.0019	−0.019	0.35	0.0008
5	0.085	0.01	0.0133	−0.045	0.05	0.0084
6	−0.001	0.98	<0.0001	−0.019	0.64	0.0059
7	0.174	<0.01	0.1346	−0.108	<0.01	0.0788
8	0.204	<0.01	0.0148	−0.076	<0.01	0.0120
9	−0.055	0.13	0.0035	0.059	<0.01	0.0110
10	−0.153	<0.01	0.1389	0.209	<0.01	0.2390
11	−0.190	<0.01	0.1038	0.197	<0.01	0.1382
12	−0.174	<0.01	0.0504	0.133	<0.01	0.0564
13	−0.183	<0.01	0.1274	0.233	<0.01	0.2274
14	0.204	<0.01	0.1666	−0.126	<0.01	0.1211

The table shows that adaptive and extrapolative behavior are generally not significant for the simple full-information experiments 1-6. For the seasonality experiments 7-8 and for the random-walk experiment 14, $\hat{\lambda}$ is positive, and $\hat{\gamma}$ is negative. For the incomplete-information experiments 10-13, the converse holds: $\hat{\lambda}$ is negative (i.e. subjects tend to "compensate" the last forecast error), and $\hat{\gamma}$ is positive (i.e. subjects extrapolate the last change of p).

As will be seen later from the analysis of influence of single variables, the adaptive and extrapolative behavior in Exp. 10-13 are well captured by past changes of the exogenous variables which are obviously replaced for the (unknown) current changes of those variables.

At this stage, an observation can already be formulated which is confirmed later: Adaptive and extrapolative coefficients in most cases have oppositve sign (here: for 12 out of 14 experiments). The reason for this, however, is presumably not psychological in nature but rather a consequence of underestimation of changes: If the last change Δp_{-1} is large, the last forecast error will tend to be negative, and if $\Delta p_{-1} << 0$, the forecast error will tend to be positive: $f_{-1} - p_{-1} > 0$. If the regressor $(f_{-1} - p_{-1})$ from the adaptive regression equation is replaced by the regressor Δp_{-1} which is negatively correlated to the former one, the corresponding slope estimate will generally have opposite sign.

For the incomplete-information experiments 10-13, the extrapolative model gives a better explanation, for the remaining experiments (where $\hat{\lambda}$ is mostly positive), the converse holds. It is impossible to state generally whether subjects tend to extrapolate (and adaptive behavior is only a consequence of underestimation of changes but does not really take place in subjects' minds) or whether adaptation is the crucial factor.

As a consequence of the negative correlation of $(f_{-1} - p_{-1})$ and Δp_{-1}, both $\hat{\lambda}$ and $\hat{\gamma}$ are significantly *positive* (i.e. $\hat{\lambda}$ changes sign) for Exp. 10-13 when adaptive and extrapolative component are *jointly* added to the regression.

In order to demonstrate the strong correlation between last forecast error and last change of p, the following table presents the results of the corresponding regression (for average forecasts):

Table 3.11: Regression $(f_{-1} - p_{-1}) = \beta_0 + \beta_1 \Delta p_{-1} + \varepsilon$
(Average Forecasts, Periods 21-end)

Exp. No.	$\hat{\beta}_0$	$\hat{\beta}_1$	R^2
1	0.151	−0.171	0.5085
2	0.102	−0.207	0.6317
3	0.089	−0.225	0.7109
4	0.259	−0.428	0.6170
5	0.361	−0.604	0.8136
6	−0.019	−0.691	0.8826
7	2.143	−0.769	0.8821
8	0.348	−0.365	0.7652
9	0.451	−0.527	0.7773

(continued)

Table 3.11 (continued)

Exp. No.	$\hat{\beta}_0$	$\hat{\beta}_1$	R^2
10	0.138	−0.878	0.8629
11	0.168	−0.719	0.7943
12	0.163	−0.702	0.7029
13	0.017	−0.788	0.7959
14	−0.531	−0.880	0.8816

All estimated slope coefficients are negative (with the level - according to a one-sided t test - far less than 1%, except for Exp. 3), all intercept coefficients (except those for Exp. 7 and 14) are not significant at the 5% level. Note that the relationship is less significant for those experiments where forecasts were "good" and underestimation of changes was less significant (Exp. 1-3 and 8). In particular, for median forecasts from Exp. 3, the negative relationship is not significant at a reasonable level, corresponding to the fact that median forecasts from Exp. 3 are nearly rational. For all other series of medians, however, the same significance results hold as for average forecasts.

3.4. "Trend-Underestimating Predictions"

The following three non-rational features of aggregate forecasts,

1. Underestimation of changes,
2. Concentration on changes, formalized by the "delta model",
3. Misspecified auxiliary models, formalized by the "misspecified delta model"

suggest the following "underestimating prediction rule"

$$f_t^U = p_{t-1} + c\,E^D \Delta p_t \quad , \quad 0 < c < 1 \tag{3.26}$$

where delta-expected changes $E^D\Delta p$ may be replaced by misspecified expected changes $E^M\Delta p$ when appropriate (for Exp. 7, 9, and 11).

The following table once again summarizes the results from the regression of observed forecasted changes $\Delta f = f - p_{-1}$ on delta-expected changes (for Periods 21-end). For the "undisturbed" experiments 1-3 and 7-12, delta-expected changes equal rationally expected changes, for Exp. 4-6, 13 and 14 they are different. For Exp. 7, 9, and 11, delta-expected changes were replaced by misspecified expected changes

$E^M\Delta p = \Delta y - \Delta z + 5sign(t\ modulo\ 4)$ (for Exp. 7),
$E^M\Delta p = \frac{1}{2}\Delta x + \Delta y - \Delta z$ (for Exp. 9), and
$E^M\Delta p = -E\Delta w$ (for Exp. 11).

For Exp. 14, delta-expected changes are always zero. Thus, for regression purposes, it had to be replaced by rationally expected changes.

The t statistic for significance of the intercept, the root mean squared regression error, and the coefficient of determination are included.

Table 3.12: OLS Regression $\Delta f = \beta_0 + \beta_1 E^D\Delta p + u$
(* = Regression on $E^M\Delta p$ (Exp. 7, 9, 11) or $E\Delta p$ (Exp. 14))
(Average Forecasts, Periods 21-end)

Exp. No.	$\hat{\beta}_0$	$\hat{\beta}_1$	t for H_0: $\beta_0 = 0$	RMSE	R^2
1	0.109	0.828	0.89	1.09	0.9621
2	0.094	0.795	1.17	0.72	0.9626
3	0.072	0.783	1.09	0.51	0.9654
4	0.253	0.691	2.56	0.89	0.9279
5	0.331	0.489	3.43	0.86	0.8242
6	−0.048	0.443	−0.45	0.83	0.7720
* 7	0.099	0.523	0.24	2.80	0.4093
8	0.295	0.644	1.20	2.19	0.9166
* 9	0.429	0.566	4.32	0.89	0.8816
10	0.120	0.404	1.34	0.69	0.5841
*11	0.146	0.509	1.15	0.99	0.5234
12	0.076	0.594	1.02	0.58	0.8457
13	0.049	0.462	0.41	0.92	0.5108
*14	−0.376	0.455	−3.89	0.74	0.4182

For Exp. 1-6, 8, 9, and 12, R^2 is more than 75%, and the root mean squared regression error (which is greater than the mean absolute regression error) is less than one for most experiments. The slope coefficient is relatively large for the simple deterministic experiments 1-3 and smaller for more "difficult" experiments. The intercept is not significant at the 5% level except for Exp. 4, 5, 9, and 14 (two-sided t test of H_0: "*intercept = 0*").

For comparison, the following two tables present mean and mean absolute deviations from rational and from underestimating predictions according to Eq. (3.26), with simple values for the constant c ($c = \frac{1}{2}$ or $\frac{3}{4}$). $E^D \Delta p$ is again replaced by rationally expected changes for Exp. 14, and by misspecified expected changes for Exp. 7, 9, and 11. The first table gives the results for average, the second one the results for median forecasts.

Table 3.13: Mean and mean absolute deviations from rational and underestimating predictions (Average Forecasts, Periods 21-end)

Exp. No.	*MD* Rat.	from Underest.	*MAD* Rat.	from Underest.	c
1	0.120	0.104	1.264	0.924	0.75
2	0.086	0.095	0.921	0.590	0.75
3	0.101	0.068	0.630	0.396	0.75
4	−0.058	0.251	1.785	0.741	0.75
5	0.038	0.331	1.889	0.734	0.50
6	−0.141	−0.041	2.031	0.663	0.50
7	2.066	0.143	5.711	2.165	0.50
8	0.282	0.301	3.598	2.070	0.50
9	0.415	0.430	2.295	0.804	0.50
10	0.120	0.120	1.192	0.560	0.50
11	0.063	0.146	1.863	0.757	0.50
12	0.049	0.082	0.836	0.483	0.50
13	0.232	0.049	1.804	0.737	0.50
14	−0.276	−0.368	0.905	0.642	0.50

Table 3.14: Mean and mean absolute deviations from rational and underestimating predictions (Median Forecasts, Periods 21-end)

Exp. No.	MD Rat.	from Underest.	MAD Rat.	from Underest.	c
1	0.200	0.184	0.538	1.078	0.75
2	0.006	0.016	0.281	0.766	0.75
3	0.025	−0.008	0.025	0.633	0.75
4	−0.169	0.141	1.731	0.778	0.75
5	−0.069	0.225	1.869	0.813	0.50
6	−0.133	−0.033	2.133	0.800	0.50
7	2.750	0.869	6.175	2.331	0.50
8	−0.150	−0.131	2.638	2.781	0.50
9	0.313	0.328	2.213	0.922	0.50
10	0.042	0.042	1.158	0.708	0.50
11	0.067	0.150	1.800	0.817	0.50
12	0.000	0.033	0.700	0.533	0.50
13	0.242	0.058	1.792	0.908	0.50
14	−0.175	−0.367	0.792	0.600	0.50

Mean absolute deviations from underestimating predictions are considerably less than those from rational predictions - except for median forecasts in Exp. 1-3 and 8. This exception is - as already mentioned - due to the fact that in these experiments many subjects succeeded in forecasting correctly which implies equality of median forecasts to rational predictions. For the remaining experiments and for average forecasts from all experiments, the underestimating rule yields the best explanation.

The tables show that deviations from "trend-underestimating predictions" are generally low. However, there is a second requirement which should be fulfilled for a "good rule": The deviations from it should be purely random, they should not be autocorrelated. An appropriate nonparametric test is the Wald-Wolfowitz iteration test:[16] The observed

---

[16] See Büning/Trenkler [8], pp 117-121, and Becker (1967 [2], pp. 253/254) for a description.

forecasts (60 or 80, resp.) are subdivided into two groups according to the sign of deviation: forecasts greater than the "underestimating prediction", and forecasts less than the "underestimating prediction" (forecasts equal to underestimating predictions are omitted). Now count how often the sign changes. This number plus one is the number of iterations (= blocks with equal signs). A low number of iterations indicates positive autocorrelation of deviations whereas a high number indicates negative autocorrelation. Under the null hypothesis that the succession is random (which should result in a medium number of iterations), the distribution of the number of iterations can be calculated. Thus, the null hypothesis may be tested. The following table presents some results:

Table 3.15:

Deviations from "underestimating predictions", Iterations of sign (Periods 21-end)

	Average Forecasts			Median Forecasts		
Exp. No.	No. of Iterations		Expected under H_0	No. of Iterations		Expected under H_0
1	42		40.10	39		37.03
2	43		39.43	39		34.88
3	30		28.49	16	xx	25.41
4	25	xx	36.64	32		36.56
5	32		34.97	31		30.71
6	29		30.28	21		24.00
7	24	xx	39.40	30		35.17
8	36		35.17	32		32.26
9	31		33.26	26		32.54
10	26		28.81	20		20.80
11	28		28.31	20		18.94
12	22		29.42	17		22.40
13	22		29.97	18		24.49
14	20		25.63	16		19.32

Notes on the table:

1. The expected value (under H_0) depends on the number of negative

and positive deviations (which is not displayed in the table) and is in general not integer.
2. x and xx mark significance at 5% and 1% level, resp., according to a two-sided test of H_0: "*succession is random*".

For medians from Exp. 3 and averages from Exp. 4 and 7, the null hypothesis of random succession is rejected (for median forecasts from Exp. 3, we already know that they are better explained by rational predictions). Apart from these cases, there are no rejections. For most experiments, however, the number of iterations is below its expected value.

To sum up this section, underestimating predictions are the best *general* concept studied here to describe aggregate forecasts. After presenting some results on learning behavior in the next section, some "improvements" of underestimating predictions are studied by considering the influence of each exogenous variable separately, and allowing for adaptive or extrapolative behavior. These results, however, are no longer general but rather special with respect to each experiment.

3.5 Learning Behavior?

Now the question arises whether deviations from rational predictions decrease during the experiment, that is, whether learning is present.

For this purpose, the time span of 80 or 100 periods, resp., is subdivided into four or five sections of 20 periods, resp. If some learning is present, mean absolute deviations from fully rational predictions (or, alternatively, mean absolute deviations from delta or misspecified predictions) should decrease from the first section to the second, or from the second to the third, and so forth.

The following table summarizes mean absolute deviations from rational (delta/misspecified) predictions for each experiment by 20-period sections (for average forecasts, the results for medians look similar). For better exposition, the first section is subdivided into (1-10) and (11-20).

Table 3.16: Mean absolute deviations from rational predictions.
(*): from delta (Exp. 4-6, 13, 14) or misspecified (Exp. 7, 9, and 11) pred.

	MAD in time section ...					
Exp. No.	1-10	11- 20	21- 40	41- 60	61- 80	81-100
1	2.329	1.107	1.214	1.125	1.400	1.317
2	2.162	0.992	0.965	0.977	0.825	0.915
3	1.525	1.000	0.854	0.454	0.581	.
4	2.958	2.250	1.646	1.904	1.921	1.671
5	3.046	1.954	2.008	1.562	1.846	2.142
6	3.136	2.164	2.514	1.786	1.794	.
7	6.231	6.582	6.692	5.173	5.581	5.396
8	5.267	5.100	4.221	3.600	3.267	3.306
9	2.993	2.112	2.617	1.859	2.314	2.390
10	0.745	0.473	1.177	1.198	1.200	.
11	1.908	1.723	2.074	1.631	1.885	.
12	1.473	1.282	0.605	1.009	0.894	.
13	2.645	1.345	1.627	1.871	1.913	.
14	1.257	1.457	1.129	0.843	0.743	.
* 4	2.658	0.950	1.296	1.438	1.179	1.404
* 5	2.992	1.454	1.477	1.292	1.827	1.769
* 6	2.773	1.474	1.632	1.550	1.660	.
*13	1.355	0.855	0.736	1.356	1.191	.
*14	1.229	1.029	1.186	0.671	0.679	.
* 7	4.508	2.385	3.385	2.108	3.238	2.577
* 9	3.243	1.229	1.729	1.612	1.386	1.710
*11	0.700	0.738	1.036	1.204	1.085	.

A first view over the table shows that, for most experiments, the deviations decrease remarkably after period 10 and again after period 20. For the experiments with "additional influence" (seasonality/autoregression) which were felt to be most difficult, this decline is observed later. Apart from this, no noticeable learning occurs after Period 20. No decline occurs in Exp. 10 and 11.

In addition, deviations slightly increase after period 60 for some experiments.

In order to analyze the significance of learning behavior, it seems appropriate to subdivide all periods into

- an "initial section" (Periods 1-10),
- a "learning section" (Periods 11-20, for the "difficult" experiments Periods 11-40), and
- a "main section" containing all remaining periods,

and to compare then the "initial section" to the "main section". There are two approaches to test the significance of learning behavior:

1st Approach: Test H_0: *"Equality of mean absolute deviations in initial and main section"* by a Wilcoxon rank sum test. If learning is present, the observations from the initial section should have high ranks after sorting all absolute deviations (i.e. from every period) in ascending order.

2nd Approach: Estimate the regression equation[17]

$$f_t - p_{t-1} = \beta \, E\Delta p_t + u_t \tag{3.27}$$

separately for "initial" and "main" section and for both sections jointly. Let $\hat{\beta}_c$ denote the estimate obtained from joint regression, $\hat{\beta}_{s1}$ the estimate for the "initial", and $\hat{\beta}_{s2}$ for the "main" section. Further, let $\hat{u}_{t,c}$ be the residuals from joint regression, and $\hat{u}_{t,s}$ the residuals from the separate regressions. Then, the Chow statistic[18]

$$F = \frac{\sum_t \hat{u}^2_{t,c} - \sum_t \hat{u}^2_{t,s}}{\frac{1}{T-12} \sum_t \hat{u}^2_{t,s}} \tag{3.28}$$

can be used to test the null hypothesis *"parameters in the two sections are equal"*. If some learning is present, the slope parameter should be greater in the main section which leads to rejection of the null hypothesis.

---

[17] Note that no intercept is included.

[18] See Chow (1960) [12]). The summation is - for our purposes - taken over $t = 1, \dots, 10, 21, \dots, T$ (initial section plus main section). Thus, the total number of periods processed is $T - 10$. Under the assumption of normality this statistic is distributed as $F(1, T-12)$ if H_0: $\beta_{s1} = \beta_{s2}$ holds. (Some care has to be taken in view of the violation of the normality assumption.)

Now let us apply the two approaches. First, the following table presents mean absolute deviations from rational predictions for initial and main section and the Wilcoxon rank sums from the initial section after sorting absolute deviations in ascending order. The last column gives the expected rank sums under H_0: *"equality of mean absolute deviatons in initial and main section"*. At the end of the table, corresponding results for delta and misspecified predictions are included - marked by (*) as in other tables above. Only results for average forecasts are tabulated, medians give similar results.

Table 3.17:
Wilcoxon rank sums for deviations from rational predictions.
(*): from delta/misspecified predictions, resp.
(1-10) vs (21-end)

Exp. No.	*MAD* (1-10)	*MAD* (21-end)	Wilcoxon rank sum		(expected under H_0)
1	2.329	1.264	684.0	xx	(455)
2	2.162	0.921	664.5	xx	(455)
3	1.525	0.630	473.0	x	(355)
4	2.958	1.785	616.0	x	(455)
5	3.046	1.889	599.5	x	(455)
6	3.136	2.031	438.0		(355)
7	6.231	**5.383	410.0		(355)
8	5.267	3.598	494.5		(455)
9	2.993	**2.188	425.5		(355)
10	0.745	1.192	223.0		(355)
11	1.908	1.863	368.0		(355)
12	1.473	0.836	451.0		(355)
13	2.645	1.804	451.5		(355)
14	1.257	0.905	410.0		(355)

(continued)

Table 3.17 (continued)

Exp. No.	*MAD* (1-10)	*MAD* (21-end)	Wilcoxon rank sum		(expected under H_0)
* 4	2.658	1.329	671.0	xx	(455)
* 5	2.992	1.591	613.0	x	(455)
* 6	2.773	1.614	406.5		(355)
*13	1.355	1.095	388.5		(355)
*14	1.229	0.845	444.0		(355)
* 7	4.508	**2.641	468.0	x	(355)
* 9	3.243	1.609	682.0	xx	(455)
*11	0.700	1.108	257.0		(355)

Notes on the table:
1. x denotes significance at 5% level, xx at 1% level, according to a one-sided test of H_0: "*equality of means*", based on the distribution of the Wilcoxon statistic under the null hypothesis.
2. ** : Comparison (1-10) to (41-end).
3. Absolute deviations were sorted in ascending order. The third column gives the rank sum of the absolute deviations in periods 1-10.
4. Midranks were used in case of ties.

For most single experiments the rank sum is not significant (in particular for the incomplete-information experiments 10-14). However, for deviations from rational predictions (first block of the table), it exceeds its expected (under H_0) value for 13 out of 14 experiments (the only exception is Exp. 10). After replacing deviations from rational predictions by deviations from delta/misspecified predictions, i.e. replacing the lines marked by (*) for the corresponding lines in the first block, one more exception occurs (Exp. 11). The proportion 12 out of 14, however, is significant at the 1% level according to a one-sided binomial test of H_0: "*equal frequencies*".

This means: although learning is not significant for many single experiments, it is present for a significant *majority* of experiments - with respect to rational as well as with respect to delta and misspecified predictions.

After these results from the Wilcoxon test, the following table presents results from the second approach, the regression (for average forecasts).

Table 3.18:
Average Forecasts, Regression $f - p_{-1} = \beta E\Delta p$ (no intercept).
(*): Regression on $E^D\Delta p$ and $E^M\Delta p$

Exp. No.	$\hat{\beta}_c$ (joint regr.)	$\hat{\beta}_{s1}$ (1-10)	$\hat{\beta}_{s2}$ (21-end)	F for H_0: $\beta_{s1} = \beta_{s2}$
1	0.809	0.731	0.827	x 5.131
2	0.755	0.552	0.795	xx 28.702
3	0.740	0.544	0.782	xx 15.077
4	0.587	0.427	0.617	x 6.427
5	0.431	0.342	0.448	2.023
6	0.311	0.053	0.365	xx 10.717
7	0.271	0.260	** 0.273	0.015
8	0.609	0.266	0.644	xx 27.791
9	0.468	0.395	** 0.485	1.045
10	0.436	0.627	0.404	3.851
11	0.348	0.383	0.343	0.114
12	0.563	0.441	0.595	3.656
13	0.229	0.010	0.265	2.544
14	0.483	0.445	0.492	0.055
* 4	0.652	0.448	0.691	xx 19.549
* 5	0.464	0.349	0.489	3.882
* 6	0.381	0.089	0.443	xx 17.919
*13	0.460	0.450	0.462	0.005
* 7	0.533	0.295	** 0.593	x 4.680
* 9	0.531	0.373	0.566	xx 8.976
*11	0.540	0.727	0.509	1.783

Notes on the table:
1. x marks significance at 5% level, xx at 1% level.
2. **= (41-end) instead of (21-end).
3. For Exp. 14, regression on $E^D\Delta p$ is not possible since $E^D\Delta p \equiv 0$.

Except for Exp. 10 and 11, i.e. for 12 out of 14 experiments, the slope parameter increases from the initial to the the main section but this is not always significant. The statements on significance as for the Wilcoxon test may be reproduced here: The slope parameter increases for a significant majority of experiments.

The increasing slope parameter indicates that subjects become more "confident" of the model.

Apart from learning behavior at the beginning of each experiment, Table 3.16 also suggests a slight "unlearning" at the end of some experiments. The following table presents mean absolute deviations from rational predictions during the section (21-60) vs. the section (61-end) and gives the rank sums of the observations from the end section.

Table 3.19: Mean absolute deviations of average forecasts from rational ((*): delta/misspec.) predictions (**): (41-60) instead of (21-60) (61-end) vs (21-60)

Exp. No.	MAD (21-60)	MAD (61-end)	Wilcoxon rank sum	(expected under H_0)
1	1.170	1.359	1725.5	(1620)
2	0.971	0.870	1585.0	(1620)
3	0.654	0.581	547.5	(610)
4	1.775	1.796	1653.0	(1620)
5	1.785	1.994	1627.5	(1620)
6	2.150	1.794	598.0	(610)
7	**5.173	5.488	1256.0	(1220)
8	3.910	3.286	1533.0	(1620)
9	**1.859	2.352	1288.5	(1220)
10	1.188	1.200	627.0	(610)
11	1.852	1.885	640.0	(610)
12	0.807	0.894	598.0	(610)
13	1.749	1.913	650.0	(610)
14	0.986	0.743	627.0	(610)

(continued)

Table 3.19 (continued)

Exp. No.	*MAD* (21-60)	*MAD* (61-end)	Wilcoxon rank sum	(expected under H_0)
* 4	1.367	1.292	1609.0	(1620)
* 5	1.385	1.798	1746.0	(1620)
* 6	1.591	1.660	648.5	(610)
*13	1.046	1.191	682.0	(610)
*14	0.929	0.679	527.5	(610)
* 7	**2.108	2.908	1278.5	(1220)
* 9	1.670	1.548	1569.5	(1620)
*11	1.120	1.085	622.0	(610)

For the comparison to rational predictions, in nine out of 14 experiments there is a slight "unlearning" (exceptions are Exp. 2, 3, 6, 8, and 14). The proportion 9 out of 14 is not significant. After replacing deviations from delta/misspecified predictions (lines marked by $*$) for deviations from rational predictions (corresponding lines in the first block), the proportion reduces to seven out of fourteen. None of the Wilcoxon rank sums is significant at the 5% level.

To summarize, learning within the first 20 periods is present for a significant majority of experiments. After the 20th period, no noticeable learning occurs. The same holds with respect to delta and misspecified models. Unlearning at the end of the experiments is not significant in any sense.

This is the reason why the time section (21-end) may be regarded as relatively stable. Thus, it seems appropriate to drop the observations from the first 20 periods. This is done throughout this chapter.

3.6 The Influence of Single Variables

So far, forecasted changes have only been compared to rationally, delta and misspecified expected changes but not to changes of the involved exogenous variables. This section presents some results on the influence of single exogenous variables which may give rise to an "improved" underestimating prediction concept

$$f^{U,impr.} = p_{-1} + \sum_{k=1}^{K} \beta_k \Delta r_k$$

($r_1, \ldots, r_k$ denote the involved exogenous variables) where the β_k are not necessarily equal to $c \cdot$*(true model coefficient)*, $0 < c < 1$, which would give underestimating delta predictions. Some variables are possibly "overvalued" with respect to others.

For better exposition, the following table once again summarizes the underlying models in each experiment and indicates for which experiments full information on exogenous variables was given.

Table 3.20: Models for each experiment

Exp. No.	Model	Full information?
1	$p = 120 + y - 2z$	yes
2	$p = -80 + x + \left[\frac{1}{2}y\right] - z$	yes
3	$p = 85 - x_{-1} + y_{-1}$	yes
4	$p = -80 + x + \left[\frac{1}{2}y\right] - z + u$	yes
5	$p = 20 + y - z + u$	yes
6	$p = 85 - x_{-1} + y_{-1} + u$	yes
7	$p = 12 + y - z + 5 \cdot (t \textit{ modulo } 4)$	yes
8	$p = 10 + y - z + 5 \cdot (t \textit{ modulo } 5)$	yes
9	$p = -7 + \left[\frac{1}{2}p_{-1}\right] + y - z$	yes
10	$p = 100 + v - w$	no
11	$p = 100 + v_{-1} - w$	no
12	$p = 100 + v - w_{-1}$	no
13	$p = 200 - w + u$	no
14	$p = 150 - v + u$	no

The method adopted in this section is regressing forecasted changes on changes of the involved exogenous variables. For this purpose, the experiments are subdivided into three groups:

Simple full-information experiments: Exp. 1-6 and 9
Experiment 9 may be included since no subject recognized the autoregressive component.
$\Delta f = f - p_{-1}$ is regressed on Δx, Δy, Δz for experiments with *contemporary* influence (Exp. 1, 2, 4, 5, and 9), and on Δx_{-1}, Δy_{-1}, Δz_{-1} for experiments with *lagged* influence (Exp. 3 and 6). In addition, for disturbed models, (Exp. 4-6), $u_{-1} = -E\Delta u$ (the last disturbance) is included in the regression in order to verify that subjects do not perceive past disturbances which corresponds to the fact that they do not care for levels (see Section 3.3 above).

Seasonality experiments: Exp. 7 and 8
Δf is regressed on Δx (for Exp. 7), Δy, Δz, and on four (for Exp. 7) or five (for Exp. 8) dummy variables, resp., depending on the length of the seasonal cycles. No intercept is included.

Incomplete-information experiments: Exp. 10-14
Δf is regressed on $E\Delta w$ (note that $E\Delta v \equiv 0$ cannot be included) and on the lagged changes Δv_{-1} and Δw_{-1} to account for the fact that subjects might replace past changes for current expected ones since the latter are not given as information. For disturbed-model experiments (Exp. 13 and 14), u_{-1} is included as in Exp. 4-6 above.

The following analysis proceeds for each of these three groups separately:

Simple Full-Information Experiments: Exp. 1-6 and 9

The following table presents the regression results. If parameter estimates are not significant according to a two-sided t test (level 5%) of H_0: "*parameter = 0*", this is indicated by "n". Only results for average forecasts are given, the results for median forecasts are similar.

Table 3.21: Regressions

$$\Delta f = \beta_0 + \beta_x \Delta x + \beta_y \Delta y + \beta_z \Delta z + \varepsilon \qquad \text{for Exp. 1, 2, and 9,}$$
$$\Delta f = \beta_0 + \beta_x \Delta x_{-1} + \beta_y \Delta y_{-1} + \beta_z \Delta z_{-1} + \varepsilon \qquad \text{for Exp. 3,}$$
$$\Delta f = \beta_0 + \beta_x \Delta x + \beta_y \Delta y + \beta_z \Delta z + \rho u_{-1} + \varepsilon \qquad \text{for Exp. 4 and 5,}$$
$$\Delta f = \beta_0 + \beta_x \Delta x_{-1} + \beta_y \Delta y_{-1} + \beta_z \Delta z_{-1} + \rho u_{-1} + \varepsilon \qquad \text{for Exp. 6.}$$

(Average Forecasts, Periods 21-end)

Exp. No.	$\hat{\beta}_0$	$\hat{\beta}_x$	$\hat{\beta}_y$	$\hat{\beta}_z$	$\hat{\rho}$	R^2
1	n 0.118	n 0.057	0.560	−1.700	·	0.9784
2	n 0.109	0.649	0.484	−0.878	·	0.9770
3	n 0.073	−0.789	0.778	n 0.009	·	0.9655
4	0.268	0.620	0.440	−0.715	n 0.026	0.9326
5	0.313	n 0.035	0.360	−0.554	n −0.079	0.8712
6	n −0.032	−0.420	0.455	n 0.057	n 0.039	0.7873
9	0.431	0.237	0.606	−0.569	·	0.8882

The following results are obtained from the regressions:

1. Where the corresponding variable is not relevant (x in Exp. 1, 5, and 9, z in Exp. 3 and 6, see Table 3.20 above), the parameter estimate is not significant except for $\hat{\beta}_x$ in Exp. 9 (see misspecified model used in previous sections!).

2. Where the corresponding variable is relevant (see Table 3.20 above), the parameter estimate is always significant and has the same sign as the coefficient in the underlying model, i.e. relevant variables were always recognized, and the direction of their influence was assessed correctly. However, the estimates are always absolutely *smaller* than the coefficient in the underlying model. This confirms the observed underestimation of changes.

3. The last disturbance u_{-1} has no significant influence on forecasts. This corresponds to the fact that subjects do not observe past disturbances which they would be able to do if they cared for levels. If they did so, they would subtract the last disturbance before adding the changes resulting from the exogenous variables, in our regression $\hat{\rho} \approx -1$ should hold. This does obviously not hold, for Exp. 4 and 6, $\hat{\rho}$ is even positive.

4. Due to the underestimation of change, the joint null hypothesis "*parameters = coefficients in the true model*" is rejected at the 1% level in all experiments. Instead, an F test of the hypotheses "*parameter relations = relations of coefficients of the true model*" is provided, i.e.

$$\begin{aligned}
&H_0 : \beta_x = 0, \quad \beta_z = -2\beta_y \quad \text{for Exp. 1,}\\
&H_0 : \beta_x = 2\beta_y, \quad \beta_z = -2\beta_y \quad \text{for Exp. 2 and 4,}\\
&H_0 : \beta_x = -\beta_y, \quad \beta_z = 0 \quad \text{for Exp. 3 and 6,}\\
&H_0 : \beta_x = 0, \quad \beta_z = -\beta_y \quad \text{for Exp. 5 and 9.}
\end{aligned}$$

Except for Exp. 3 and 6, even this hypothesis is rejected at the 5% level. The rejection is partly due to an obvious "overvaluation" of the variable z relative to the other variables (note that z is irrelevant in Exp. 3 and 6 where H_0 was not rejected). This in turn may be a consequence of the fact that z is more volatile than x and y, implying that the (negative) influence of z can easily be seen from the graph. This observation is confirmed by studying individual forecasts and questionnaires (see Chapters 4 and 5).

Seasonality Experiments: Exp. 7 and 8

The regressions for these experiments include four or five dummy variables, resp., depending on the cycle length. More specifically,

$$D_{t,k} = \begin{cases} 1 & \text{if } t \textit{ modulo } 4 = k \\ 0 & \text{else} \end{cases} \qquad k = 0, \ldots, 3 \quad \text{(for Exp. 7)} \qquad (3.29)$$

$$D_{t,k} = \begin{cases} 1 & \text{if } t \textit{ modulo } 5 = k \\ 0 & \text{else} \end{cases} \qquad k = 0, \ldots, 4 \quad \text{(for Exp. 8)} \qquad (3.30)$$

D_0 equals one for the "crash" periods ($0, 4, 8, \ldots$ for Exp. 7, $0, 5, 10, \ldots$ for Exp. 8) and zero else; the dummies D_1, D_2, D_3 (for Exp. 7) and $D_1, \ldots, D_4$ (for Exp. 8) correspond to the "growth" periods. Now, the following table presents the regression results (note that, in Exp. 8, the irrelevant variable x was not displayed, thus, it is not included in the regression). As above, non-significance is indicated by "n".

Table 3.22: Regressions
$\Delta f = \beta_x \Delta x + \beta_y \Delta y + \beta_z \Delta z + \delta_0 D_0 + \delta_1 D_1 + \delta_2 D_2 + \delta_3 D_3 + \varepsilon$
for Exp. 7,
$\Delta f = \beta_y \Delta y + \beta_z \Delta z + \delta_0 D_0 + \delta_1 D_1 + \delta_2 D_2 + \delta_3 D_3 + \delta_4 D_4 + \varepsilon$
for Exp. 8.
(Average Forecasts, Periods 21-end)

Coefficient	Exp. 7	Exp. 8
$\hat{\beta}_x$	n −0.087	.
$\hat{\beta}_y$	0.450	0.648
$\hat{\beta}_z$	−0.424	−0.400
$\hat{\delta}_0$	n −1.089	−13.220
$\hat{\delta}_1$	4.096	5.015
$\hat{\delta}_2$	3.074	4.078
$\hat{\delta}_3$	2.174	2.745
$\hat{\delta}_4$	.	2.845
R^2	0.6250	0.9418
$Prob. > F$	0.76	0.048

Note on the F test:
As above for simple full-information experiments, the hypothesis "*parameter relations = relations of coefficients in the true model*" is tested (but not for the dummy variables), i.e.
$H_0 : \beta_x = 0, \beta_y = -\beta_z$ in Exp. 7, and
$H_0 : \beta_y = -\beta_z$ in Exp. 8.

As far as the exogenous variables x, y, and z are concerned, the influence is assessed correctly by aggregate forecasts. For the relevant variables y and z, the parameter estimate is again absolutely smaller than the coefficient of the true model.

The null hypothesis of "correct" parameter relations is not rejected for Exp. 7, but for Exp. 8, it is rejected at the 5% level although forecasts were much better in this experiment. In contrast to simple full-information experiments, the highly volatile variable z is *undervalued* which may be due to the volatility of the p series (from seasonality): The short-term fluctuations induced by z are covered by the seasonal volatility.

As far as the dummy variables are concerned, the "crash-period" dummy D_0 is not significant for Exp. 7 implying that subjects fail to forecast the crashes (see misspecified model for Exp. 7 above). For Exp. 8, subjects forecasted the crash but underestimated it (the crash was -20). During the other periods, the growth of $+5$ per period is generally underestimated in both experiments, and, what is more interesting, it is *increasingly* underestimated: ($\hat{\delta}_1 > \hat{\delta}_2 > \hat{\delta}_3$ for both experiments, and $\hat{\delta}_4 \approx \hat{\delta}_3$ for Exp. 8. Some subjects expected the next crash too early, before the end of the growth phase.

Incomplete-Information Experiments: Exp. 10-14

The situation is quite complicated here because of incomplete information and, in addition, partly lagged influence (Exp. 11 and 12). For better exposition, the underlying models are reproduced from above:

Table 3.23: Underlying models in Exp. 10-14

Exp. No.	Model
10	$p = 100 + v - w$
11	$p = 100 + v_{-1} - w$
12	$p = 100 + v - w_{-1}$
13	$p = 200 - w + u$
14	$p = 150 - v + u$

Actual changes Δv and Δw (which are unknown at the forecasting time) have to be replaced by $E\Delta v$ and $E\Delta w$ (but $E\Delta v \equiv 0$ cannot be included in the regression). As stated above, lagged changes Δv_{-1} and Δw_{-1} are included in the regressions. For disturbed-model experiments (Exp. 13 and 14), the last disturbance u_{-1} is included.

Table 3.24: Regressions

$$\Delta f = \beta_0 + \beta_w E\Delta w + \beta_{vlag}\Delta v_{-1} + \beta_{wlag}\Delta w_{-1} + \varepsilon$$

for Exp. 10-12,

$$\Delta f = \beta_0 + \beta_w E\Delta w + \beta_{vlag}\Delta v_{-1} + \beta_{wlag}\Delta w_{-1} + \rho u_{-1} + \varepsilon$$

for Exp. 13 and 14

(Average Forecasts, Periods 21-end)

Exp. No.	$\hat{\beta}_0$	$\hat{\beta}_w$	$\hat{\beta}_{vlag}$	$\hat{\beta}_{wlag}$	$\hat{\rho}$	R^2
10	0.128	−0.200	0.148	−0.304	·	0.8682
11	0.153	−0.228	0.258	−0.413	·	0.8614
12	n 0.105	n −0.020	0.168	−0.620	·	0.9008
13	n −0.024	−0.238	n −0.071	−0.340	0.202	0.7477
14	−0.331	n 0.084	0.171	n 0.077	−0.504	0.6868

Note: Testing the null hypotheses "*parameter relations* = *coefficient relations in the true model*", i.e.

$H_0 : \beta_{vlag} = 0, \beta_{wlag} = 0$ for Exp. 10,
$H_0 : \beta_{wlag} = 0, \beta_w = -\beta_{vlag}$ for Exp. 11,
$H_0 : \beta_w = 0, \beta_{vlag} = 0$ for Exp. 12,
$H_0 : \beta_{vlag} = 0, \beta_{wlag} = 0$ for Exp. 13,
$H_0 : \beta_w = 0, \beta_{vlag} = 0, \beta_{wlag} = 0$ for Exp. 14,

yields F values beyond the 1% significance bound for alle five experiments considered.

The reason for this is the "overvaluation" of lagged changes:

In all experiments where w is relevant, $\hat{\beta}_{wlag}$ is absolutely greater (and more significant) than $\hat{\beta}_w$, even in those experiments where w has contemporary influence (Exp. 10, 11, and 13). According to experimental design (for Exp. 10 and 13)[19] and to the questionnaires (for Exp. 11), resp., this is not due to erroneous presumption of lagged influence. Subjects obviously replace the last change of w for $E\Delta w$. One might argue that it is impossible to assess $E\Delta w$ correctly, but there are two

---

[19] Note that in Exp. 10 and 13 no lagged influence occurs at all, and subjects were told that the influence is contemporary.

participants in Exp. 10 and 11 who succeeded in forecasting nearly rationally.

The same observation can be made with respect to v for Exp. 10 and 12: v has positive contemporary influence, and $\hat{\beta}_{vlag}$ is significant and positive.

The fact that subjects replace past changes for current expected ones exactly corresponds to the extrapolative (and, thus, negative adaptive) behavior observed in Section 3.3 above. The next section will show that, after including past changes of v and w, extrapolative and adaptive components added to the regression are much less significant than in the simple regressions $\Delta f = \beta_0 + \beta_1 E^D \Delta p$ + *adaptive/extrapolative component*.

For Exp. 14, the result is contrary: v has negative contemporary influence, but $\hat{\beta}_{vlag}$ was significant and positive. This, however, corresponds to the negative extrapolation observed for this experiment in Section 3.3.

The last disturbance u_{-1} gives no conclusive results: $\hat{\rho}$ is significant and negative for Exp. 14 (which corresponds to rationality) but significant and positive for Exp. 13.

The following points will summarize this section:

1. Relevant variables are recognized by aggregate forecasts, and the sign of influence is assessed correctly.

2. In absence of additional influence (e.g. seasonality), more volatile variables (z in Exp. 1-9, w in Exp. 10-14) tend to be overvalued relative to other variables.

3. Without full information on exogenous variables, subjects tend to replace past changes of involved variables for current expected ones.

4. Past disturbances are generally not perceived which may be a consequence of caring for changes rather than levels. This contradicts rationality.

3.7 Psychological Factors

This section once again briefly takes up adaptive and extrapolative behavior and accounts for two more psychological factors: bang-bang movements and long-run trends.

Adaptive and Extrapolative Behavior

First, the following table presents the results from adding the adaptive component $\lambda(f_{-1} - p_{-1})$ and the extrapolative component $\gamma \Delta p_{-1}$, resp., to the regression equations estimated in the previous section. It gives the estimates $\hat{\lambda}$ and $\hat{\gamma}$ (non-significance at the 5% level according to a two-sided t test is denoted by "n") and the improvement in determination (R^2) compared to the regression without adaptive/extrapolative component, resp. The remaining estimates are not given here since they closely resemble those obtained in the previous section.

Table 3.25: Significance of adaptive/extrapolative behavior (Average Forecasts, Periods 21-end)

	Adaptive Behavior		Extrapolative Behavior	
Exp. No.	$\hat{\lambda}$	Impr. R^2	$\hat{\gamma}$	Impr. R^2
1	0.132	0.0013	n−0.009	<0.0001
2	n0.012	<0.0001	n0.018	0.0004
3	n−0.103	0.0010	n0.019	0.0004
4	n0.066	0.0022	n−0.018	0.0007
5	0.082	0.0090	n−0.040	0.0060
6	n0.010	0.0002	n−0.034	0.0043
7	0.381	0.0834	n−0.140	0.0153
8	n0.056	0.0005	n−0.013	0.0001
9	n−0.062	0.0039	0.063	0.0331
10	0.302	0.0434	.	.
11	n−0.038	0.0028	0.092	0.0188
12	n−0.051	0.0012	0.077	0.0095
13	n−0.025	0.0009	n0.103	0.0111
14	0.244	0.0574	n0.025	0.0011

Note: In Exp. 10, $\Delta p_{-1} = \Delta v_{-1} - \Delta w_{-1}$, thus, an extrapolative component cannot be added to the model.

Added to a model which accounts for single exogenous variables, adaptive and extrapolative components are much less significant than in context with the simple model including only expected changes of p (See Section 3.3). In particular, for Exp. 11-13, extrapolative behavior is partly captured by past changes of the exogenous variables. Correspondingly, adaptive behavior fails to be significant.

Three remarkable cases remain: the significant and positive adaptive coefficient in Exp. 7, 10, and 14.

For Exp. 7 and 14, the result corresponds to that obtained from the simple regression in Section 3.3.

For Exp. 10, the sign is opposite to that obtained from the simple regression $\Delta f = \beta_0 + \beta_1 E\Delta p + \lambda(f_{-1} - p_{-1})$. The reason for this, however, is merely statistical: Since $\Delta p_{-1} = \Delta v_{-1} - \Delta w_{-1}$ (see note on the table), an extrapolative component is already incorporated in the regression. Thus, the adaptive regression approach contains both adaptive and extrapolative components which are highly correlated (see Section 3.3 above). This explains the remarkable result for λ in Exp. 10.[20]

Similar to the simpler regressions in Section 3.3, $\hat{\lambda}$ and $\hat{\gamma}$ have opposite signs for 11 out of 13 experiments.[21]

To summarize, after accounting for the influence of single exogenous variables, adaptive and extrapolative components have no longer been found to be significant independent features of aggregate forecasts.

Bang-bang and Past Trends

Viewing plots of p against forecasts suggests that for some individuals there is an influence of bang-bang movements and past trends. This can be verified by adding (separately) the following components to the regression equations estimated in Section 3.6:

---

[20] See remark in Section 3.3 about joint regression on adaptive and extrapolative components.

[21] Note that Exp. 10 is not included.

1. a "bang-bang" component $\beta_{bb}(E\Delta p - \Delta p_{-1})$,
2. a "short-trend" component $\beta_{st}(p_{-1} - p_{-3})$,
3. a "long-trend" component $\beta_{lt}(p_{-1} - p_{-5})$.

The following table gives, for each of the three regressions, the parameter estimate of the added component (non-significance according to a two-sided t test at level 5% is marked by "n") and the improvement in determination compared to the regressions in Section 3.6.

Table 3.26:
"Psychological components" added to the regressions from Section 3.6 (Average Forecasts, Periods 21-end)

	"Bangbang"		"Short trend"		"Long trend"	
Exp. No.	$\hat{\beta}_{bb}$	Impr. R^2	$\hat{\beta}_{st}$	Impr. R^2	$\hat{\beta}_{lt}$	Impr. R^2
1	n0.010	0.0001	n−0.018	0.0007	−0.020	0.0018
2	n−0.016	0.0003	n0.005	<0.0001	n0.000	<0.0001
3	n−0.019	0.0004	n0.009	0.0003	n0.009	0.0008
4	n0.020	0.0009	−0.030	0.0036	−0.031	0.0090
5	n0.040	0.0060	−0.044	0.0127	−0.041	0.0260
6	n0.035	0.0043	−0.068	0.0405	n−0.017	0.0072
7	n0.140	0.0153	−0.154	0.0353	−0.159	0.0881
8	n0.013	0.0001	n−0.052	0.0017	−0.063	0.0064
9	−0.144	0.0157	n0.023	0.0044	n0.006	0.0012
10	·	·	0.066	0.0224	n0.020	0.0078
11	−0.092	0.0188	0.072	0.0267	n0.018	0.0044
12	−0.077	0.0095	n0.027	0.0037	n0.009	0.0012
13	n−0.103	0.0111	n0.008	0.0002	n−0.020	0.0057
14	n−0.025	0.0011	n−0.031	0.0065	n−0.024	0.0063

Note: For Exp. 10, $E\Delta p - \Delta p_{-1} = -E\Delta w - \Delta v_{-1} + \Delta w_{-1}$, i.e. the bangbang component is a linear combination of other regressors and, thus, cannot be included in the regression.

The following conclusions can be drawn from the table:

Bang-bang component: This component is not significant, with the exception of Exp. 9, 11, and 12. For Exp. 11 and 12, the results are doubtful since for these experiments, the bang-bang component is nearly a linear combination of the other regressors (in Exp. 10: a full linear combination, see note on the table). Thus, we may conclude that bang-bang movements have no systematic influence on average forecasts (in Chapter 5, however, it will be seen that they do have an influence on the dispersion of forecasts). For median forecasts, the bang-bang component is significant only for Exp. 9.

"Past bang-bang" components like $(\Delta p_{-1} - \Delta p_{-2})$ do not yield significance, either.

Trend components: Trends generally have a significant and *negative* influence on average forecasts in the disturbed simple full-information experiments and in the seasonality experiments. The influence, however, is small: Consider, for example, $\hat{\beta}_{st}$ in Exp. 6: After a short-term trend of -20, average forecasts are shifted by $-0.068 \cdot (-20) = 1.36$.

For the incomplete-information experiments, trends seem to have a positive influence but this is significant only for short-term trends in Exp. 10 and 11.

These results seem quite plausible:

The exogenous variable w in the incomplete-information experiments 10-14 has 10-period trend segments which were easily seen by subjects from the graphical representation. Since v has no trend, these trend segments of w induce corresponding segments of p - when w is relevant (in Exp. 10-13). This causes subjects to "continue" past trends - estimates $\hat{\beta}_{st}$ and $\hat{\beta}_{lt}$ are positive. Note that for Exp. 14 where w is irrelevant, both estimates are negative.

In Exp. 9, the autoregressive component induced long (more than 10 periods) trend segments and, correspondingly, both estimates are postive.

For Exp. 7 and 8, the seasonal fluctuations induce four-period (for Exp. 7) and five-period (for Exp. 8) segments, resp., which are interrupted by the crashes. Thus, subjects are more likely to "interrupt" past trends in those experiments. This is matched by the strong negative influence of past trends in Exp. 7. In Exp. 8, subjects captured the model relatively well, so that their behavior is captured by dummies and changes of the exogenous variables y and z, and the influence of past trends is less significant than in Exp. 7.

After these considerations, seven experiments remain which are "neutral" with respect to trends: Exp. 1-6, and 14. Within this group, negative signs occur more often, but the negative influence is significant in only three experiments (for short as well as for long trends). The improvement-of-determination figures as well as the t statistics (which are not tabulated) indicate that the influence of "long trends" is slightly more significant. However, results become less and less conclusive when regressing on trends longer than five periods.

For median forecasts, similar results are obtained with respect to the trend components.

To summarize, relevance of bang-bang movements can be denied, whereas past trends are partly significant: The influence is positive in presence of long (at least 10 periods) trend segments, and negative for the seasonality experiments. If trends are not apparent, negative influence of past trends is prevailing but not significant.

The next chapter will pass to individual forecasts: It will be shown that most features found for aggregate forecasts hold for a significant majority of individual forecasts, too.

3.8 Concluding Remarks on Average Forecasts

The basic criterion applied in this chapter for comparing various prediction concepts to observed aggregate forecasts is the mean absolute deviation. The results are summarized in the following tables (the first two tables for all periods, the third and fourth for Periods 21-end). Note that "underestimating predictions" are given by

$$f^U = p_{-1} + c\,E^D \Delta p$$

with $c = 0.75$ for Exp. 1-4 and $c = 0.50$ for the remaining experiments, and delta-expected changes $E^D \Delta p$ are replaced by misspecified expected changes in Exp. 7, 9, and 11. Some comments are given after presenting the tables.

Table 3.27: Average Forecasts,
mean absolute deviations from various prediction concepts
(All Periods)

Exp. No.	p	Mean absolute deviation from ... f^R	f^{LSL1}	f^{LSL2}	f^D	f^M	f^U
1	1.355	[1]	[1]	[1]	[1]	–	0.926
2	1.052	[1]	1.067	1.058	[1]	–	0.668
3	0.788	[1]	[1]	[1]	[1]	–	0.488
4	2.163	1.949	1.863	1.677	1.424	–	1.016
5	2.417	2.012	1.997	1.968	1.718	–	0.822
6	2.530	2.186	2.154	1.876	1.741	–	0.743
7	5.828	[1]	[1]	[1]	[1]	*3.041	*2.155
8	3.915	[1]	[1]	[1]	[1]	–	2.096
9	2.246	[1]	2.255	2.230	[1]	*1.734	*0.808
10	2.075	1.046	–	–	[2]	–	0.545
11	2.025	1.851	–	–	[2]	*1.011	*0.755
12	1.888	0.971	–	–	[2]	–	0.509
13	2.163	1.852	–	–	1.097	–	0.795
14	2.248	1.017	–	–	0.916	–	*0.779

[1] equal to MAD from p

[2] equal to MAD from f^R

* Comparison to
$f_t^M = p_{t-1} + \Delta y_t - \Delta z_t + 5\text{sign}(t\ modulo\ 4)$,
and $f^U = p_{t-1} + \frac{1}{2} \cdot (\Delta y_t - \Delta z_t + 5\text{sign}(t\ modulo\ 4))$ (for Exp. 7),
$f_t^M = p_{t-1} + \frac{1}{2}\Delta x_t + \Delta y_t - \Delta z_t$
and $f_t^U = p_{t-1} + \frac{1}{2} \cdot (\frac{1}{2}\Delta x_t + \Delta y_t - \Delta z_t$ (for Exp. 9),
$f_t^M = p_{t-1} - E\Delta w_t$ and $f_t^U = p_{t-1} - \frac{1}{2} \cdot E\Delta w_t$ (for Exp. 11),
$f_t^U = p_{t-1} + \frac{1}{2} \cdot E\Delta p_t$ (for Exp. 14).

Table 3.28: Median forecasts,
mean absolute deviations from various prediction concepts
(All Periods)

Exp. No.	p	f^R	f^{LSL1}	f^{LSL2}	f^D	f^M	f^U
		Mean absolute deviation from ...					
1	0.675	[1]	[1]	[1]	[1]	–	1.078
2	0.520	[1]	0.637	0.614	[1]	–	0.808
3	0.169	[1]	[1]	[1]	[1]	–	0.688
4	2.105	1.915	1.807	1.625	1.365	–	0.858
5	2.335	1.985	1.940	1.905	1.605	–	0.840
6	2.588	2.213	2.246	1.964	1.763	–	0.875
7	6.240	[1]	[1]	[1]	[1]	*3.130	*2.350
8	3.170	[1]	[1]	[1]	[1]	–	2.730
9	2.190	[1]	2.213	2.176	[1]	*1.590	*0.890
10	2.119	0.994	–	–	[2]	–	0.656
11	1.963	1.800	–	–	[2]	*1.025	*0.825
12	1.813	0.813	–	–	[2]	–	0.538
13	2.094	1.844	–	–	0.944	–	0.981
14	2.269	0.919	–	–	0.794	–	*0.750

[1], [2], *: see Table 3.27 above.

Table 3.29: Average Forecasts,
mean absolute deviations from various prediction concepts
(Periods 21-end)

Exp. No.	p	f^R	f^{LSL1}	f^{LSL2}	f^D	f^M	f^U
		Mean absolute deviation from ...					
1	1.264	[1]	[1]	[1]	[1]	–	0.924
2	0.921	[1]	0.936	0.928	[1]	–	0.590
3	0.630	[1]	[1]	[1]	[1]	–	0.396
4	1.990	1.785	1.727	1.598	1.329	–	0.741
5	2.223	1.889	1.895	1.876	1.591	–	0.734
6	2.415	2.031	1.974	1.577	1.614	–	0.663
7	5.711	[1]	[1]	[1]	[1]	*2.939	*2.165
8	3.598	[1]	[1]	[1]	[1]	–	2.070
9	2.295	[1]	2.281	2.264	[1]	*1.609	*0.804
10	2.253	1.192	–	–	[2]	–	0.560
11	2.009	1.863	–	–	[2]	*1.108	*0.757
12	1.834	0.836	–	–	[2]	–	0.483
13	2.071	1.804	–	–	1.095	–	0.737
14	2.307	0.905	–	–	0.845	–	*0.642

[1], [2], *: see Table 3.27 above.

Table 3.30: Median Forecasts,
mean absolute deviations from various prediction concepts
(Periods 21-end)

Exp. No.	p	Mean absolute deviation from ... f^R	f^{LSL1}	f^{LSL2}	f^D	f^M	f^U
1	0.538	[1]	[1]	[1]	[1]	–	1.078
2	0.281	[1]	0.425	0.404	[1]	–	0.766
3	0.025	[1]	[1]	[1]	[1]	–	0.633
4	1.894	1.731	1.649	1.532	1.244	–	0.778
5	2.156	1.869	1.874	1.851	1.519	–	0.813
6	2.517	2.133	2.133	1.715	1.667	–	0.800
7	6.175	[1]	[1]	[1]	[1]	*3.000	*2.331
8	2.638	[1]	[1]	[1]	[1]	–	2.781
9	2.213	[1]	2.220	2.203	[1]	*1.444	*0.922
10	2.342	1.538	–	–	[2]	–	0.708
11	1.933	1.800	–	–	[2]	*1.150	*0.817
12	1.800	0.700	–	–	[2]	–	0.533
13	1.958	1.792	–	–	0.958	–	0.908
14	2.292	0.792	–	–	0.692	–	*0.600

[1], [2], *: see Table 3.27 above.

The following observations follow from the tables without exception:

1. The (mean absolute) deviation from rational predictions is smaller than the (mean absolute) forecast error (for all experiments where different).

2. Comparing the two implementations of LSL, the deviations from Implementation 2 (only last 15 observations processed) are smaller than those from Implementation 1 (all past observations processed).

3. The deviations from delta predictions are less than the deviations from rational predictions (where delta predictions differ from rational predictions).

For average forecasts, underestimating predictions provide the best description in all experiments.

The next section will start with verifying these statements at the individual level.

4. Sum Results on Individual Forecasts

This chapter presents some results which lend support to the statements on aggregate forecasts in Chapter 3: Comparison of observed forecasts to various prediction concepts, non-rational features, learning, and "improvements" of underestimating predictions (regression on single exogenous variables and psychological components).

The basic method is counting the number of individuals for whom a certain feature holds (e.g. upward bias, learning behavior) and testing (by a one-sided binomial test) if this number is significantly high. As in Chapter 3, the first 20 periods are dropped, but this is no longer indicated in the tables.

4.1 Comparison to Various Prediction Concepts

From Chapter 3, we know that for average and median forecasts from most experiments, the following inequalities generally hold:[1]

Mean absolute forecast error > MAD from rational predictions,
MAD from LSL (Implementation 1) > MAD from LSL (Implement. 2),
MAD from rational predictions > MAD from delta predictions >
> MAD from underestimating predictions

In order to study whether this also holds true at the individual level, mean absolute errors and mean absolute deviations from rational predictions, LSL predictions, and so forth, can be listed for each individual and for average and median forecasts. The results for all subjects are given in the appendix. The table for Experiment 4 is presented as an example:

[1] (if the involved concepts differ from one another)

Table 4.1:
Experiment 4, Mean absolute deviations from ...
(Periods 21-end)

Subj. No.	p	f^R	f^{LSL1}	f^{LSL2}	f^D	f^U
1	2.71	2.40	2.50	2.45	2.28	2.10
2	3.05	3.07	3.00	3.03	2.69	2.52
3	3.06	3.05	2.88	2.85	2.80	2.36
4	2.80	2.64	2.58	2.57	2.29	1.87
5	2.49	2.25	2.21	2.16	1.88	2.05
6	3.99	3.73	3.79	3.46	3.55	3.09
7	2.01	1.88	1.75	1.79	1.20	1.51
8	2.11	1.98	1.91	1.85	1.55	1.15
9	2.69	2.58	2.53	2.37	2.15	1.52
10	2.55	2.26	2.24	2.22	2.04	2.05
11	1.98	1.66	1.51	1.65	1.11	1.18
12	2.19	1.90	1.88	1.81	1.53	1.21
Average	1.990	1.785	1.727	1.598	1.329	0.740
Median	1.894	1.731	1.649	1.532	1.244	0.778

First note that all inequalities from above hold for average and median forecasts. On the individual level, each inequality holds for a majority of subjects: For 11 out of 12 subjects, the mean absolute forecast error is greater than the mean absolute deviation from rational predictions, for 9 out of 12 subjects, the MAD from LSL(1) is greater than the MAD from LSL(2), all subjects are more "close" to delta than to rational predictions, and the MAD from delta predictions is grater than the MAD from underestimating predictions for 8 out of 12 subjects.

However, mean absolute deviations from underestimating predictions are quite large for many subjects. Thus, although it is the "best" prediction concept considered here, underestimating predictions may not be regarded as a good description of *individual* forecasting behavior - in contrast to the results at the aggregate level.

Looking at the "columns" of the table suggests that individuals generally forecast worse than the aggregate. There is some "gain in rationality" from aggregation.[2]

The results from Exp. 4 prove quite typical. Simple counting yields the following results:

1. Comparison of mean absolute errors (MAE) to mean absolute deviations from fully rational predictions (MAD^R):

$p \neq f^R$ for Exp. 4-6 and 10-14.
$MAE > MAD^R$ for average and median forecasts from all eight experiments considered.

Exp. No.	No. of Subjects	$MAE > MAD^R$ for ... subjects	$MAE < MAD^R$ for ... subjects
4	12	11	1
5	13	13	0
6	11	11	0
10	11	11	0
11	13	9	2
12	11	11	0
13	11	10	0
14	7	7	0
Total	89	83	3

In all eight experiments, for a majority of subjects $MAE > MAD^R$ holds. The proportion 8 out of 8 is significant at the 1% level as well as the proportion 83 out of 86 for all individuals.[3]

2. Comparison of mean absolute deviations from LSL predictions - Implementation 1 (all past observations processed) - to mean absolute deviations from LSL - Implementation 2 (only last 15 observations processed).

---

[2] This has to be expected since the MAD of average forecasts is always smaller than the average of individual MAD's. Thus, for most samples, the majority of individuals "deviates more than the average".

[3] If not indicated otherwise, throughout this chapter "significant" is meant with respect to a one-sided binomial test of H_0: "equal frequencies".

$f^{LSL1} \neq f^{LSL2}$ for Exp. 2, 4, 5, 6, 9.
$MAD^{LSL1} > MAD^{LSL2}$ for average and median forecasts from all five experiments considered.

Exp. No.	No. of Subjects	$MAD^{LSL1} > MAD^{LSL2}$ for ... subj.	$MAD^{LSL1} > MAD^{LSL2}$ for ... subj.
2	13	10	3
4	12	9	3
5	13	9	4
6	11	10	1
9	14	9	5
Total	63	47	16

In all five experiments, for a majority of subjects $MAD^{LSL1} > MAD^{LSL2}$ holds (5 out of 5: significant at the 5% level). The total proportion 47 out of 63 is significant at the 1% level.

3. Comparison of mean absolute deviations from LSL(2) (MAD^{LSL2}) to mean absolute deviations from delta predictions (MAD^D).
$f^{LSL2} \neq f^D$ for Exp. 4-6.
$MAD^{LSL2} > MAD^D$ for median forecasts from all three experiments considered and for average forecasts from Exp. 4 and 5.

Exp. No.	No. of Subjects	$MAD^{LSL2} > MAD^D$ for ... subjects	$MAD^{LSL2} < MAD^D$ for ... subjects
4	12	11	1
5	13	11	2
6	11	5	6
Total	36	27	9

In Exp. 6, the claimed inequality does not hold for a majority of subjects. But anyway, for three experiments, no proportion is significant. The total proportion 27 out of 36, however, is significant at the 1% level.

4. Comparison of mean absolute deviations from rational predictions (MAD^R) to mean absolute deviations from delta predictions (MAD^D).

$f^R \neq f^D$ for Exp. 4, 5, 6, 13, 14
$MAD^R > MAD^D$ for average and median forecasts from all five experiments considered.

Exp. No.	No. of Subjects	$MAD^R > MAD^D$ for ... subjects	$MAD^R < MAD^D$ for ... subjects
4	12	12	0
5	13	11	2
6	11	9	2
13	11	11	0
14	7	3	4
Total	54	46	8

In four out of five experiments, the claimed inequality $MAD^R > MAD^D$ holds for a majority of subjects. The proportion 4 out of 5 is not significant. However, the total proportion 46 out of 54 is significant at the 1% level.

5. Comparison of mean absolute deviations from fully rational predictions (MAD^R) to mean absolute deviations from underestimating predictions (MAD^U), where $f^U = p_{-1} + c\,E^D\Delta p$, with $c = 0.75$ for Exp. 1-4 and $c = 0.50$ for Exp. 5-14. For Experiment 7, 9, and 11, underestimating predictions are based on a misspecified model (see Chapter 3): Delta-expected changes $E^D\Delta p$ are replaced by misspecified expected changes $E^M\Delta p$ which gives (see Section 3.3):
$f^U = p_{-1} + 0.5 \cdot (\Delta y - \Delta z + 5sign(t\ modulo\ 4))$ for Exp. 7,
$f^U = p_{-1} + 0.5 \cdot (\frac{1}{2}\Delta x + \Delta y - \Delta z)$ for Exp. 9, and
$f^U = p_{-1} + 0.5 \cdot (-E\Delta w)$ for Exp. 11.

For Exp. 14, $f^U = p_{-1} + 0.5 \cdot E\Delta p$ ($E\Delta p$ replaced for $E^D\Delta p$).

$f^R \neq f^U$ for all 14 experiments. $MAD^R > MAD^U$ for average forecasts from all 14 experiments and for median forecasts from Exp. 4-7, 9-14. For median forecasts from Exp. 1-3 and 8, the converse inequality holds.

Exp. No.	No. of Subjects	$MAD^R > MAD^U$ for ... subjects	$MAD^R < MAD^U$ for ... subjects
1	14	6	8
2	13	5	8
3	12	1	11
4	12	12	0
5	13	13	0
6	11	9	2
7	13	12	1
8	12	7	5
9	14	13	1
10	11	8	3
11	13	11	2
12	11	5	6
13	11	10	1
14	7	5	2
Total for			
Exp. 1-3	39	12	27
Exp. 4-14	128	105	23

For Exp. 1-3, the results are not in favor of underestimating predictions. This is due to the high proportion of subjects who predicted nearly rationally.

For the remaining 11 experiments, there is only one "exception" (Exp. 12) where the claimed inequality $MAD^R > MAD^U$ holds only for a minority of subjects. The proportion 10 out of 11 is significant at the 1% level as well as the total proportion 105 out of 128 (for Exp. 4-14).

6. Comparison of mean absolute deviations from delta predictions (MAD^D) to mean absolute deviations from underestimating predictions (MAD^U).

Results differ from comparison MAD^R to MAD^U for Exp. 4-6, 13, and 14 (since $f^R \neq f^D$ for these experiments).

$MAD^D > MAD^U$ for average and median forecasts from all five experiments considered.

Exp. No.	No. of Subjects	$MAD^D > MAD^U$ for ... subjects	$MAD^D < MAD^U$ for ... subjects
4	12	8	4
5	13	12	1
6	11	8	3
13	11	6	4
14	7	5	2
Total	54	39	14

In all five experiments, the inequality $MAD^D > MAD^U$ holds for a majority of subjects. This proportion is significant at the 5% level. The total proportion 39 out of 53 is significant at the 1% level.

7. Comparison of mean absolute deviations from fully rational predictions (MAD^R) to mean absolute deviations from misspecified predictions (MAD^M) for
Exp. 7 ($f^M = p_{-1} + \Delta y - \Delta z + 5sign(t\ modulo\ 4)$),
Exp. 9 ($f^M = p_{-1} + \frac{1}{2}\Delta x + \Delta y - \Delta z$), and
Exp. 11 ($f^M = p_{-1} - E\Delta w$).
$MAD^R > MAD^M$ for average and median forecasts from all three experiments considered.

Exp. No.	No. of Subjects	$MAD^R > MAD^M$ for for ... subjects	$MAD^R < MAD^M$ for for ... subjects
7	13	12	1
9	14	13	1
11	13	11	2

For every single experiment, the proportion of individuals who fulfil the claimed inequality $MAD^R > MAD^M$ is significant at the 5% level. Summing up over the three experiments does not make sense since the misspecified models differ.

The tables show that the claimed inequalities $MAE > MAD^R$, $MAD^{LSL1} > MAD^{LSL2}$, $MAD^R > MAD^D$, $MAD^R > MAD^U$, and $MAD^D > MAD^U$ hold for a significant majority of individuals. Thus, underestimating predictions are the best concept for aggregate as well as for most individual forecasts. However, for many subjects, the deviations from underestimating predictions are quite high. Moreover, the reduction of *MAD* by passing to underestimating predictions is not as high for many individuals as for average and median forecasts.

Comparing individual mean absolute deviations from underestimating predictions ($MAD_i^U, i = 1, \ldots, N$) to aggregate ones ($MAD_A^U, MAD_M^U$), the inequality

$$MAD_i^U > MAD_A^U \tag{4.1}$$

holds for 166 out of 167 individuals in from all 14 experiments (one exception in Exp. 14). The corresponding inequality for median forecasts,

$$MAD_i^U > MAD_M^U \tag{4.2}$$

holds with only four exceptions (three subjects in Exp. 3 and one in Exp. 13). For comparison, the following table gives, for each experiment, the number of individuals where

$$MAD_i^R > MAD_A^R \;, \tag{4.3}$$

$$\text{or} \qquad MAD_i^R > MAD_M^R \;, \qquad \text{resp.} \tag{4.4}$$

holds, i.e. the number of individuals who forecast less rational than the corresponding group average or median. (only for periods 21-end).

Table 4.2:
Comparison of MAD's from rational predictions (Periods 21-end)
Number of subjects where

Exp. No.	No. of Subj.	Eq.(4.3) holds	Eq.(4.4) holds
1	14	8	9
2	13	8	12
3	12	5	9
4	12	11	11
5	13	12	12
6	11	10	10
7	13	12	12
8	12	9	10
9	14	12	12
10	11	8	9
11	13	11	11
12	11	9	10
13	11	9	9
14	7	6	6
Total for			
Exp. 1-3	39	21	30
Exp. 4-14	128	109	112

There are some exceptions from Eq. (4.3) and (4.4), i.e. some individuals forecast more "rationally" than the group average or median.[4] The fact that much less exceptions are observed for deviations from underestimating predictions stresses the conclusion that the latter concept fails to describe individual forecasting behavior sufficiently.

---

[4] Note that $MAD_i > MAD_A$ has to be expected to hold for a majority of individuals, see Footnote 2 above.

4.2 Non-Rational Features of Forecasts

This section presents, at the individual level, some evidence on possible reasons for the observed lack of rationality at the individual level which are already known from Chapter 3. Concentration on changes and misspecified models have already been analyzed in Section 4.1 by comparing rational to delta predictions and to misspecified predictions at the individual level. This section investigates

1. Upward bias
2. Underestimation of changes

Upward Bias

For this purpose, an individual's forecasts are called *upward biased* if the mean deviation from rational predictions is positive, $MD^R > 0$. The following table presents, for each experiment, the number of individuals whose forecasts are upward biased. At the end of the table, the results from comparing to delta (for Exp. 4-6, 13 and 14) and misspecified (for Exp. 9 and 11) predictions are presented. Experiments 7 and 8 are excluded from consideration as in Chapter 3.

Table 4.3: Sum results on Upward Bias
(Comparison to fully rational predictions,
(*) to delta predictions (for Exp. 4-6),
and to misspecified predictions(for Exp. 9 and 11), resp.)
Number of individuals with ...

Exp. No.	No. of Subjects	$MD^R > 0$	$MD_R < 0$
1	14	9	5
2	13	7	6
3	12	6	3
4	12	3	9
5	13	5	8
6	11	4	7
9	14	11	3

(continued)

Table 4.3 (continued)
Number of individuals with ...

Exp. No.	No. of Subjects	$MD^R > 0$	$MD^R < 0$
10	11	8	3
11	13	7	6
12	11	7	4
13	11	11	0
14	7	3	4
		$MD^D > 0$	$MD^D < 0$
* 4	12	11	1
* 5	13	11	2
* 6	11	5	6
*13	11	7	4
*14	7	2	5
		$MD^M > 0$	$MD^M < 0$
** 9	14	11	3
**11	13	9	4
Total(1)	142	81	58
Total(2)	142	93	46

Remark:
Total(1) = Sum over the first block (concerning MD^R only).
Total(2): calculated as Total (1), but the results for delta and misspecified predictions (*) have been adopted for Exp. 4-6, 13, 14, 9, and 11.

As stated earlier in Chapter 3, Experiments 7 and 8 are not suitable to test for bias. Therefore, these experiments have been excluded.

In eight out of twelve experiments, a majority of subjects revealed an upward bias. When comparing to delta/misspecified predictions instead of rational predictions for Exp. 4-6, 9, 11, 13, and 14, this proportion is higher (10 out of 12). The latter proportion is significant at the 5% level.

For Total (1) (Comparison to rational predictions), the number of individuals with positive MD^R is significant at the 5% level, for Total (2), it is significant at the 1% level.

Since most individuals tend to calculate delta or misspecified changes, Total(2) is more conclusive. Upward bias is present for a highly significant majority of subjects.

Underestimation of Changes

As in Chapter 3, forecasted changes ($f - p_{-1}$) are compared to rationally expected changes, delta-expected changes, and misspecified expected changes. There are two ways to analyze underestimation of changes:
(1) Counting the number of under- and overestimations of changes for each individual, and (2) estimating the regression

$$f - p_{-1} = \beta_0 + \beta_1 E\Delta p + u \ , \tag{4.5}$$

and testing $H_0 : \beta_1 = 1$ against $H_1 : \beta_1 < 1$. More striking results are obtained if counting and regression, resp., are restricted to such periods where the absolute expected change is relatively large, for example $|E\Delta p| > 2$.

The following tables summarize the sum results: For each experiment, the number of individuals is listed for whom the number of underestimations of change (#UEC) exceeds the number of overestimations of change (#OEC). In the first table the results from considering all periods (after Period 20) are presented, the second table gives the results from omitting those periods where the expected change $E\Delta p$ of p is absolutely less than or equal 2. At the end of both tables, the results from comparing to delta-expected changes and to misspecified expected changes are given (*).

Table 4.4: Counting results on underestimation of change

Exp. No.	No. of Sub-jects	Number of individuals with ... #UEC > #OEC signif. (1%)	#UEC > #OEC signif. (5%)	#UEC > #OEC	#UEC < # OEC
1	14	2	4	9	3
2	13	3	3	10	3
3	12	0	0	3	9
4	12	6	7	12	0
5	13	4	7	13	0
6	11	1	3	6	5
7	13	2	4	11	2
8	12	7	7	12	0
9	14	7	7	12	1
10	11	5	5	6	4
11	13	5	7	13	0
12	11	6	7	8	3
13	11	2	4	9	2
14	7	0	2	2	5
* 4	12	3	5	8	3
* 5	13	4	5	12	1
* 6	11	0	3	5	5
*13	11	3	3	6	5
* 7	13	0	2	4	9
* 9	14	4	6	8	6
*11	13	2	3	5	8
Total(1)	167	50	67	126	37
Total(2)	160	39	53	96	59

Note on the table: In Exp. 14, delta-expected changes are always zero. Thus, Exp. 14 is omitted in Total (2). Apart from this, Total(1) and Total(2) were calculated as in Table 4.3 above.

In 12 out of 14 experiments (this proportion is significant at the 1% level), a majority of subjects reveals more under- than overestimations of *rationally* expected changes. Replacing rationally expected by delta or misspecified expected changes for Exp. 4-6, 7, 9, 11, and 13, this proportion reduces to 9 out of 13 which is no longer significant at the 5% level. The total proportions (126 out of 163, 96 out of 155, resp.), however, are significant at the 1% level.

The next table presents the results from omitting "small" changes:

Table 4.5: Counting results on underestimation of changes, only absolute expected changes > 2 considered.

		Number of individuals with ...			
Exp. No.	No. of Sub- jects	#UEC > #OEC signif. (1%)	#UEC > #OEC signif. (5%)	#UEC > #OEC	#UEC < # OEC
1	14	5	5	11	1
2	13	5	7	12	1
3	12	0	2	3	2
4	12	8	11	12	0
5	13	12	13	13	0
6	11	4	6	9	2
7	13	4	6	11	1
8	12	8	10	12	0
9	14	10	12	14	0
10	–	–	–	–	–
11	13	12	12	13	0
12	11	8	8	10	1
13	11	10	11	11	0
14	–	–	–	–	–

(continued)

Table 4.5 (continued)

Number of individuals with ...

Exp. No.	No. of Subjects	#UEC > #OEC signif. (1%)	#UEC > #OEC signif. (1%)	#UEC > #OEC	#UEC < # OEC
* 4	12	6	9	12	0
* 5	13	10	11	13	0
* 6	11	5	6	7	3
** 7	13	3	3	9	3
** 9	14	8	9	13	1
Total(1)	149	86	103	131	8
Total(2)	125	58	70	102	8

Note: In Exp. 10 and 14, only absolute expected changes ≤ 2 occur, and these experiments are missing in Total (1). Misspecified expected changes for Exp. 11 and delta-expected changes for Exp. 13 are also absolutely ≤ 2. Thus, in Total (2), Exp. 10, 11, 13, and 14 are missing.

Now, in all experiments for a majority of subjects the number of underestimations exceeds that of overestimations. The number of exceptions in the total proportions is very small, far below the 1% significance bound.

Note that underestimation is less significant when comparing to delta and misspecified predictions (compare Total(1) to Total(2)). This corresponds to the fact that regressions of Δf on $E^D\Delta p$ and $E^M\Delta p$, resp., result in higher slope estimates than regression on $E\Delta p$.

The regressions $f - p_{-1} = \beta_0 + \beta_1 \mathrm{E}[\Delta p] + u$ yield even more impressive results which are given in the following table:

Table 4.6: Sum results on regression $\Delta f = \beta_0 + \beta_1 E\Delta p + u$,
($* = E\Delta p$ replaced by $E^D\Delta p$ and $E^M\Delta p$, resp.)
(All Periods)
Number of individuals with ...

Exp. No.	No. of Subjects	$\hat{\beta}_1 < 1$ signif.[1] (1%)	$\hat{\beta}_1 < 1$ signif.[1] (5%)	$\hat{\beta}_1 < 1$	$\hat{\beta}_1 > 1$
1	14	6	7	12	2
2	13	7	9	12	1
3	12	3	4	8	1
4	12	11	11	12	0
5	13	13	13	13	0
6	11	9	9	11	0
7	13	12	12	13	0
8	12	9	10	11	1
9	14	14	14	14	0
10	11	9	9	10	1
11	13	12	12	13	0
12	11	11	11	11	0
13	11	10	10	11	0
14	7	6	6	7	0
* 4	12	9	10	12	0
* 5	13	12	13	13	0
* 6	11	8	8	9	2
*13	11	10	10	10	1
* 7	13	8	9	10	3
* 9	14	11	11	14	0
*11	13	11	11	12	1
Total(1)	167	132	137	158	6
Total(2)	160	114	122	144	13

[1]: with respect to a one-sided t test of $H_0 : \beta_1 = 1$ against $H_1 : \beta_1 < 1$.

For more than 90% of the individuals, the estimated slope coefficient $\hat{\beta}_1$ is less than one, for more than two thirds significantly at the 1% level (according to a one-sided t test of $H_0 : \beta_1 = 1$). Underestimation is again less significant when comparing to delta or misspecified predictions.

Altogether, these regression results are striking enough. Thus, the results from restricting regression to "large-change" periods need not be presented here.

Both approaches (regression and counting) show that underestimation of changes is present for a highly significant majority of subjects.

To summarize, two sources of non-rational behavior have been found significant at the individual level: upward bias and underestimation of changes. These features are already known from Chapter 3. Two more features from Chapter 3 - concentration on changes rather than on levels and misspecified auxiliary models - have already been studied in Section 4.1 when comparing various prediction concepts: Delta predictions and misspecified predictions (for Exp. 7, 9, and 11) perform better than rational predictions for a highly significant majority of individuals.

Other non-rational features like adaptive or extrapolative behavior are studied in Section 4.5 below.

4.3 Learning Behavior

If learning is present on the individual level, one should expect that, for a majority of individuals, the mean absolute deviation from rational predictions decreases from the initial section (1-10) to the main section (21-end).

The following table shows that this indeed holds true. It summarizes the number of individuals #L for whom the mean absolute deviation from rational predictions decreases from (1-10) to (11-20), from (11-20) to (21-end), from (1-10) to (21-end), and the number #NL of individuals for whom the mean absolute deviation increases from (1-10) to (21-end).

Table 4.7: Sum results on learning
(* = with respect to delta predictions (Exp. 4-6, 13 and 14)
or misspecified predictions (Exp. 7, 9, and 11), resp.)

Exp. No.	No. of Sub-jects	#L (1-10) to (11-20)	#L (11-20) to (21-end)	#L (1-10) to (21-end)	#NL (1-10) to (21-end)
1	14	11	8	9	5
2	13	13	8	13	0
3	12	10	8	11	0
4	12	9	7	11	1
5	13	10	9	13	0
6	11	9	6	8	3
d 7	13	7	9	9	4
8	12	7	10	9	3
d 9	14	13	5	12	2
10	11	5	3	2	9
11	13	7	8	7	4
12	11	9	9	10	1
13	11	11	4	9	2
14	7	2	5	7	0
* 4	12	12	5	11	1
* 5	13	13	10	13	0
* 6	11	10	5	9	2
* 13	11	8	3	8	3
* 14	7	3	5	6	1
*d 7	13	9	8	12	1
* 9	14	13	5	14	0
* 11	13	9	3	4	4
Total(1)	167	123	99	130	34
Total(2)	167	132	90	131	30

Notes on the table:
Total (1) = sum over first block of the table (learning with respect to

rational predictions).
Total (2) = sum, with (*) lines replaced for the corresponding lines in the first block.
d = (11-40) and (41-end) instead of (11-20) and (21-end), resp.

With respect to rational predictions, there are more "learning" than "unlearning" subjects (from (1-10) to (21-end)) in 13 out of 14 experiments. This proportion is significant at the 1% level according to a one-sided binomial test of H_0 : "$proportion = \frac{1}{2}$" (which would correspond to no learning). When comparing to delta/misspecified predictions for Exp. 4-6, 13, 14, 7, 9, and 11, a tie is observed in Exp. 13, and more "unlearning" occurs in Exp. 11.

For the totals, a significant (at the 1% level) majority learns according to comparison of (1-10) to (11-20) and to (21-end).

In the analysis of aggregate behavior also some unlearning at the end of the experiments has been observed. The following table gives, for each experiment, the number #U of individuals where the mean absolute deviation from rational (* = from delta/misspecified predictions) increases from (21-60) to (61-end). #NU denotes the number where the converse holds.

Table 4.8: Sum results on unlearning
(* = for delta predictions (Exp. 4-6, 13, 14),
and misspecified predictions (Exp. 7, 9, and 11), resp.)

Exp. No.	No. of Subjects	#U	#NU
1	14	7	7
2	13	4	9
3	12	4	5
4	12	5	7
5	13	8	5
6	9	2	7
7	13	8	3
8	12	3	9
9	14	12	2

(continued)

Table 4.8 (continued)

Exp. No.	No. of Subjects	#U	#NU
10	11	5	5
11	13	6	7
12	11	5	6
13	11	7	4
14	7	3	4
* 4	12	4	8
* 5	13	9	4
* 6	9	3	4
* 13	11	7	4
* 14	7	2	5
* 7	13	9	3
* 9	14	5	9
* 11	13	3	10
Total(1)	165	79	80
Total(2)	165	70	88

Notes on the table:
Total(1) and Total(2) calculated as in Table 4.7.
For Exp. 6, two subjects stopped participating after Period 60. Therefore, only nine subjects could be evaluated for this table.

As already stated in the Chapter 3, unlearning is obviously not significant, there is even a majority who "improved" forecasting after Period 60.

4.4 Regression on Single Exogenous Variables

This section corresponds to Section 3.6 which presented regressions of average forecasted changes on changes of involved exogenous variables.

Strictly speaking, counting over individual regression results is trivial: Since regression estimates from average forecasts equal the average of individual regression estimates,[5] counting over individual regressions will generally confirm the results from average forecasts. The only goal of counting is to find - based on a large number of independent subjects - more significance of those results already obtained for aggregate forecasts.

Since Section 3.6 was not designed to find significance of certain phenomena, this section does not give sum results but only briefly reports some highlights from studying individual regression results (for the exact regression equations estimated see Section 3.6):

Simple full-information Experiments: 1-6 and 9

The overvaluation of the highly volatile variable z in Exp. 1, 2, 4, 5, and 9 (in Exp. 3 and 6, z was irrelevant) is impressively confirmed: Without any exception, subjects' behavior (regression results) matched the negative influence of z whereas some exceptions from correct assessing are observed for the other variables. The null hypothesis H_0: "*parameter relations equal coefficient relations in the true model*" is rejected for 38 out of 66 participants in Exp. 1, 2, 4, 5, and 9.[6] Among those 38 rejections, z is overvalued with respect to all other relevant variables[7] in 23 cases. This means: overvaluation of z contributes to significant deviations from the "correct" coefficient relation (which would give delta or underestimating delta predictions) for more than one third of subjects in those experiments.

The last disturbance u_{-1} (in Exp. 4-6) has significant influence for only 6 out of 36 subjects, for three of them the (significant) influence of u_{-1} is negative which is the implication of rationality. With respect to the exogenous variables x, y, and z, however, these three subjects are far away from rationality.

Seasonality experiments: 7 and 8

An overvaluation of z is not apparent in these experiments.

---

[5] With the exception of regressions containing an adaptive component, i.e. an individual component among the regressors.

[6] H_0 is rejected for only 4 out of 23 participants in Exp. 3 and 6.

[7] I.e. the absolute relation of parameter estimates exceeds the absolute coefficient relation in the true model.

In Exp. 7, a majority of subjects completely fails to forecast the "crashes": The estimate $\hat{\delta}_0$ of the "crash-period" coefficient (see Section 3.6) is positive for 7 out of 13 subjects (and for two of them even significant). This result corresponds to the misspecified model used in Chapter 3.

Incomplete-information experiments: 10-14

The most striking phenomenon in these experiments is the replacement of past changes of the exogenous variables v and w for conditional expected changes of these variables.

Only 3 subjects (in Exp. 10-12 where the underlying model was undisturbed) succeeded in forecasting rationally, i.e. guessed rationally expected changes of v and w correctly. Apart from this, for 20 out of 35 subjects in Exp. 10, 11, and 13 (where w had negative contemporary influence), Δw_{-1} has a significant and negative influence but not $E\Delta w$. Among the remaining 15 cases, there are only four subjects for whom the converse holds ($E\Delta w$ had significant and negative influence but not Δw_{-1}). For the exogenous variable v, results are weaker: Δv_{-1} has a significant influence for 13 out of 29 subjects in Exp. 10, 12, and 14 (where v has contemporary influence). In Exp. 14, the sign of influence is positive in spite of the negative influence of v.

4.5 Psychological Factors

In Chapter 3, the significance of adaptive and extrapolative components (last forecast error and last change of p, resp.) and of two more psychological factors (bang-bang movements and past trends) were investigated for aggregate forecasts. The basic method was adding a component to regressions on single exogenous variables and testing its significance by a simple t test.

This section presents some counting results on individual forecasts, i.e. the number of subjects with negative and positive adaptive/extrapolative/bang-bang/trend coefficients in the regression equations obtained by adding

an adaptive component $\lambda(f_{-1} - p_{-1})$, or
an extrapolative component $\gamma \Delta p_{-1}$, or
a bang-bang component $\beta_{bb}(E\Delta p - \Delta p_{-1})$, or
a short-trend component $\beta_{st}(p_{-1} - p_{-3})$, or
a long-trend component $\beta_{lt}(p_{-1} - p_{-5})$, resp.

to the regression equations from section (3.6).

Since only sign and significance of the coefficients in the added component are of interest, the basic regression equations from Section 3.6 need not be reproduced here.

Adaptive and Extrapolative Components

The following two tables show the frequencies of negative and positive adaptive and extrapolative coefficients for each experiment:

Table 4.9: Adaptive Behavior

Number of subjects with ...

Exp. No.	No. of Subjects	$\hat{\lambda} < 0$, signif.	$\hat{\lambda} < 0$	$\hat{\lambda} = 0$	$\hat{\lambda} > 0$	$\hat{\lambda} > 0$, signif.
1	14	0	5	1	8	3
2	13	0	6	0	7	1
3	12	0	6	4	2	1
4	12	0	5	0	7	1
5	13	0	2	0	11	3
6	11	0	4	0	7	1
7	13	0	4	0	9	5
8	12	0	4	0	8	2
9	14	1	9	0	5	0
10	11	0	0	1	10	5
11	13	0	4	0	9	3
12	11	1	6	0	5	2
13	11	2	6	0	5	1
14	7	0	1	0	6	5
Total	167	4	62	6	99	33

Note: "significant" means: level 5% according to a two-sided t test of $H_0 : \lambda = 0$.

In contrast to the summing in Section 4.4, the number of subjects with $\hat{\lambda} < 0$ includes those subjects with $\hat{\lambda} < 0$ significantly (and analogously for positive $\hat{\lambda}$).

Table 4.10: Extrapolative Behavior
Number of subjects with ...

Exp. No.	No. of Subjects	$\hat{\gamma} < 0$, signif.	$\hat{\gamma} < 0$	$\hat{\gamma} = 0$	$\hat{\gamma} > 0$	$\hat{\gamma} > 0$, signif.
1	14	1	4	1	9	0
2	13	0	5	0	8	1
3	12	0	3	4	5	0
4	12	1	7	0	5	0
5	13	1	9	0	4	0
6	11	0	8	0	3	0
7	13	0	9	0	4	1
8	12	0	6	0	6	0
9	14	0	1	0	13	3
11	13	0	5	0	8	3
12	11	1	2	0	9	2
13	11	0	3	0	8	3
14	7	1	2	0	5	1
Total	156	5	64	5	87	14

Note: Exp. 10 is missing since Δp_{-1} is a linear combination of Δv_{-1} and Δw_{-1} (see Section 3.7).

The following conclusions can be drawn from the tables:

1. Adaptive and extrapolative behavior are significant only for very few subjects.

2. For both adaptive and extrapolative component, the positive sign dominates: The total proportion of positive adaptive coefficient estimates $\hat{\lambda}$ is significant at the 1% level, the proportion of positive extrapolative coefficient estimates $\hat{\gamma}$ is significant at the 5% level. However, there are large differences among experiments: For some experiments (e.g. Exp. 9) negative adaptive behavior is prevailing. Simliar differences among experiments can be found for extrapolative behavior.

3. Although this is not seen from the totals, a negative correlation between λ and γ is apparent: Where the number of subjects with negative $\hat{\lambda}$ is high (e.g. Exp. 9) the number of subjects with positive $\hat{\gamma}$ is high, and vice versa (e.g. Exp. 5). To confirm this observation, the following table summarizes the joint frequency distribution of estimated adaptive and extrapolative coefficients.

Table 4.11: Joint frequencies of negative and positive adaptive/extrapolative coefficients

		Number of subjects with ...			
Exp. No.	No. of Subjects	$\hat{\lambda} < 0$, $\hat{\gamma} < 0$	$\hat{\lambda} < 0$, $\hat{\gamma} > 0$	$\hat{\lambda} > 0$, $\hat{\gamma} < 0$	$\hat{\lambda} > 0$, $\hat{\gamma} > 0$
1	14	1	4	3	5
2	13	2	4	3	4
3	12	2	4	1	1
4	12	1	4	6	1
5	13	0	2	9	2
6	11	1	3	7	0
7	13	3	1	6	3
8	12	1	3	5	3
9	14	0	9	1	4
11	13	0	4	5	4
12	11	0	6	2	3
13	11	0	6	3	2
14	7	0	1	2	4
Total	156	11	51	53	36

Note: For Exp. 1 and 3, the row sum is not 14 and 12, resp., since for some individuals $\hat{\lambda} = 0$ and $\hat{\gamma} = 0$. Thus, the totals do not sum up to 156.

Exp. 10 is missing (see Note on Table 4.10).

In 12 out of 13 experiments, $\hat{\lambda}$ and $\hat{\gamma}$ have opposite sign for a majority of subjects.[8] For Exp. 1-3, the results are less conclusive than for the

[8] (after excluding those subjects in Exp. 1 and 3 where $\hat{\lambda}$ or $\hat{\gamma}$ are equal to zero)

remaining experiments.

The totals indicate a significant negative correlation: The χ^2 statistic for testing the null hypothesis H_0: "*signs are independent*" (i.e. joint relative frequencies = product of marginal relative frequencies) is 26.152, with one degree of freedom (2 x 2 contingency table). This is far beyond the 1% significance bound which is 6.63.

As already stated in Chapter 3, the reason for this negative correlation is presumably not psychological in nature but rather a consequence of underestimation of changes which causes negative correlation between last forecast error and lagged changes of p. The regression $(f - p_{-1}) = \beta_0 + \beta_1 \Delta p_{-1}$ impressively confirms this negative correlation: The estimate $\hat{\beta}_1$ is positive for only three out of 167 subjects (those three subjects are among the participants in Exp. 1, 2, and 8 and forecasted nearly perfectly). The slope coefficient is significantly negative at the 1% level for 143 subjects and at the 5% level for 150 subjects.

Bang-Bang and Trend Components

The following three tables show the number of subjects with negative and positive parameter estimates for bang-bang and trend components.

Table 4.12:
Counting results for bang-bang component $\beta_{bb}(E\Delta p - \Delta p_{-1})$.
Number of subjects with ...

Exp. No.	No. of Subjects	$\hat{\beta}_{bb} < 0$, signif.	$\hat{\beta}_{bb} < 0$	$\hat{\beta}_{bb} = 0$	$\hat{\beta}_{bb} > 0$	$\hat{\beta}_{bb} > 0$, signif.
1	14	0	9	1	4	1
2	13	1	8	0	5	0
3	12	0	6	3	3	0
4	12	0	5	0	7	1
5	13	0	5	0	8	1
6	11	0	3	0	8	0

(continued)

Table 4.12 (continued)

Number of subjects with ...

Exp. No.	No. of Subjects	$\hat{\beta}_{bb} < 0$, signif.	$\hat{\beta}_{bb} < 0$	$\hat{\beta}_{bb} = 0$	$\hat{\beta}_{bb} > 0$	$\hat{\beta}_{bb} > 0$, signif.
7	13	0	4	0	9	2
8	12	0	7	0	5	0
9	14	3	12	0	2	0
11	13	3	8	0	5	0
12	11	2	9	0	2	1
13	11	3	8	0	3	0
14	7	1	5	0	2	1
Totals:						
1-9	114	4	59	4	51	5
11-14	42	9	30	0	12	2
1-14	156	13	89	4	63	7

Note on the table:
Exp. 10 is missing since the bang-bang component is a linear combination of other regressors (see Section 3.7).

For a majority of subjects, $\hat{\beta}_{bb}$ is negative. This majority is significant at the 1% level (one-sided binomial test) for the incomplete-information experiments. From Section 3.7, however, we know that this is possibly due to "almost" multicollinearity. Only for few *single* subjects significance of $\hat{\beta}_{bb}$ is observed.

The following two tables summarize the results for past trends. The totals are calculated according to the three groups found in Section 3.7:

1. Long trend segments prevailing: Exp. 9-13,
2. Seasonality: Exp. 7 and 8,
3. "Trend-neutral" experiments: Exp. 1-6 and 14.

Table 4.13: Counting results for short-trend component $\beta_{st}(p_{-1} - p_{-3})$.

Number of subjects with ...

Exp. No.	No. of Subjects	$\hat{\beta}_{st} < 0$, signif.	$\hat{\beta}_{st} < 0$	$\hat{\beta}_{st} = 0$	$\hat{\beta}_{st} > 0$	$\hat{\beta}_{st} > 0$, signif.
1	14	1	7	1	6	0
2	13	0	6	0	7	0
3	12	1	2	3	7	0
4	12	2	7	0	5	0
5	13	3	10	0	3	0
6	11	2	9	0	2	0
7	13	3	12	0	1	0
8	12	1	11	0	1	1
9	14	0	4	0	10	3
10	11	0	1	1	9	3
11	13	0	0	0	13	3
12	11	0	3	0	8	2
13	11	0	5	0	6	0
14	7	1	5	0	2	0
Totals:						
1-6,14	82	10	46	4	32	0
7,8	25	4	23	0	2	1
9-13	60	0	13	1	46	11

Table 4.14: Counting results for long-trend component $\beta_{st}(p_{-1} - p_{-5})$.

Number of subjects with ...

Exp. No.	No. of Subjects	$\hat{\beta}_{lt} < 0$, signif.	$\hat{\beta}_{lt} < 0$	$\hat{\beta}_{lt} = 0$	$\hat{\beta}_{lt} > 0$	$\hat{\beta}_{lt} > 0$, signif.
1	14	3	9	1	4	0
2	13	1	7	0	6	1
3	12	0	2	3	7	1
4	12	3	9	0	3	0
5	13	5	11	0	2	0
6	11	1	7	0	4	0

(continued)

Table 4.14 (continued)

Exp. No.	No. of Subjects	$\hat{\beta}_{lt} < 0$, signif.	$\hat{\beta}_{lt} < 0$	$\hat{\beta}_{lt} = 0$	$\hat{\beta}_{lt} > 0$	$\hat{\beta}_{lt} > 0$, signif.
7	13	5	13	0	0	0
8	12	3	11	0	1	0
9	14	0	5	0	9	1
10	11	0	2	1	8	4
11	13	1	2	0	11	2
12	11	0	4	0	7	1
13	11	1	6	0	5	1
14	7	1	5	0	2	1
Totals:						
1-6,14	82	14	50	4	28	3
7-8	25	8	24	0	1	0
9-13	60	2	19	1	40	9

The results found in Section 3.7 are confirmed by the figures in the tables:

Positive influence of past trends in presence of long trend segments (Exp. 9-13): The majority of positive signs of is significant (1% level) for $\hat{\beta}_{st}$ and $\hat{\beta}_{lt}$. The majority is more striking for short trends.

Negative influence of past trends in presence of seasonality (Exp. 7 and 8): The majority of negative signs is highly significant (1% level).

Negative influence of past trends prevails for "neutral" experiments (Exp. 1-6 and 14): The majority is highly significant (1% level) for "long trends" but not significant for "short trends".

So far, individual forecasts have only been used for confirming (by a large number of independent observations) some results found for aggregate forecasts. The next chapter will deal with merely individual features of forecasts such as preference for round numbers and time spent for forecasting.

5. Features of Individual Forecasts

This chapter analyzes some features of individual forecasts which cannot be discussed in context with aggregate forecasts. In most sections of this chapter, the analysis is subdivided according to three groups which we already know from Sections 3.6 and 4.4 on influence of single exogenous variables:

- Simple full-information experiments (Exp. 1-6 and 9),
- Seasonality experiments (Exp. 7 and 8),
- Incomplete-information experiments (Exp. 10-14).

For better exposition, at the beginning of each of these sub-sections, the underlying models of the involved experiments are tabulated.

Again for all tests based on linear regression, some care has to be taken concerning violation of the normality assumption (individual forecasted changes often have a nearly symmetric distribution but the support consists of integer numbers only).

Before starting analysis, the plots of Exp. 5 and 7 are shown as examples. These plots contain individual forecasts (marked by squares). The size of the squares indicates the frequency of the marked values.

Figure 5.1 Plot of Exp. 5 - including forecasts

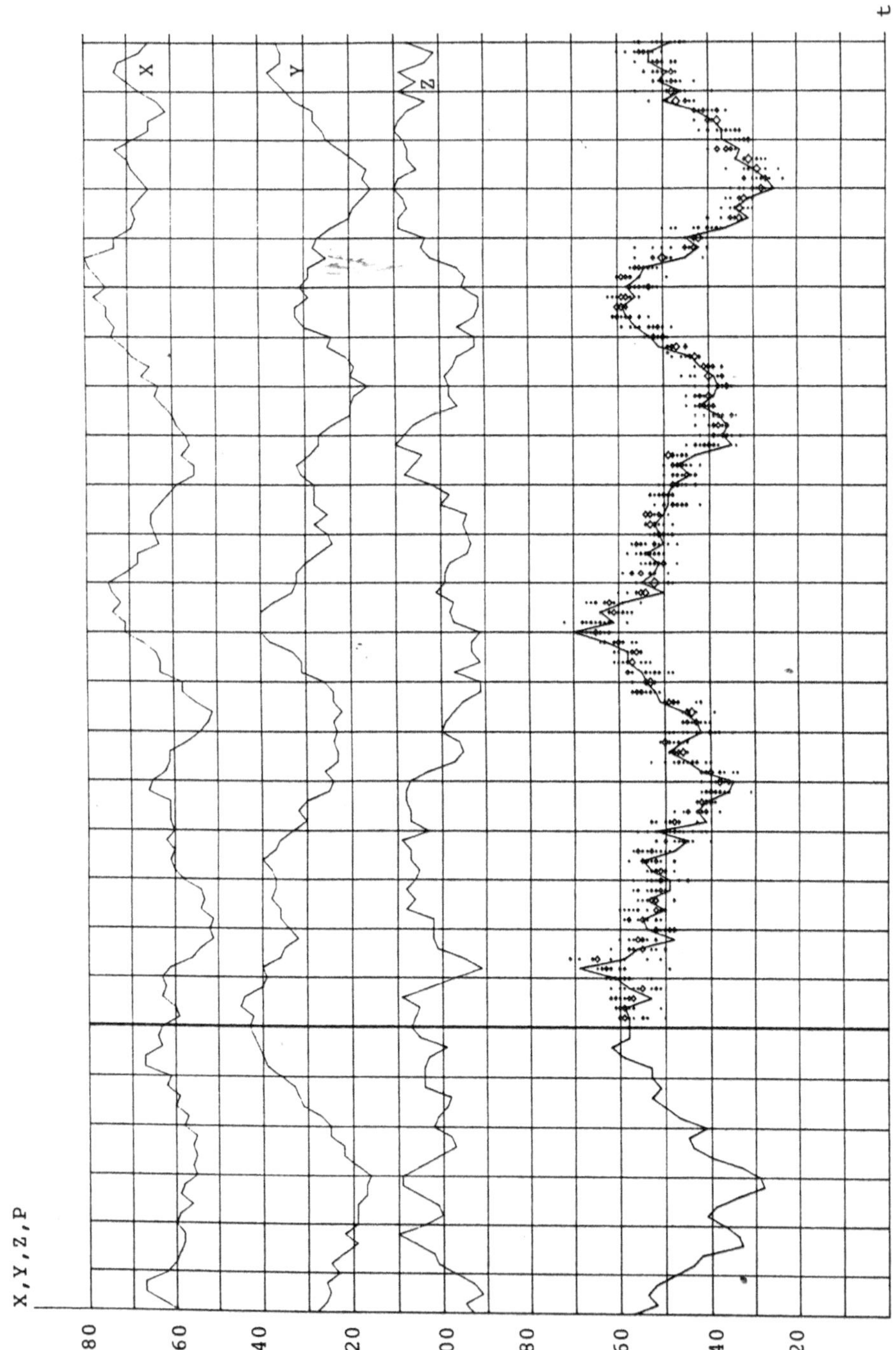

Figure 5.2 Plot of Exp. 7 - including forecasts

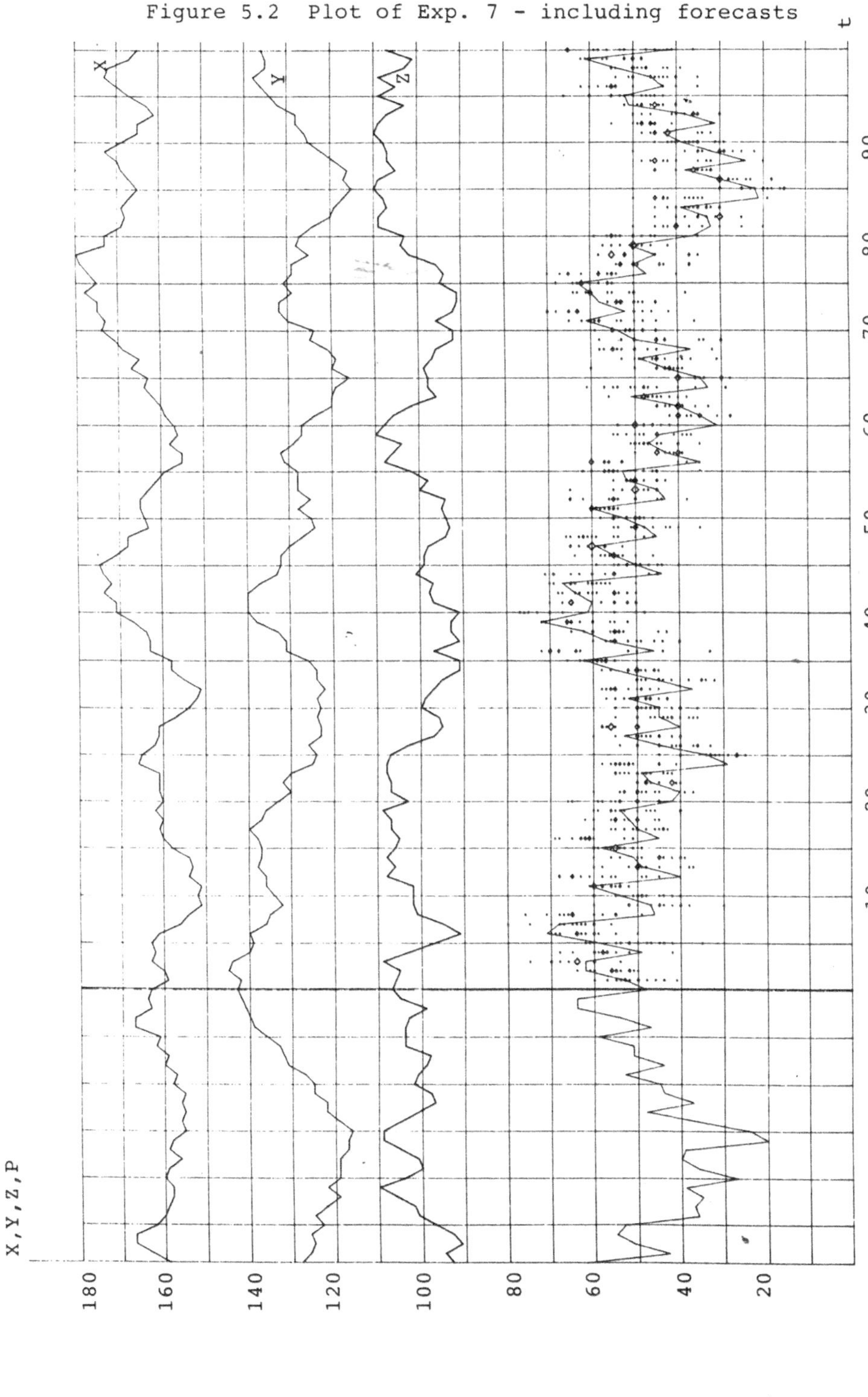

5.1 The Questionnaires

As stated above in the description of the experimental design, all subjects were asked to fill out a questionnaire after Period 20, 40, 60, and so on. In these questionnaires, they were asked for a qualitative statement on the influence of each exogenous variable ("no influence", "negative influence", or "positive influence"). In addition, they had the opportunity to give some comments on their opinion about the model. Some subjects gave quantitative statements, but the majority confined itself to the required qualitative statements.

Simple Full-Information Experiments: 1-6 and 9

Table 5.1: Models in Exp. 1-6 and 9

Exp. No.	Model
1	$p = 120 + y - 2z$
2	$p = -80 + x + \left[\frac{1}{2}y\right] - z$
3	$p = 85 - x_{-1} + y_{-1}$
4	$p = -80 + x + \left[\frac{1}{2}y\right] - z + u$
5	$p = 20 + y - z + u$
6	$p = 85 - x_{-1} + y_{-1} + u$
9	$p = -7 + y - z + \left[\frac{1}{2}p_{-1}\right]$

Concerning the questionnaires, subjects had to state whether x has a negative, a positive, or no influence on p, and the same for y and z.

Qualitative Statements

The first question that arises is: Are the qualitative statements correct in terms of the underlying model? This question cannot be answered easily for those subjects who changed their opinion during the experiment.[1] Therefore, the first analysis is restricted to those subjects who did not change their opinion.

---

[1] Note that subjects were asked for statements every 20 periods, i.e. 4 or 5 times depending on the total number of periods (80 or 100, resp.).

Definition 5.1: An individual's opinion on the influence of a variable is *unchanged* if the following holds:

1. At most one answer (out of 4 or 5, resp., see Footnote 1) is missing for that variable.
2. All nonmissing answers agree.

The following table gives, for each experiment and each variable, the number of subjects who had unchanged opinions and, among those, the proportion of "+" (opinion "positive influence), "−" ("negative influence"), and "n" ("no influence"). The "correct" answer (see above Table on the underlying models) is included.

The last column of the second part of the table gives the number of individuals whose opinion was unchanged with respect to all three variables jointly, and (in brackets) the number of *correct* unchanged opinions with respect to all variables jointly.

Table 5.2: Number of unchanged opinions with respect to ...

Exp. No.	Correct Answer	No. of Subjects	x	y
1	xn, y+, z−	14	9 (6n, 3+)	10 (9+,1n)
2	x+, y+, z−	13	12 (11+, 1−)	12 (12+)
3	x−, y+, zn	12	9 (9−)	10 (10+)
4	x+, y+, z−	12	9 (9+)	11 (10+, 1n)
5	xn, y+, z−	13	7 (4n, 2+, 1−)	6 (6+)
6	x−, y+, zn	11	6 (4−, 2n)	7 (7+)
9	xn, y+, z−	14	2 (2+)	6 (6+)

(continued)

Table 5.2 (continued)
Number of unchanged opinions with repect to ...

Exp. No.	z	x, y, and z jointly
1	14 (14–)	7 (5)
2	13 (13–)	10 (9)
3	10 (10n)	9 (9)
4	12 (12–)	8 (7)
5	8 (8–)	3 (2)
6	4 (2n, 1–, 1+)	4 (1)
9	7 (7–)	2 (0)

For Exp. 1-4, a majority of subjects has unchanged opinions with respect to all three exogenous variables separately and jointly. For the remaining experiments, the proportion of unchanged opinions is smaller which obviously corresponds to higher deviations from rational predictions in these experiments (see Section 3.1).

With respect to relevant variables (correct answer is "+" or "–"), the proportion of "correct" among unchanged opinions is very high, always more than two thirds. With respect to sunspot variables, however, things look different: The number of unchanged opinions is very small, and among them, there is a relatively great number of "incorrect" opinions (in Exp. 9, for example, both subjects with unchanged opinion on x thought that x has positive influence).

Note that in those experiments where z is relevant (Exp. 1, 2, 4, 5, and 9), the proportion of unchanged opinions is higher than for the two other variables x and y, and all unchanged opinions on z were correct! This corresponds to the observation from the regressions on single exogenous variables in Section 3.6: z was "overvalued" relative to the other variables, possibly due to its high volatility which facilitates the recognition of its influence.

Among the "incorrect" opinions, only one case occurs where opinion and correct answer have *opposite* sign: Subject 8 in Exp. 2 stated that x had negative influence. This subject even gave a quantitative statement on the model: $\Delta p = -\frac{1}{3}\Delta x + 2\Delta y - \Delta z$.

Conformity of qualitative statements and forecasting behavior

One may now ask whether unchanged opinions are matched by observed forecasting behavior. To answer this question, the regression equations

$$\Delta f = \beta_0 + \beta_x \Delta x + \beta_y \Delta y + \beta_z \Delta z + \varepsilon \qquad \text{(for Exp. 1, 2, and 9)},$$

$$\Delta f = \beta_0 + \beta_x \Delta x_{-1} + \beta_y \Delta y_{-1} + \beta_z \Delta z_{-1} + \varepsilon \qquad \text{(for Exp. 3)},$$

$$\Delta f = \beta_0 + \beta_x \Delta x + \beta_y \Delta y + \beta_z \Delta z + \rho u_{-1} + \varepsilon \qquad \text{(for Exp. 4 and 5)},$$

$$\Delta f = \beta_0 + \beta_x \Delta x_{-1} + \beta_y \Delta y_{-1} + \beta_z \Delta z_{-1} + \rho u_{-1} + \varepsilon \qquad \text{(for Exp. 6)}.$$

(which are already known from Section 3.6) were estimated. Now, $\hat{\beta}_x, \hat{\beta}_y, \hat{\beta}_z$ can be compared to the qualitative statements on the corresponding variable.

Definition 5.2: A slope estimate $\hat{\beta}$ for a variable is said to *contradict* an unchanged opinion if
opinion "+" and $\hat{\beta} \leq 0$, or
opinion "n" and $\hat{\beta}$ is significant (two-sided t test, level 5%), or
opinion "−" and $\hat{\beta} \geq 0$.

The comparison of unchanged opinions to actual behavior (slope estimates) yields conformity for most subjects and variables. The following contradictions occur:

Exp. 1:
x: Subj. 14: Opinion "n", $\hat{\beta}_x < 0$ (significant).
y and z: no contradictions.

Exp. 2:
x and z: no contradictions.
y: Subj. 13: Opinion "+", $\hat{\beta}_y < 0$ (but not significant).

Exp. 3 and 4: No contradictions.

Exp. 5:
x: Subj. 1: Opinion "n", $\hat{\beta}_y < 0$ (significant).
y and z: no contradictions.

Exp. 6:
x and z: no contradictions.
y: Subj. 9 and 10: Opinion "+", $\hat{\beta}_y < 0$ (but not significant).

Exp. 9:
No contradictions.

The analysis shows that the number of contradictions is small, and no case occurs where the parameter estimate has opposite sign *and* is significant.

Comparative statements

In some cases subjects gave comparative statements like "z has a stronger influence than y". These statements may be compared to the estimates $\hat{\beta}_x$, $\hat{\beta}_y$, $\hat{\beta}_z$ from the regressions above. For the example given, the estimates *correspond* to the statement if $|\hat{\beta}_z| > |\hat{\beta}_y|$.

In all seven experiments considered, 16 subjects gave such comparative statements. In only one case, the regression results contradict the comparative statements: Subject 1 in Exp. 4 stated "z has a stronger influence than x, and x has a stronger influence than y", but the regression results are $(\hat{\beta}_x, \hat{\beta}_y, \hat{\beta}_z) = (0.236, 0.402, -1.133)$. However, $\hat{\beta}_x$ is not significantly smaller than $\hat{\beta}_y$ according to a one-sided t test.

So far, it may be concluded that the qualitative statements given in the questionnaires are generally matched by observed forecasting behavior.

Quantitative Statements

Some subjects even gave quantitative statements like "the model is $\Delta p = -\frac{1}{3}\Delta x + 2\Delta y - \Delta z$". (Exp. 2, Subj. 8). Apart from subjects who comprehended the model and forecasted perfectly, such statements were always given in terms of changes.

One might expect that these precise statements are matched by observed forecasts. Here are some results (for simplicity, the subjects' statements are given here in terms of the parameters β_x, β_y, and β_z):

Exp. 1

Subj. 1, 2, 3, 5, and 6 (they were *not* placed next to each other!) succeeded in comprehending the true model ($p = 120 + y - 2z$) and forecasted nearly perfectly (some small deviations are presumably due to typing errors). The estimates $(\hat{\beta}_x, \hat{\beta}_y, \hat{\beta}_z)$ do not differ significantly from $(0, 1, -2)$ according to an F test (level 5%).

Exp. 2

Subj. 4: Statement $(\beta_x, \beta_y, \beta_z) = (1, \frac{1}{2}, -1)$.
  Estimates $(\hat{\beta}_x, \hat{\beta}_y, \hat{\beta}_z) = (0.946, 0.570, -0.835)$.
  Prob. $> F$ for H_0: $(\beta_x, \beta_y, \beta_z) = (1, \frac{1}{2}, -1)$ is 0.0544.
Subj. 6: Statement as Subj. 4.
  Estimates $(\hat{\beta}_x, \hat{\beta}_y, \hat{\beta}_z) = (0.667, 0.552, -0.935)$.
  Prob. $> F$ for H_0: $(\beta_x, \beta_y, \beta_z) = (1, \frac{1}{2}, -1)$ is 0.0473.
  Prob. $> F$ for H_0: $(\beta_x = 2\beta_y, \beta_z = -2\beta_y)$ is 0.2990.
Subj. 8: Statement $(\beta_x, \beta_y, \beta_z) = (-\frac{1}{3}, 2, -1)$.
  Estimates $(\hat{\beta}_x, \hat{\beta}_y, \hat{\beta}_z) = (-0.394, 1.497, -0.982)$.
  Prob. $> F$ for H_0: $(\beta_x, \beta_y, \beta_z) = (-\frac{1}{3}, 2, -1)$ is < 0.001.
  Prob. $> F$ for H_0: $(\beta_y = -6\beta_x, \beta_z = 3\beta_x)$ is 0.0228.
Subj. 9: Statement $(\beta_y, \beta_z) = (\frac{1}{2}, -1)$.
  Estimates $(\hat{\beta}_y, \hat{\beta}_z) = (0.436, -0.815)$.
  Prob. $> F$ for H_0: $(\beta_y, \beta_z) = (\frac{1}{2}, -1)$ is 0.0033.
  Prob. $> F$ for H_0: $(\beta_z = -2\beta_y)$ is 0.6784.

Exp. 3:

Subj. 1, 6, 8, 11, and 12 comprehended the true model and forecasted nearly perfectly. The estimates $(\hat{\beta}_x, \hat{\beta}_y, \hat{\beta}_z)$ did not differ significantly from (-1,1,0).

Exp. 4:
Subj. 7: Statement $(\beta_x, \beta_y, \beta_z) = (1, 1, -1)$.
Estimates $(\hat{\beta}_x, \hat{\beta}_y, \hat{\beta}_z) = (0.989, 0.749, -0.829)$.
Prob. $> F$ for H_0: $(\beta_x, \beta_y, \beta_z) = (1, 1, -1)$ is 0.0010.
Prob. $> F$ for H_0: $(\beta_x = \beta_y, \beta_z = -\beta_y)$ is 0.0980.

Exp. 5:
Subj. 5: Statement $(\beta_x, \beta_y, \beta_z) = (\frac{3}{4}, \frac{3}{4}, -1)$.
Estimates $(\hat{\beta}_x, \hat{\beta}_y, \hat{\beta}_z) = (0.536, 0.645, -0.829)$.
Prob. $> F$ for H_0: $(\beta_x, \beta_y, \beta_z) = (\frac{3}{4}, \frac{3}{4}, -1)$ is < 0.001.
Prob. $> F$ for H_0: $(\beta_x = \beta_y, \beta_z = -\frac{4}{3}\beta_y)$ is 0.4401.

Only few subjects gave precise quantitative statements. For most of them (except for those subjects in Exp. 1 and 3 who forecasted perfectly), observed forecasting behavior (regression results) does *not* match the quantitative statement. The regression estimates are generally *absolutely smaller* than the stated values. However, the *relation* between the estimates in most cases does not differ significantly from the stated relation.

This suggests that these subjects apply their stated rule but tend to reduce (absolutely) the forecasted change obtained from this calculation. This corresponds to the observed underestimation of changes.

Changing Opinions

So far, individuals who changed their opinion have been omitted. For the purpose of studying conformity of statements to observed behavior, there is good reason to do so: If, for example, the statement on y after Period 40 differs from that after Period 20, the change in opinion may have taken place after Period 21 as well as it may have taken place after Period 40. Thus, it is not possible to find "analogous" sections for regression.[2]

One may, however, be interested in whether changing opinions indicate some "learning". For this purpose, consider - for each experiment and each exogenous variable - the subjects who changed their statements.

---

[2] The same reasoning may apply to apparently unchanged opinions: It is well possible that a subject always gave the same statements but had another opinion somewhere in between. This may be the reason for some "contradictions" above.

Table 5.3: Subjects with Changing Opinion (in Exp. 5)

Exp. No.	Subj.	x	y	z
5	1		+ n n n n	
	3	+ + + n −		
	6	n + + + +		
	7		+ − + + +	
	8	+ + n − −	+ − + − +	− − − + −
	10	n + + + +	n + + + +	
	11		− + + + +	+ − − − −
	12	+ + + + −		− − − − n

This table is only an example. Note that some subjects changed their opinion only for one variable, others for two or three variables. Comparing the first and the last nonmissing statement to the correct answers xn, y+, z−[3] yields that some individuals "learned" (for example, Subject 11 with respect to y) while others "unlearned" (Subject 1 with respect to y). Sometimes the same subject learned with respect to one and unlearned with respect to another variable (for example Subject 10: learning with respect to y and unlearning with respect to x).

More precisely, the first and last nonmissing statements are said to indicate learning if the last nonmissing statement is "more close" to the correct answer than the first nonmissing one according to the following tables:

Table 5.4: Learning and Unlearning for correct answer = "n"

↓ first st.	last st. →	−	n	+
−			Learning	
n		Unlearn.		Unlearn.
+			Learning	

[3] The true model is $p = 20 + y - z + u$, see Table 5.1.

Table 5.5: Learning and Unlearning for correct answer = "−"

↓ first st.	last st. →	−	n	+
−			Unlearn.	Unlearn.
n		Learning		Unlearn.
+		Learning	Learning	

For correct answer = "+", learning and unlearning are defined analogously. Counting over all experiments the number of cases of learning and unlearning yields that for sunspot variables (correct answer = "n"), unlearning occurs more often than learning (6 cases of unlearning, 3 cases of learning). For relevant variables (correct answer is "−" or "+"), more learning occurs but the number of "unlearning" cases remains considerable (17 cases of learning, 11 cases of unlearning). Altogether, changing opinions indicate some learning only with respect to *relevant* variables, but not with respect to irrelevant ones. The proportion of "n" answers shrinks during the experiment, i.e. subjects try to find relevance for each variable.

Seasonality Experiments: 7 and 8

Table 5.6: Models in Exp. 7 and 8

Exp. 7	$p = 12 + y - z + 5(t\ modulo\ 4)$
Exp. 8	$p = 10 + y - z + 5(t\ modulo\ 5)$

In Exp. 7, the exogenous variables x, y, and z were displayed, in Exp. 8, only y and z were displayed.

The following table summarizes, as Table 5.2 above, the number of unchanged opinions (on each variable separately and on all variables jointly, for the jointly unchanged opinions, the number of correct ones is again given in brackets), and gives the correct answers.

Table 5.7: Number of subjects who had unchanged opinions with respect to ...

Exp. No.	Correct Answer	No. of Subjects	x	y
7	xn,y+, $z-$	13	4 (2+, 1−, 1n)	7 (6+, 1n)
8	y+, $z-$	12	·	6 (6+)

Table 5.7 (continued)
Number of unchanged opinions with respect to ...

Exp. No.	z	All Var. jointly
7	7 (6−, 1+)	4 (0)
8	4 (4−)	3 (3)

The proportion of unchanged opinions is only about halfth of the number of participants for each variable. In particular, the proportion for z is much lower than in the simple full-information experiments. This corresponds to the observation (see Section 3.6) that z tends to be undervalued in these experiments.

The seasonality pattern was (qualitatively) detected by only three participants in Exp. 7 (two of them already within the first 20 periods, one of them within the last 20 periods), but by 9 subjects in Exp. 8 (seven of them within the first 20 periods, one within the last 20 periods, and one between the 40th and 60th period).

Conformity of qualitative statements and observed behavior

As above for simple full-information experiments, the contradictions between unchanged opinions and the parameter estimates $\hat{\beta}_x$ (only for Exp. 7), $\hat{\beta}_y$, and $\hat{\beta}_z$ from the regressions

$$\Delta f = \beta_x \Delta x + \beta_y \Delta y + \beta_z \Delta z + \delta_0 D_0 + \delta_1 D_1 + \delta_2 D_2 + \delta_3 D_3 + \varepsilon \quad \text{(for Exp. 7)},$$

and

$$\Delta f = \beta_y \Delta y + \beta_z \Delta z + \delta_0 D_0 + \delta_1 D_1 + \delta_2 D_2 + \delta_3 D_3 + \delta_4 D_4 + \varepsilon \quad \text{(for Exp. 8)}.$$

(for the dummy variables $D_0, D_1, \ldots$ see Section 3.6) are listed below. In addition, for those subjects who mentioned the seasonal pattern in their questionnaires, sign of influence and significance of the dummy variables are verified. The following contradictions occur:

Exp. 7:
x and z: no contradictions;
y: Subj. 3: Opinion "+", but $\hat{\beta}_y < 0$ (not significant).

Exp. 8:
y: no contradictions;
z: Subj. 1: Opinion "−", but $\hat{\beta}_z > 0$ (not significant).

As far as the statements on seasonality are concerned, no contradictions occurred: For those subjects who recognized seasonality, the coefficient of the "crash-period" dummy D_0 was significant and negative (but in most cases absolutely smaller than -15 (for Exp. 7) or -20 (for Exp. 8)), and the parameter estimates of the remaining dummies were positive and, in most cases, significant.

Comparative statements

Only one comparative statement occurs: Subject 6 in Exp. 7 claimed that "y has the strongest influence" among the tabulated exogenous variables. This is not matched by the regression results, but the null hypothesis corresponding to the statement could not been rejected at a reasonable level.

Quantitative statements

occur only in Exp. 8. They are given in the sequel (translated into our parameters $\beta_y, \beta_z, \delta_0, \ldots, \delta_4$):

Subj. 1: Statement $(\delta_0, \delta_1, \delta_2, \delta_3, \delta_4) = (-20, 5, 5, 5, 5)$.
Estimates $(\hat{\delta}_0, \hat{\delta}_1, \hat{\delta}_2, \hat{\delta}_3, \hat{\delta}_4) = (-18.273, 5.662, 4.735, 2.583, 5.186)$
Prob. $> F$ for H_0: $(\delta_0, \delta_1, \delta_2, \delta_3, \delta_4) = (-20, 5, 5, 5, 5)$ is 0.0327
Prob. $> F$ for H_0: $(\delta_0 = -4\delta_1, \delta_1 = \delta_2 = \delta_3 = \delta_4)$ is 0.2178

Subj. 5: Wrote down the correct model
Estimates $(\hat{\beta}_y, \hat{\beta}_z, \hat{\delta}_0, \hat{\delta}_1, \hat{\delta}_2, \hat{\delta}_3, \hat{\delta}_4)$
$= (1.063, -0.998, -19.989, 4.663, 5.618, 4.865, 4.701)$
Prob. $> F$ for H_0: $(\beta_y, \beta_z, \delta_0, \delta_1, \delta_2, \delta_3, \delta_4) = (1, -1, -20, 5, 5, 5, 5)$ is 0.5801

Subj. 10: Statement $(\beta_y, \beta_z) = (1, -1)$.
Estimates $(\hat{\beta}_y, \hat{\beta}_z) = (0.645, -0.829)$.
Prob. $> F$ for H$_0$: $(\beta_y, \beta_z) = (1, -1)$ is 0.3076.
Prob. $> F$ for H$_0$: $\beta_z = -\beta_y$ is 0.8980.

The quantitative statements listed are mostly matched by regression results, in particular for the seasonal pattern.

Changing Opinions

As above, for each subject who changed opinion, the first and the last nonmissing statement are compared in order to verify some learning. For the irrelevant variable x in Exp. 7, one case of unlearning (Subj. 9: first statement "n", last statement "+"), and no case of learning occurs. For the relevant variables y and z (in both experiments), 4 cases of unlearning and 11 cases of learning occur. This confirms the impression from above that some learning occurs with respect to relevant variables but not with respect to irrelevant ones.

Incomplete-Information Experiments: 10-14

Table 5.8: Models in Exp. 10-14

10	$p = 100 + v - w$
11	$p = 100 + v_{-1} - w$
12	$p = 100 + v - w_{-1}$
13	$p = 200 - w + u$
14	$p = 150 - v + u$

Only two exogenous variables are involved. However, in Exp. 11 and 12, partly lagged influence occurs (v in Exp. 11, w in Exp. 12). In these experiments, subjects were not only asked for the *sign* of influence of each variable but also for the *time relation*: For a variable presumed to be relevant, they had to state whether its influence is contemporary or lagged (by 1 period).

As far as unchanged opinions are concerned, they are hardly observed in Exp. 11 and 12 when answers on sign of influence and time relation are considered *jointly*. Thus, these topics are studied separately. The following table gives, for each experiment, the number of unchanged opinions with respect to v and w (separately and jointly, for jointly unchanged opinions, the number of correct ones among them is again given in brackets).

Table 5.9: Number of subjects who had unchanged opinions concerning the sign of influence with respect to ...

Exp. No.	Correct Answer	No. of Subjects	v	w	v and w jointly
10	$v+$, $w-$	11	10 $(9+, 1-)$	9 $(9-)$	9 (9)
11	$v+$, $w-$	13	3 $(2+, 1-)$	11 $(10-, 1+)$	3 (2)
12	$v+$, $w-$	11	9 $(7+, 2n)$	9 $(8-, 1n)$	9 (7)
13	vn, $w-$	11	1 $(1n)$	9 $(9-)$	1 (1)
14	$v-$, wn	7	6 $(6-)$	5 $(5n)$	5 (5)

The proportion of unchanged opinions is quite high with respect to single variables, in particular for relevant ones (with the exception of v in Exp. 11). Among the unchanged opinions, there are at most two "incorrect" opinions, in three cases with opposite sign (v and w in Exp. 11 - from the same subject -, and v in Exp. 10).

Now, the following table gives the number of unchanged opinions concerning the time relation for Exp. 11 and 12 ("l" stands for "lagged", and "c" for "contemporary"), again for v and w separately and jointly.

Table 5.10: Number of subjects who had unchanged opinions concerning the time relation with respect to ...

Exp. No.	Correct Answer	No. of Subjects	v	w	v and w jointly
11	vl, wc	13	9 $(7l, 2c)$	10 $(9c, 1l)$	5 (4)
12	vc, wl	11	5 $(4c, 1l)$	7 $(6l, 1c)$	5 (4)

In all cases, a majority of unchanged opinions is correct (at most two exceptions).

Conformity of qualitative statements and observed behavior

Unchanged opinions (with respect to the sign of influence) were viewed for contradictions to parameter estimates $\hat{\beta}_w$, $\hat{\beta}_{vlag}$, and $\hat{\beta}_{wlag}$ from the regressions

$$\Delta f = \beta_0 + \beta_w E\Delta w + \beta_{vlag}\Delta v_{-1} + \beta_{wlag}\Delta w_{-1} + \varepsilon \qquad \text{(for Exp. } 10-12\text{)},$$

and

$$\Delta f = \beta_0 + \beta_w E\Delta w + \beta_{vlag}\Delta v_{-1} + \beta_{wlag}\Delta w_{-1} + \rho u_{-1} + \varepsilon$$

(for Exp. 13 and 14).

Due to statements on time relation and regression lagged changes, the notion of "contradiction" needs to be redefined. The following table gives the definition:

Definition 5.3: (Contradiction of statements to regression estimates)

for v:

All statements on sign	Majority of st. on time relation	Contradiction if ...
$-$	"lagged"	$\hat{\beta}_{vlag} \geq 0$
$+$	"lagged"	$\hat{\beta}_{vlag} \leq 0$
n	·	$\hat{\beta}_{vlag}$ signif.
$+$ or $-$	"contemp."	$\hat{\beta}_{vlag}$ signif.

for w:

All statements on sign	Majority of st. on time relation	Contradiction if ...
$-$	"lagged"	$\hat{\beta}_{wlag} \geq 0$ or $\hat{\beta}_w$ signif.
$+$	"lagged"	$\hat{\beta}_{wlag} \leq 0$ or $\hat{\beta}_w$ signif.
n	·	$\hat{\beta}_{wlag}$ signif. or $\hat{\beta}_w$ signif.
$-$	"contemp."	$\hat{\beta}_{wlag}$ signif. or $\hat{\beta}_w \geq 0$
$+$	"contemp."	$\hat{\beta}_{wlag}$ signif. or $\hat{\beta}_w le 0$

For Exp. 10, 13, and 14, no statements on time relation were required. Since no lagged influence occurred, subjects' opinions on time relation are treated as "contemporary" for these experiments, i.e. a contradiction is registered for all cases where the opinion on sign was unchanged and and at least one of the lagged-change variables is found to have significant influence. The contradictions can now be listed:

Exp. 10 (only contemporary influence)

Subj. 1, 4, 8: Unchanged opinion on v ("+"), $\hat{\beta}_{vlag} > 0$ (signif.)
Subj. 6: Unchanged opinion on v ("n"), $\hat{\beta}_{vlag} > 0$ (signif.)
Subj. 1, 3-8: Unchanged opinion on w ("−"), $\hat{\beta}_{wlag} < 0$ (signif.)
Subj. 1 and 5: Opinion "$w-$", but $\hat{\beta}_w > 0$ (not signif.)
Subj. 10: Opinion "$w-$", but $\Delta f \equiv 0$, thus $\hat{\beta}_w = 0$.

Exp. 11

Subj. 2, 3, 7, 8, 12, 13: Opinion "$w-$, contemp.", but $\hat{\beta}_{wlag} < 0$ (signif.)
Subj. 2 Opinion "$w-$, contemp.", but $\hat{\beta}_w > 0$ (not signif.)
Subj. 5: Opinion "$w+$, contemp.", but $\hat{\beta}_w < 0$ (not signif.)
and $\hat{\beta}_{wlag} < 0$ (signif.)

Exp. 12

Subj. 1: Opinion "vn, wn", but $\hat{\beta}_{vlag} > 0$ (signif.) and $\hat{\beta}_{wlag} < 0$ (signif.)
Subj. 2: Opinion "$v+$, contemp.", but $\hat{\beta}_{vlag} > 0$ (signif.)
Subj. 11: Opinion "$w-$, contemp.", but $\hat{\beta}_w > 0$ (not signif.)
and $\hat{\beta}_{wlag} < 0$ (signif.).

Exp. 13 (only contemporary influence)

Subj. 2, 3, 6-11: Unchanged opinion on w ("−"), $\hat{\beta}_{wlag} < 0$ (signif.)

Exp. 14 (only contemporary influence)

Subj. 2, 4, 6: Unchanged opinion on v ("−"), $\hat{\beta}_{vlag} > 0$ (signif.)

The listing shows that most "contradictions" are due to extrapolation: Subjects presume contemporary influence of a variable (or only contemporary influence occurs in the experiment), but the lagged change of this variable has significant influence, with the sign of that influence equal to the sign stated by the subject. Lagged changes are used as a proxy for current expected changes.

The contradictions in Exp. 14, however, suggest the contrary: In spite of the opinion "$v-$", Δv_{-1} had a significant positive influence on forecasted changes of three subjects.

Apart from extrapolation (positive in Exp.10-13, negative in Exp. 14) there are only few contradictions: Subj. 10 in Exp. 10 assessed the influence of v and w correctly but always forecasted naively $f = p_{-1}$, presumably due to the erroneous assumption that both v and w have no trend. Subj. 5 in Exp. 11 and Subj. 1 in Exp. 12 presumably did not really understand the meaning of "positive" and "negative" influence.

Comparative statements and *quantitative statements* were not given by any participant in these experiments.

Changing opinions

Among those cases where subjects changed their opinion on a variable, the first and last nonmissing statements are again compared. The results from above are confirmed: In those cases where the corresponding variable is irrelevant (v in Exp. 13, w in Exp. 14, three cases of unlearning occur (subjects initially stated "no influence", and later "positive" or "negative" influence), and two cases of learning. With respect to relevant variables, however, the relation is much more in favor of learning: 13 cases of learning, 6 cases of unlearning.

As far as the time relation is concerned (Exp. 11 and 12), in 8 cases there was learning whereas unlearning occurred in 4 cases.

This section on questionnaires has shown that, for those subjects who did not change their opinion during the experiment, qualitative statements on the sign of influence for each variable are broadly matched by observed forecasting behavior (regression results). The same holds true for comparative statements on the strength of influence of involved variables but not for statements on time relation: Subjects tend to replace past changes for current expected ones.

Only few subjects gave quantitative statements on the model. Some quantitative statements are not matched by the regression results: the forecasted changes are absolutely smaller than those obtained by applying the forecasting rule following from the quantitative statements.

Finally, changing opinions indicate some learning with respect to relevant variables but not with respect to irrelevant ones. Subjects tend to look for relevance during the experiment.

5.2 Categories of Individual Forecasts

This section presents an approach to find some categories of typical forecasting behavior. Viewing the questionnaires and the plots of observed individual forecasts suggests that most subjects forecast according to

$$f = p_{-1} + \sum_{k=1}^{K} \beta_k \Delta r_k$$

where $r_1, \ldots, r_K$ denote the involved exogenous variables. For lagged influence, the changes $\Delta r_k, k = 1, \ldots, K$, have to be replaced by lagged changes, for incomplete-information experiments, they may be replaced by either current expected changes or lagged changes.

If the underlying model is[4]

$$p = \alpha_0 + \sum_{k=1}^{K} \alpha_k r_k + u \ , \tag{5.1}$$

the special case $\beta_k = \alpha_k, k = 1, \ldots, K$, gives delta predictions, and if

$$(\beta_1, \ldots, \beta_K) = q(\alpha_1, \ldots, \alpha_K) \quad , \quad 0 < q < 1 \quad , \tag{5.2}$$

we obtain underestimating delta predictions. However, viewing the regression results suggests that a majority of subjects implements neither delta nor underestimating delta predictions. For example, they "overvalue" one exogenous variable relative to others or neglect a relevant variable, i.e. the *relations* between the β_k's differ from those between the true model coefficients α_k.

According to these considerations, it seems appropriate to look for categories of typical behavior by studying the regression results.

The regression results on psychological components (adaption, extrapolation, bang-bang movements and past trends) were also viewed but no apparent relation between those phenomena and the categories was

---

[4] For the case of lagged influence replace r_k by $r_{-1,k}$, $k = 1, \ldots, K$.

found. For example, the adaptive component was found significant for some subjects who forecasted nearly rationally but was not found significant for those subjects where none of the exogenous variables are significant at all.

As in previous sections based on regression results, the analysis is split up according to the three groups already known:

1. Simple full-information experiments (Exp. 1-6 and 9),
2. Seasonality experiments (Exp. 7-8),
3. Incomplete-information experiments (Exp. 10-14).

For better exposition, the underlying models and the regression equations estimated are reproduced at the beginning of each sub-section.

Simple Full-Information Experiments: Exp. 1-6 and 9

Table 5.11: Underlying Models

Exp. No.	Model
1	$p = 120 + y - 2z$
2	$p = -80 + x + \left[\frac{1}{2}y\right] - z$
3	$p = 85 - x_{-1} + y_{-1}$
4	$p = -80 + x + \left[\frac{1}{2}y\right] - z + u$
5	$p = 20 + y - z + u$
6	$p = 85 - x_{-1} + y_{-1} + u$
9	$p = -7 + y - z + \left[\frac{1}{2}p_{-1}\right]$

Regression equations estimated:

$$\Delta f = \beta_0 + \beta_x \Delta x + \beta_y \Delta y + \beta_z \Delta z + \varepsilon \qquad \text{(for Exp. 1, 2, and 9)}$$

$$\Delta f = \beta_0 + \beta_x \Delta x_{-1} + \beta_y \Delta y_{-1} + \beta_z \Delta z_{-1} + \varepsilon \qquad \text{(for Exp. 3)}$$

$$\Delta f = \beta_0 + \beta_x \Delta x + \beta_y \Delta y + \beta_z \Delta z + \rho u_{-1} + \varepsilon \qquad \text{(for Exp. 4 and 5)}$$

$$\Delta f = \beta_0 + \beta_x \Delta x_{-1} + \beta_y \Delta y_{-1} + \beta_z \Delta z_{-1} + \rho u_{-1} + \varepsilon \qquad \text{(for Exp. 6)}$$

The follwing six categories of typical behavior were found:

(1) Delta predictions.

(2) Underestimating delta predictions.

(3) Overvaluation of z relative to other relevant variables (only for those experiments where z is relevant: Exp. 1, 2, 4, 5, and 9).

(4) Neglection of y.

(5) Inclusion of an irrelevant variable (only for those experiments where irrelevant variables occur: Exp. 1, 5, and 9 (x irrelevant), Exp. 3 and 6 (z irrelevant), in most cases observed in combination with overvaluation of z.

(6) "Chaotic" behavior, i.e. the exogenous variables obviously have no influence on forecasts, but the forecasted changes are not equal to zero.

For Exp. 9, the neglection of the autoregressive part gives "misspecified" and "underestimating misspecified" instead of delta and underestimating delta predictions (see Chapter 3).

With the exception of category (6) and β_y in category (4), only those subjects were included in categories who correctly assessed the *sign* of influence for all relevant variables (this was the majority in all experiments). This fact is very important for understanding the table below which gives the formal expressions.

Let $\alpha_x, \alpha_y, \alpha_z$ denote the true model coefficients (for example: $\alpha_x = 0$, $\alpha_y = 1$, $\alpha_z = -1$ for Exp. 5), and let β_x, β_y, β_z the individual forecasting parameters estimated in the regressions above. Using this notation, the following table summarizes the formal expressions and gives an example for each category.

Note once again that (except for category 6 and for β_y in category 4), $\text{sign}(\beta_x)\cdot\text{sign}(\alpha_x) \neq -1$, $(\beta_y)\cdot\text{sign}(\alpha_y) \neq -1$, $(\beta_z)\cdot\text{sign}(\alpha_z) \neq -1$ is implicitly assumed. For the formal expression of category (3) - "overvaluation of z" - the overvaluation factor chosen was $\frac{3}{2}$, i.e. $\frac{\beta_z}{\beta_x} = \frac{3}{2}\frac{\alpha_z}{\alpha_x}$ (if $\alpha_x \neq 0$), and $\frac{\beta_z}{\beta_y} = \frac{3}{2}\frac{\alpha_z}{\alpha_y}$.

Table 5.12: Formal expression of Categories (1)-(6)

Cat.	$\alpha_x = 0,$ $\alpha_y \neq 0, \alpha_z \neq 0$ (Exp. 1, 5, 9)	$\alpha_x \neq 0,$ $\alpha_y \neq 0, \alpha_z \neq 0$ (Exp. 2, 4)	$\alpha_z = 0,$ $\alpha_x \neq 0, \alpha_y \neq 0$ (Exp. 3, 6)
(1)	$(\beta_x, \beta_y, \beta_z)$ $= (\alpha_x, \alpha_y, \alpha_z)$	$(\beta_x, \beta_y, \beta_z)$ $= (\alpha_x, \alpha_y, \alpha_z)$	$(\beta_x, \beta_y, \beta_z)$ $= (\alpha_x, \alpha_y, \alpha_z)$
Ex.	$(\beta_x, \beta_y, \beta_z)$ $= (0, 1, -2)$ in Exp. 1	$(\beta_x, \beta_y, \beta_z)$ $= (1, \frac{1}{2}, -1)$[1] in Exp. 2	$(\beta_x, \beta_y, \beta_z)$ $= (-1, 1, 0)$ in Exp. 3
(2)	$\beta_x = 0, \frac{\beta_z}{\beta_y} = \frac{\alpha_z}{\alpha_y}$	$\frac{\beta_x}{\beta_y} = \frac{\alpha_x}{\alpha_y}, \frac{\beta_z}{\beta_y} = \frac{\alpha_z}{\alpha_y}$	$\frac{\beta_x}{\beta_y} = \frac{\alpha_x}{\alpha_y}, \beta_z = 0$
Ex.	$\beta_x = 0, \frac{\beta_z}{\beta_y} = -2$ in Exp. 1	$\frac{\beta_x}{\beta_y} = 2, \frac{\beta_z}{\beta_y} = -2$ in Exp. 2	$\frac{\beta_x}{\beta_y} = -1, \beta_z = 0$ in Exp. 3
(3)	$\beta_x = 0, \frac{\beta_z}{\beta_y} = \frac{3}{2}\frac{\alpha_z}{\alpha_y}$	$\frac{\beta_x}{\beta_y} = \frac{\alpha_x}{\alpha_y}, \frac{\beta_z}{\beta_y} = \frac{3}{2}\frac{\alpha_z}{\alpha_y}$	.
Ex.	$\beta_x = 0, \frac{\beta_z}{\beta_y} = -3$ in Exp. 1	$\frac{\beta_x}{\beta_y} = 2, \frac{\beta_z}{\beta_y} = -3$ in Exp. 2	. in Exp. 3
(4)	$\beta_x = 0, \beta_y = 0,$ $\beta_z \neq 0$	$\beta_y = 0, \frac{\beta_x}{\beta_z} = \frac{3}{2}\frac{\alpha_x}{\alpha_z}$	$\beta_x \neq 0, \beta_y = 0,$ $\beta_z = 0$
Ex.	trivial	$\beta_y = 0, \frac{\beta_x}{\beta_z} = -1$	trivial
(5)	$\beta_x = \beta_y$ or $\beta_x = -\beta_y,$ $\frac{\beta_z}{\beta_y} = \frac{3}{2}\frac{\alpha_z}{\alpha_y}$	.	$\beta_z = \frac{3}{2}\beta_y$ or $\beta_z = -\frac{3}{2}\beta_y,$ $\frac{\beta_x}{\beta_y} = \frac{\alpha_x}{\alpha_y}$
Ex.	$\beta_x = \pm\beta_y$ $\beta_z = -3\beta_y$ in Exp. 1	. in Exp. 2	$\beta_z = \pm\frac{3}{2}\beta_y$ $\beta_x = -\beta_y$ in Exp. 3
(6)	$(\beta_x, \beta_y, \beta_z)$ $= (0, 0, 0)$	$(\beta_x, \beta_y, \beta_z)$ $= (0, 0, 0)$	$(\beta_x, \beta_y, \beta_z)$ $= (0, 0, 0)$
Ex.	trivial	trivial	trivial

Notes on the table:

[1]: Rounding (see true model) is neglected.

For disturbed-model experiments (Exp. 4-6), $\rho = 0$ (no influence of past disturbance) has to be included in the stated equations.

Now the procedure was essentially as follows: Where plausible, subjects are assigned to categories by simple viewing of regression results, and the equations corresponding to the chosen category are tested by an F test.[5] If the null hypothesis is rejected at the 10% level, the subject is excluded from the category.

The following table presents the "members" for each category (subject numbers) so that the regression results given in the appendix can be viewed for each category.

Table 5.13: Sum results on Categories
Subjects in Category ...

Exp. No.	No. of Subj.	(1)	(2)	(3)	(4)	(5)
1	14	1-3,5,6	–	8	9-11	4,7,13
2	13	7,10	1,4,6,9	12	–	·
3	12	1,4,6-8,11,12	3,5,9,10	·	–	–
4	12	–	4,8	5	6,10	·
5	13	–	11	3,6,9	10,13	1,5,12
6	11	5	1	·	3	8,11
9	14	8	2,4,5,6,9	–	–	11,14
Total Number	89	16	17	6	8	10

(continued)

[5] Recall that $\rho = 0$ is included in the tested equation for Exp. 4-6. Furthermore, note that the inequality statements (like $\beta_z \neq 0$) cannot be tested. These inequalities are rather a criterion at the stage of viewing the regression results and grouping individuals.

Table 5.13 (continued)
Subjects in Category ...

Exp. No.	(6)	No category
1	–	12,14
2	–	2,3,5,8,11,13
3	–	2
4	–	1-3,7,9,11,12
5	8	2,4,7
6	7,9,10	2,4,6
9	–	1,3,7,10,12,13
Total Number	4	28

Almost two thirds of subjects (57 out of 89) can be assigned to "non-chaotic" categories. Only a minority of subjects implements delta or underestimating delta predictions. This is due to under- or overvaluation of variables: z tends to be overvalued, possibly due to its high volatility, and y tends to be undervalued. In some cases, irrelevant variables are included by subjects.

Note that "overvaluation of z" appears in two categories: (3) and (5). Even some more subjects overvalue z and undervalue y. The reason why they are not assigned to a category is that the relation between the coefficients of the other variables does not fit to the relations required by the category. If however, no exact relations for the other variables were specified, one could hardly speak of "typical behavior".

For non-disturbed experiments (where the majority of "delta-forecasting" subjects occurred), delta predictions equal perfect predictions. Indeed, the mean absolute forecast error for those subjects in Exp. 1-3 is below one, some of them forecasted perfectly. In the disturbed-model experiments, delta predictions are hardly observed.

For all categories except delta predictions, underestimation of changes is prevailing. Correspondingly, the regression estimates $\hat{\beta}_x, \hat{\beta}_y, \hat{\beta}_z$ are absolutely smaller than the model coefficients $\alpha_x, \alpha_y, \alpha_z$, even in those cases where a variable is overvalued.

Now one might presume that significance of psychological components (adaptive behavior, extrapolation, bang-bang movements, short and long trends) added to the regression is related to some categories, in particular to those categories which are "far away" from rational behavior (neglection of y, or "chaotic" behavior).

Viewing the regression results, however, suggests that no relation is present: There are some "delta-forecasting" individuals with highly significant extrapolation, and for all "chaotic" forecasters, psychological components are not significant.

In order to verify that no relation is present, the following procedure (for each component separately) was adopted: A (2 x 7) contingency table was calculated (2 features concerning the additional component: significant/not significant, and 7 features concerning "categories": the six categories from above, and those subjects who cannot be categorized). This table contains the joint frequencies. Then, a χ^2 test for independence was performed. Indeed, the null hypothesis of independence is not rejected (at the 10% level) for all five contingency tables.[6]

Thus, we may conclude that psychological factors are not related to the categories found above. Viewing the regression results from adding a component also suggests that the parameter estimates are only slightly altered, thus, the categories are not affected.

Seasonality Experiments: Exp. 7 and 8

Table 5.14: Underlying Models

Exp. No.	Model
7	$p = 12 + y - z + 5(t \textit{ modulo } 4)$
8	$p = 10 + y - z + 5(t \textit{ modulo } 5)$

Regression equations estimated:

$$\Delta f = \beta_x \Delta x + \beta_y \Delta y + \beta_z \Delta z + \delta_0 D_0 + \delta_1 D_1 + \delta_2 D_2 + \delta_3 D_3 + \varepsilon$$

[6] 5 contingency tables = one for each psychological factor: Adaption, extrapolation, bang-bang, short trend, long trend.

where

$$D_{t,k} = \begin{cases} 1 & \text{if } t \textit{ modulo } 4 = k \\ 0 & \text{else} \end{cases} \quad , \; k = 0,1,2,3 \qquad \text{(for Exp. 7)}$$

and

$$\Delta f = \beta_y \Delta y + \beta_z \Delta z + \delta_0 D_0 + \delta_1 D_1 + \delta_2 D_2 + \delta_3 D_3 + \delta_4 D_4 + \varepsilon$$

where

$$D_{t,k} = \begin{cases} 1 & \text{if } t \textit{ modulo } 5 = k \\ 0 & \text{else} \end{cases} \quad , \; k = 0,\ldots,4 \qquad \text{(for Exp. 8)}$$

The method adopted is essentially the same as above for simple full-information experiments: Subjects are assigned to categories by viewing regression results, and the corresponding linear hypothesis is tested. In case of rejection at the 10% level, the subject is excluded from the category.

Only a small number of subjects fully comprehends the influence of the exogenous variables and the seasonality pattern *jointly*. Thus, delta predictions[7]

$$f = p_{-1} + E\Delta p = p_{-1} + \Delta y - \Delta z + s_t \;,$$

$$s_t = \begin{cases} -15 & t \textit{ modulo } 4 = 0 \\ 5 & \text{else} \end{cases} \qquad \text{(for Exp.7)}$$

and

$$f = p_{-1} + E\Delta p = p_{-1} + \Delta y - \Delta z + s_t \;,$$

$$s_t = \begin{cases} -20 & t \textit{ modulo } 5 = 0 \\ 5 & \text{else} \end{cases} \qquad \text{(for Exp.8)}$$

[7] Equal to rational predictions in these experiments.

are observed for only one subject in Exp. 7 (Subj. 5) and for one subject in Exp. 8 (Subj. 5). Underestimating delta predictions are observed for one subject in Exp. 7 (Subj. 3) and for no subject in Exp. 8. For the remaining 22 subjects (from both experiments together), it does not make sense to study the exogenous variables and the seasonality pattern jointly since no reasonably large categories can be drawn from this small number of subjects.

Restricting to the tabulated exogenous variables x (only for Exp. 7), y, and z, the relation $\beta_z = -\beta_y$ (and $\beta_x = 0$ in Exp. 7) - which means matching the coefficient relations in the true model - is plausible and not rejected for five subjects in Exp. 7 (Subj. 4,7,11-13) and for six subjects in Exp. 8 (Subj. 3,4,8,10-12). If those subjects who approximately implement delta or misspecified delta predictions are added, we obtain seven subjects (i.e. a majority) in both experiments who assessed the coefficient relation between the tabulated exogenous variables nearly correctly.

In Exp. 7, two subjects "neglect" all exogenous variables (Subj. 2 and 6), and one subject neglects y (Subj. 1). But there are too few subjects as to form categories of them.

Restricting to the seasonality pattern, the first observation made is that most subjects underestimate the growth as well as the crashes. Thus, in order to find categories, it is advisable to study the *relations* of the seasonal dummies in the same way as *relations* of β_x, β_y, β_z were studied. The following four categories have been found, in terms of the regression parameters $\delta_0, \delta_1, \delta_2, \ldots$.

(1) "Correct relation": The forecasted crash after 4 periods (for Exp. 7) or after 5 periods (for Exp. 8), resp., is, in absolute terms, three times (Exp. 7) or four times (Exp. 8) as large as the foregoing growth per period:

$$\delta_0 = -3\delta_1, \delta_1 = \delta_2 = \delta_3 \qquad \text{(for Exp. 7)}$$

$$\delta_0 = -4\delta_1, \delta_1 = \delta_2 = \delta_3 = \delta_4 \qquad \text{(for Exp. 8)}$$

(2) "Underestimated crash": The forecasted crash has (absolutely) the same amount as the foregoing growth per period:

$$\delta_0 = -\delta_1, \delta_1 = \delta_2 = \delta_3 (= \delta_4 \text{ for Exp. 8})$$

(3) "Growth interrupted": Subjects fail to forecast the crashes and realize zero growth in the crash periods:

$$\delta_0 = 0, \delta_1 = \delta_2 = \delta_3 (= \delta_4 \text{ for Exp. 8})$$

(4) "Growth continued": Subjects continue to forecast growth in the crash periods:

$$\delta_0 = \delta_1 = \delta_2 = \delta_3 (= \delta_4 \text{ for Exp. 8})$$

The following table now gives the sum results:

Table 5.15: Categories concerning seasonality pattern
Subject numbers

Category	Exp. 7	Exp. 8
"Correct"	–	1,2,3,6,9,10
"Crash underest."	8,10	8
"Growth interrupted"	12	–
"Growth continued"	2,6,7,13	–

Note that this table does *not* contain those subjects who were already assigned to delta and underestimating delta predictions above (Subj. 3 and 5 in Exp. 7, Subj. 5 in Exp. 8). These subjects would belong to the category "correct relation" here. For Exp. 7, no more subjects belong to this category, and five out of seven categorized subjects failed to forecast the crashes. This corresponds to the misspecified model used in Chapter 3 which also neglected the crashes. In Exp. 8, behavior is much "better": No categorized subject fails to forecast the crashes.

The number of subjects in the seasonality experiments is too small as to test for independence of categories and psychological factors.

Incomplete-Information Experiments: Exp. 10-14

Table 5.16: Underlying Models

Exp. No.	Model
10	$p = 100 + v - w$
11	$p = 100 + v_{-1} - w$
12	$p = 100 + v - w_{-1}$
13	$p = 200 - w + u$
14	$p = 150 - v + u$

Regression equations estimated:

$$\Delta f = \beta_0 + \beta_w E\Delta w + \beta_{vlag}\Delta v_{-1} + \beta_{wlag}\Delta w_{-1} + \varepsilon$$

(for Exp. 10-12),

$$\Delta f = \beta_0 + \beta_w E\Delta w + \beta_{vlag}\Delta v_{-1} + \beta_{wlag}\Delta w_{-1} + \rho u_{-1} + \varepsilon$$

(for Exp. 13 and 14).

The following five categories were found:

(1) Delta predictions.

(2) Underestimating Delta predictions.

(3) Neglection of v, combined with replacing current expected changes $E\Delta w$ of w by lagged changes Δw_{-1}.

(4) Replacing $E\Delta w$ and $E\Delta v$ by lagged changes Δv_{-1} and Δw_{-1}.

(5) "Chaotic" behavior, i.e. neither current expected nor lagged changes influence forecasts, but the forecasted change is not equal to zero.

As above, only those subjects are assigned to categories who correctly assess the sign of influence for all exogenous variables.

As will be seen below in Section 5.5, the dispersion of forecasts is relatively small in the incomplete-information experiments. As a consequence, there is a strongest category, namely Category (4). The following table gives, for each experiment, the formal expression of each category, with the exception of category (5) (chaotic behavior: all parameters = 0).

Table 5.17: Formal expressions for Categories (1)-(5)

Exp. No.	(1) Delta pred.	(2) Underest. Delta Pr.
10	$(\beta_w, \beta_{vlag}, \beta_{wlag}) = (-1, 0, 0)$	$\beta_w < 0, \beta_{vlag} = 0, \beta_{wlag} = 0$
11	$(\beta_w, \beta_{vlag}, \beta_{wlag}) = (-1, 1, 0)$	$\beta_w = -\beta_{vlag}, \beta_{wlag} = 0$
12	$(\beta_w, \beta_{vlag}, \beta_{wlag} = (0, 0, -1)$	$\beta_w = 0, \beta_{vlag} = 0, \beta_{wlag} < 0$
13	$(\beta_w, \beta_{vlag}, \beta_{wlag}, \rho) = (-1, 0, 0, 0)$	$\beta_w < 0, \beta_{vlag} = 0, \beta_{wlag} = 0, \rho = 0$
14	$(\beta_w, \beta_{vlag}, \beta_{wlag}, \rho) = (0, 0, 0, 0)$	$(\beta_w, \beta_{vlag}, \beta_{wlag}, \rho) = (0, 0, 0, 0)$

Table 5.17 (continued)

Exp. No.	(3) v neglected	(4) Lagged changes for current expected ch.
10	$\beta_w = 0, \beta_{vlag} = 0, \beta_{wlag} < 0$	$\beta_w = 0, \beta_{wlag} = -\beta_{vlag}$
11	$\beta_w = 0, \beta_{vlag} = 0, \beta_{wlag} < 0$	$\beta_w = 0, \beta_{wlag} = -\beta_{vlag}$
12	$\beta_w = 0, \beta_{vlag} = 0, \beta_{wlag} < 0$	$\beta_w = 0, \beta_{wlag} = -\beta_{vlag}$
13	.	$\beta_w = 0, \beta_{vlag} = 0, \beta_{wlag} < 0, \rho = 0$
14	$(\beta_w, \beta_{vlag}, \beta_{wlag}, \rho) = (0, 0, 0, 0)$	$\beta_w = 0, \beta_{vlag} < 0, \beta_{wlag} = 0, \rho = 0$

Notes on the table:

In Exp. 12, underestimating delta predictions and neglection of v cannot be discerned.

In Exp. 14, delta predictions, underestimating delta predictions, neglections of v, and "chaotic behavior" cannot be discerned. Those subjects were not regarded as "chaotic".

Now, the following table gives the sum results:

Table 5.18: Sum results on categories
Subjects in category ...

Exp. No.	No. of Subjects	(1)	(2)	(3)	(4)	(5)	No cat.
10	11	9	–	5,7	1,3,4,6	11	2,8,10
11	13	6	–	5,10	3,4,8,11	1	2,7,9,12,13
12	11	8	4-6, 7,9,10		1,3,11	–	2
13	11	4	–4	·	1-3,7,8,10	–	5,6,9,11
14	7		3,7		–	–	1,2,4-6
Total	53	?	?	?	17	12	18

Since some categories are undistinguishable in Exp. 12 and 14, no summing over the first three categories is possible. However, category (4) is obviously the strongest category, and, except for Exp. 14, a majority of subjects could be assigned to a "non-chaotic" category.

In Exp. 10, there is one interesting case: Subject No. 10 always predicted naively $f = p_{-1}$ in spite of having recognized the negative influence of w, possibly due to the erroneous assumption that w has no trend. This subject is not assigned to the "chaotic" category since his prediction rule is obvious.

In Exp. 13, some assignments to categories are cut off due to obvious *positive* influence of the last disturbance u_{-1}, and in Exp. 14, assignments are hindered because of *negative* influence of u_{-1} and *positive* influence of v_{-1} (in spite of negative influence of v in the true model, i.e. there is a contradiction in sign).

Concerning the relation between categories and psychological factors, a (2 x 4) contingency table[8] was established for each factor. The χ^2 statistics are again insignificant at the 10% level for all five psychological factors.

The following summary on categories can be given:

---

[8] (Categories (1)-(3) have to be put together due to indiscernabilities, so that the "combined" categories (1-3), (4), (5) result, and the set of "non-categorized" subjects has to be added.

The regressions on single exogenous variables suggest some categories of typical forecasting behavior. Only a minority of subjects approximately follow delta or underestimating delta predictions.

In the full-information experiments, overvaluation of the highly volatile exogenous variable z and undervaluation of the relatively stable variable y contribute to deviations from delta and underestimating delta predictions.

Similar behavior is found in the incomplete-information experiments: The random-walk variable v which is relatively stable compared to the variable w was often undervalued or neglected.

Another phenomenon is remarkable in the incomplete-information experiments: Subjects tend to extrapolate the last change of involved exogenous variables in order to forecast the change of p.

In the seasonality experiments, many subjects fail to forecast the crashes or even continue the foregoing growth in their forecasts.

5.3 Preference for "Round" Numbers

Numbers divisible by 2, 5, and 10 are regarded as "round" numbers. One may ask whether individuals "prefer" such numbers, e.g. forecast "45" rather than "46" although they consider 46 as the most probable value. Such behavior seems plausible in particular under two circumstances:

when the volatility of the p series is high,
when the individual is not sure about the true model.

In order to make sure that rounding is not induced by observed values of p ("subjects have no reason to prefer round numbers"), the following table shows, for each experiment, the frequencies of round values of p over the whole time horizon to be forecasted. The range covered by the p series (smallest and largest value) is included.

Table 5.19: Frequency of p values divisible by ...

Exp. No.	No. of observ.	2	5	10	Range
1	100	* 59	20	12	15-78
2	100	46	23	11	29-71
3	80	43	17	8	32-75
4	100	51	* 12	x 5	27-71
5	100	47	19	7	25-70
6	80	37	15	5	31-76
7	100	46	24	12	21-72
8	100	50	23	11	22-75
9	100	53	20	7	2-76
10	80	42	12	8	41-71
11	80	40	13	7	39-71
12	80	36	11	6	40-72
13	80	37	16	x 4	41-65
14	80	40	13	6	39-59

Note:
x marks significance at 10% level, * marks significance at 5% level (for a two-sided binomial test of H_0: *"values divisible by k occcur with relative frequency $1/k, k = 2, 5, 10$, resp."*).
No significance at 1% level occurrs.

The number of round values generally does no deviate significantly from the "expected" frequency $T/k, k = 2, 5, 10$, and the range is large enough for all experiments to expect this. For subsections of 20 periods, significance is not found either. Thus, subjects have no reason to avoid or to prefer round numbers.

Prominence analysis[9] seems to provide a suitable tool to analyze preference for "round" numbers. The method is described here for the case where only integer numbers occur.

A *prominence level* Δ is a "round" number, i.e. a number from the set $N_0 = \{1, 2, 5, 10, 20, 25, 50, \ldots\}$. The *prominence level* $\delta(n)$ of a number $n \in \mathrm{N}$ is the largest $\Delta \in N_0$ such that n is divisible by Δ without

[9] Selten (1987, [27]).

remainder. For example, $\delta(3) = 1$, $\delta(4) = 2$, $\delta(10) = 10$, $\delta(17) = 1$, $\delta(40) = 20$, $\delta(75) = 25$, $\delta(85) = 5$.

Now consider a time series of forecasts $f_1, \ldots, f_T$. Let k denote the frequency distribution of forecasts, i.e. $k(n)$ is the number of forecasts equal to n. Then

$$\sum_{n \in \mathrm{N}} k(n) = T \tag{5.3}$$

where T is the total number of forecasts. Let

$$S := \{n \in \mathrm{N} \mid k(n) > 0\} \tag{5.4}$$

be the support of k. Further, for every prominence level Δ, let

$$m(\Delta) = \#\{n \in S \mid \delta(n) = \Delta\} \tag{5.5}$$

be the *number of values* on the prominence level Δ, and let

$$h(\Delta) = \sum_{n:\delta(n)=\Delta} k(n) \tag{5.6}$$

the *number of observations* (forecasts) on level Δ. From m and h we may define the cumulative functions H and M by

$$M(\Delta_0) = \sum_{\Delta \geq \Delta_0} m(\Delta)\ , \tag{5.7}$$

(the number of values at least on level Δ_0), and

$$H(\Delta_0) = \sum_{\Delta \geq \Delta_0} h(\Delta)\ , \tag{5.8}$$

(the number of observations at least on level Δ_0). Obviously, $\#S = \sum_{\Delta \in N_0} m(\Delta) = M(1)$, and $T = \sum_{\Delta \in N_0} h(\Delta) = H(1)$. If the functions M and H are divided (normalized) by $\#S$ and T, resp., one obtains distribution functions on the set N_0 of prominence levels.

If no preference for prominent numbers is present, these two distribution functions should nearly coincide. If, to the contrary, preference for such numbers is present, $H(\cdot)/T$ should exceed $M(\cdot)/\#S$ significantly on a subset of N_0.

The procedure thus resembles to the one-sided Kolmogorov-Smirnov one-sample test. The *estimated prominence level* Δ^* for our time series of forecasts is that level where the difference $D(\cdot)$ of these two distribution function is maximized, i.e.

$$\Delta^* = \text{argmax}_{\Delta \in N_0} D(\Delta) = \text{argmax}_{\Delta \in N_0} \left(\frac{H(\Delta)}{T} - \frac{M(\Delta)}{\#S} \right) \quad (5.9)$$

The significance of "rounding" can then be tested using $D(\Delta^*)$ as Kolmogorov-Smirnov statistic.

Before giving an example, the following remark on the prominence analysis as performed here will be made:

Although forecasts roughly range from 30 to 70, the prominence levels 20, 25, and 50 are excluded. Instead, 10 is selected as maximal level for the following reason: Since mean absolute changes of p are between 2 and 8 for all experiments, it seems very unlikely that subjects prefer numbers divisible by 20, 25, or 50. 10 is the highest plausible prominence level. Within the range (30-70), however, no number at prominence level 10 occurs, with the exception of the boundaries 30 and 70 themselves. Level 10 is "covered" by the levels 20 and 50. Indeed, starting with level 50 yields an estimated prominence level of 20 or 50 (but not significant) for many subjects although it is very likely that they preferred 40, 50, or 60 not because of divisibility by 20 or 50, but rather because of divisibility by 10.

Now let us consider the prominence analysis for the forecasts of Subject 12 in Exp. 7 (Periods 21-100, i.e. $T = 80$) as an example:

Table 5.20: Prominence Analysis for Subj. 12 in Exp. 7

Δ	$h(\Delta)$	$m(\Delta)$	$H(\Delta)$	$M(\Delta)$	$\frac{H(\Delta)}{T}$	$\frac{M(\Delta)}{\#S}$	$D(\Delta)$
10	34	5	34	5	0.4250	0.26316	0.16184
5	29	4	63	9	0.7875	0.47368	0.31382
2	14	7	77	16	0.9625	0.84211	0.12039
1	3	3	80	19	1.0000	1.00000	0.00000

In the given example, the difference between the two distribution functions is positive on all levels. The maximal difference occurs at level 5, i.e. $\Delta^* = 5$ is the estimated prominence level for this subject. The difference $D(5) = 0.31382$ is far beyond the Kolmogorov-Smirnov 1% significance bound (0.16965), thus, preference for prominent numbers is highly significant for this subject.

The prominence analysis was applied on all 167 time series of individual forecasts, for all periods, for Periods 1-20, 21-end, and 61-end. In most cases, rounding was not found significant (in contrast to the example). The following two tables summarize, for each experiment, the number of subjects with estimated prominence levels 1, 2, 5, ... and the number of subjects where these levels are significant (for all periods). As mentioned above, 10 was selected as maximal level.

Table 5.21: Prominence Analysis (Periods 21-end)
Number of Subjects with Prominence Level ...

Exp. No.	No. of Subjects	1	2	5	10
1	14	0	2	3	9
2	13	3	3	2	5
3	12	1	1	9	1
4	12	3	7	2	0
5	13	2	3	5	3
6	11	4	0	3	4
7	13	0	1	10	2
8	12	1	3	7	1
9	14	2	5	3	4
10	11	3	2	2	4
11	13	5	4	4	0
12	11	4	2	1	4
13	11	5	4	2	0
14	7	1	0	6	0
Total	167	34	37	59	37

The results from this table may be somewhat misleading since higher estimated prominence levels do not imply more significant preference for prominent numbers. Therefore, the following table restricts to those individuals where the Kolmogorov-Smirnov statistic $D(\Delta^*)$ is significant (at the 5% level):

Table 5.22: Prominence Analysis (Periods 21-end), Significant Cases
Number of Subjects with significant Prominence Level ...

Exp. No.	No. of Subjects	1	2	5	10
4	1	.	.	1	.
7	6	.	.	6	.
8	2	.	1	1	.
11	1	.	1	.	.
14	1	.	.	1	.
Total	11	.	2	9	.

Preference for prominent numbers is significant for only 11 out of 167 subjects, six out of 11 significant cases occur in the seasonality experiment 7. This experiment has exactly those two features stated above as possible reasons for rounding: high volatility of p and uncertainty of subjects about the model.[10] The most frequent level is 5 which seems quite plausible.

Considering all periods yields slightly more significant results (19 "significant subjects") but this is due to the higher number of observations. For many subjects, the estimated prominence level changed when all periods are considered, but the totals do not indicate a systematic "shift" of prominence levels. Therefore, the results from all periods are not given here. From the first 20 periods alone, no significance can be expected due to the small number of observations.

Now, it is advisable to proceed in the same way as for "upward bias":[11] The phenomenon is significant only for very few single subjects, but it may be present for a significant majority of subjects. For this purpose,

---

[10] See deviations from rational predictions in Section 3.1, and Section 5.1 on the questionnaires.

[11] See Section 4.2.

the following table lists, for each experiment, the number of subjects with negative and positive difference D of the two distribution functions (see above),

$$D(\Delta) = \frac{H(\Delta)}{T} - \frac{M(\Delta)}{\#S} , \tag{5.10}$$

for the levels $\Delta = 2, 5, 10$. Positive $D(\Delta)$ indicates preference for numbers at least on prominence level Δ.

Table 5.23: Sum results from Prominence Analysis
(Periods 21-end)
Number of Subjects with ...

Exp. No.	No. of Subjects	$D(10) < 0$	$D(10) > 0$	$D(5) < 0$	$D(5) > 0$	$D(2) < 0$	$D(2) > 0$
1	14	2	12	7	7	3	11
2	13	4	9	8	5	7	6
3	12	4	8	1	11	5	7
4	12	7	4	6	6	3	9
5	13	3	10	4	8	5	8
6	11	5	6	6	5	7	4
7	13	4	9	2	11	0	13
8	12	5	7	3	9	5	7
9	14	5	9	4	10	3	11
10	11	4	7	6	5	8	3
11	13	6	6	6	7	5	8
12	11	6	5	7	4	7	4
13	11	8	3	8	2	6	5
14	7	3	4	1	6	2	5
Totals:							
(1)-(6),(9)	89	30	58	36	52	33	56
(7),(8)	25	9	16	5	20	5	20
(10)-(14)	53	27	25	28	24	28	25
(1)-(14)	167	66	99	69	96	66	101

Note:
$D(\Delta) = 0$ may occur, thus, the equality *(Number of subjects with $D(\Delta) < 0$) + (number of subjects with $D(\Delta) > 0$) = (number of subjects in the experiment)* does not generally hold.

According to a one-sided binomial test of H_0: "*equal frequencies of negative and positive sign of D*" against H_1: "*positive signs occur more frequently*", the following results are obtained from the table:

For the group of Exp. 1-6 and 9, the null hypothesis of equal frequencies is not rejected at the 5% level for $\Delta = 5$, but is rejected at the 1% level for $\Delta = 2$ and $\Delta = 10$.

For Exp. 7 and 8, H_0 is not rejected at the 5% level for $\Delta = 10$, but is rejected at the 1% level for $\Delta = 5$ and $\Delta = 2$.

For Exp. 10-14, no proportion is significant.

For the total from all experiments (last line of the table), the majority of positive signs is significant at the 5% level for $\Delta = 5$ and significant at the 1% level for $\Delta = 2$ and $\Delta = 10$.

For Periods 61-end, the proportions are less significant. For the results from Periods 1-20 see below.

Note that the highest *proportion* of positive D values occurs in case of the seasonality experiments. For comparison, the following table gives, for each experiment, the mean absolute expected change,

$$MAEC = \frac{1}{T-20} \sum_{t=21}^{T} |Ep_t - p_{t-1}| , \tag{5.11}$$

as a measure for the "volatility" of the p series, and the *average* of mean absolute deviations from rational predictions,

$$AvMAD^R = \frac{1}{N} \sum_{i=1}^{N} MAD_i^R = \frac{1}{N} \sum_{i=1}^{N} \left(\frac{1}{T-20} \sum_{t=21}^{T} |f_{t,i} - f_t^R| \right) , \tag{5.12}$$

as a measure for subjects' uncertainty about the model.

Table 5.24: Mean absolute expected change and average mean absolute deviations from rational predictions.

Exp. No.	$MAEC$	$AvMAD^R$
1	5.45	1.796
2	3.63	1.404
3	2.55	0.767
4	4.09	2.448
5	3.37	2.584
6	2.825	3.056
7	7.97	7.447
8	8.54	4.681
9	3.66	2.980
10	2.00	1.450
11	2.275	2.174
12	1.925	1.229
13	2.1125	2.052
14	1.1375	1.264

It is obvious that the volatility of p is much higher for the first nine experiments (where the majority of positive differences was significant) than for the incomplete-information experiments.[12] Correspondingly, the average mean absolute deviation from rational predictions is higher for the first nine experiments (except Exp. 1-3). We may conclude that preference for prominent numbers is popular only in presence of high volatility of the p series.

One might think that, corresponding to higher errors at the beginning of the experiments, rounding occurs more often within the first 20 periods. The following table shows that *the contrary* holds:

---

[12] Lower volatility was chosen for those experiments in order to compensate the additional difficulty resulting from incomplete information.

Table 5.25: Sum results from Prominence Analysis (Periods 1-20)
Number of Subjects with ...

Exp. No.	No. of Subjects	$D(10) < 0$	$D(10) > 0$	$D(5) < 0$	$D(5) > 0$	$D(2) < 0$	$D(2) > 0$
1	14	7	6	6	8	4	10
2	13	8	4	8	5	2	11
3	12	11	0	12	0	9	3
4	12	3	7	3	9	6	6
5	13	6	6	6	6	4	9
6	11	3	7	7	4	6	4
7	13	6	6	4	8	3	8
8	12	7	4	6	6	6	5
9	14	5	8	7	7	10	4
10	11	2	9	4	7	6	2
11	13	3	10	2	11	3	8
12	11	8	1	8	1	5	5
13	11	7	2	10	1	7	4
14	7	0	7	0	7	5	1
Totals:							
(1)-(6),(9)	89	43	38	49	39	41	47
(7),(8)	25	13	10	10	14	9	13
(10)-(14)	53	20	29	24	27	26	20
(1)-(14)	167	76	77	83	80	76	80

Within the first 20 periods, the proportion of subjects with positive difference D is not significant for any level and any group of experiments! A possible reason for this may be that most subjects spend more time at the beginning of the experiment (see Section 5.4 below).

Now, one may ask: Who are the individuals preferring prominent numbers? First, one should look at those 11 subjects (see Table 5.22 above) for whom that preference is significant. Their individual MAD from rational predictions was compared to the median and average of MAD^R

from all subjects within the same experiment. The results are quite clear: For 9 out of 11 "significant subjects", the individual MAD^R was greater than the group median, for 10 out of 11 greater than the group average. This lends support to the plausible presumption that subjects who prefer prominent numbers are "bad" forecasters.

To investigate this phenomenon more systematically, consider, for each subject, the difference $D(2)$ between the two distribution functions (at level $\Delta = 2$) and the MAD from rational predictions. For each experiment, one obtains as many pairs $(D(2), MAD^R)$ as there are subjects in the experiment. Thus, one may calculate, for each experiment, the correlation coefficient between $D(2)$ and MAD^R. The same can be done for $(D(5), MAD^R)$ and $(D(10), MAD^R)$. The following table summarizes the results:

Table 5.26: Correlation between "rounding" and "bad forecasting"
Pearson Correlation Coefficients Between ...

Exp. No.	$D(2)$ and MAD^R	$D(5)$ and MAD^R	$D(10)$ and MAD^R
1	0.566	0.628	0.134
2	0.401	0.740	0.605
3	−0.574	−0.416	−0.329
4	−0.388	−0.039	−0.124
5	0.072	0.204	0.174
6	0.190	0.134	0.024
7	0.208	0.184	0.403
8	0.310	0.225	0.167
9	0.456	0.342	0.569
10	−0.346	0.154	0.162
11	0.679	0.596	0.577
12	−0.395	−0.513	−0.381
13	−0.232	0.133	−0.409
14	−0.052	0.021	−0.012

For each level Δ, the correlation is positive for a majority of experiments. However, this majority is significant only for $\Delta = 5$ (level 5% according to a one-sided binomial test of H_0: "*equal frequencies*"). Positive correlation between preference for prominent numbers and deviation from rationality is apparent but not significant for all prominence levels.

To sum up the prominence results, preference for prominent numbers has generally not been found significant for single individuals, but, after the 20th period, it is present for a significant majority of subjects. Within the first 20 periods, however, even summing does not yield significance. There is some evidence in favor of the hypothesis that subjects who prefer prominent numbers are "bad forecasters".

5.4 The Time Spent for Forecasting

For 6 out of 11 subjects in Exp. 6 as well as for all participants in Exp. 12-14, the time spent from entering a forecast to entering the next one was recorded. The following results give some impression on how much time subjects spend for each forecast and on "learning" within the experiment.

Although data from every single period are available, only results from 20-period sections are presented since they reveal more structure. The whole time horizon is subdivided into four 20-period sections.[13] In the sequel, let $D_i(m,n)$ denote the time (in seconds) that subject i needed from entering the mth forecast to entering the nth one. Then,

$$DPF_i(m,n) := \frac{1}{n-m} D_i(m,n) \qquad (5.13)$$

is i's *duration per forecast* in Section (m-n). For each experiment, averages from $DPF_1, \ldots, DPF_N$ (N = number of subjects in the experiment) can be taken:

$$AvDPF(m,n) := \frac{1}{N} \sum_{i=1}^{N} DPF_i(m,n) \ . \qquad (5.14)$$

[13] Note that all involved experiments had 80 periods.

The following table summarizes, for each experiment, the averages from individual durations per forecast for the sections (0-20),[14] (20-40), (40-60), and (60-80). In addition, the smallest and largest individual DPF, i.e. the *range* of individual DPF, is given for each section.

Table 5.27: Average and range of individual durations per forecast (in seconds)

Exp. No.		Sections: (0-20)	(20-40)	(40-60)	(60-80)
6	Average	106.96	53.74	43.14	38.33
	(Range)	(54-204)	(43-80)	(27-60)	(16-62)
12	Average	67.45	37.05	26.94	23.78
	(Range)	(25-152)	(19-66)	(14-62)	(12-50)
13	Average	50.11	35.60	25.97	20.40
	(Range)	(31-80)	(22-49)	(18-37)	(15-29)
14	Average	75.11	42.85	21.65	15.20
	(Range)	(32-142)	(20-96)	(12-31)	(10-18)

The table shows that the average duration per forecast as well as the range of durations decrease monotonically[15] (according to the chosen 20-period sections) in all four experiments.

The sharpest decline is observed in Exp. 14: The average duration per forecast in the last section is only slightly above one fifth of that in the first section. For all 4 experiments involved, the observed decline is more than 50%.

Comparison of the different experiments yields the longest durations for Exp. 6 (3 exogenous variables, 2 of them relevant, lagged influence), and the shortest for Exp. 13 and 14 (2 exogenous variables, only one of them

---

[14] (0-20) means the time from switching from initial instructions to the first period until entering the 20th forecast.

[15] For the range, this means: the lower as well as the upper bound decrease monotonically. In Exp. 6, the upper bound is not monotonic.

relevant, only contemporary influence, but incomplete information on exogenous variables).

Summing over individual durations confirms the observed "monotonicity": (0-20) is the longest section for 33 out of 35 individuals, for the remaining two subjects, (20-40) is the longest section. (60-80) is the shortest section for 28 subjects, 40-60 is the shortest one for 4 subjects, and (20-40) the shortest one for 3 subjects. In no case (0-20) is the shortest section.

As stated above in Section 5.3, the long duration within the first periods may be a reason for the fact that preference for prominent numbers is not observed within that time section.

Similar to prominence analysis, one may now investigate the correlation between the time spent and the deviation from rational predictions. The following table summarizes, for each of the four experiments involved, the correlations between the duration $D(20,80)$ from the 20th to the 80th period and MAD^R:

Table 5.28:
Pearson Correlation Coefficients Between $D(20,80)$ and MAD^R

Exp. No.	Corr. Coeff.
6	−0.448
12	−0.303
13	−0.335
14	0.021

Due to the small number of experiments, no significance can be expected. However, the table suggests that those subjects who spend more time are better forecasters.

To summarize this section, the time spent per forecast decreases remarkably during the experiment. A negative correlation between time spent and absolute deviation from rational predictions is apparent, i.e. "faster" subjects are worse forecasters.

5.5 The Dispersion of Forecasts

This section analyzes the time series $\{\sigma_t\}$ of standard deviations of individual forecasts,

$$\sigma_t = \text{Standard Dev.}\left[f_{t,1},\ldots,f_{t,N}\right] \ . \tag{5.15}$$

A view over the data for each experiment suggests that the dispersion of forecasts is positively related to the volatility of the exogenous variables and increases in times of "bang-bang" movements of p. In order to verify this, the standard deviation was regressed, for each experiment, on the absolute change of each exogenous variable, on the lagged absolute disturbance (only for Exp. 4-6, 13, and 14), and on three more variables:

1. BB, defined as $BB_t = |E\Delta p_t - \Delta p_{t-1}|$. This "bangbang" variable takes large values if the expected change of p is extremely opposite to the last change of p.

2. TR, defined as $TR_t = |p_{-1} - p_{-3}|$, accounts for past trends of p.

3. t, i.e. the dispersion is simply regressed on the period number in order to verify whether there is a downward (or upward) trend of σ during the experiment.

It is presumed that the absolute change of each exogenous variable as well as the "bangbang" and the "trend" variable have a *positive* influence on σ. Thus, in the regressions, the null hypothesis H_0 : "*Parameter* = *0*" is tested against H_1: "*Parameter* > 0" for each of these variables and for the intercept. In addition, it is presumed that the dispersion shrinks during the experiment, i.e. for the parameter belonging to t, the null hypothesis is tested against H_1 : "*parameter* < 0".

The results are presented separately for the groups of Exp. 1-6 and 9/ Exp. 7 and 8 / Exp. 10-14 which are already known. Note that the test results are somewhat doubtful since the normality assumption is violated (standard deviations are always nonnegative).

Exp. 1-6 and 9

The following regression equations were estimated (the time index is dropped for simplicity):

$$\sigma = \beta_0 + \beta_x|\Delta x| + \beta_y|\Delta y| + \beta_z|\Delta z| + \beta_{bb}BB + \beta_{tr}TR + \gamma t + \varepsilon \quad (5.16)$$

for Exp. 1, 2, and 9, and

$$\sigma = \beta_0 + \beta_x|\Delta x_{-1}| + \beta_y|\Delta y_{-1}| + \beta_z|\Delta z_{-1}| + \beta_{bb}BB + \beta_{tr}TR + \gamma t + \varepsilon \quad (5.17)$$

for Exp. 3. For Exp. 4, 5, and 6, $\rho|u_{-1}|$ is added to Eq. (5.16) and (5.17), resp. The following table presents the results for this group of seven experiments. The last column of the table gives the range of σ (smallest and largest value within periods (21-end)).

Table 5.29: Regression results for dispersion, Exp. 1-6 and 9
* [**] mark significance at 5% [1%] level according to
one-sided t test of H_0 : "*Parameter* = 0"
against H_1 : "*Parameter* > 0" for $\beta_0, \beta_x, \beta_y, \beta_z, \rho, \beta_{bb}, \beta_{tr}$
and against H_1 : "*Parameter* < 0" for γ.

Exp. No.	$\hat{\beta}_0$	$\hat{\beta}_x$	$\hat{\beta}_y$	$\hat{\beta}_z$	$\hat{\rho}$
1	*0.941	*0.142	**0.206	**0.448	.
2	**1.148	**0.298	0.039	**0.193	.
3	*0.731	**0.265	**0.360	−0.003	.
4	**1.389	*0.113	**0.210	**0.260	−0.141
5	**1.009	**0.197	*0.103	**0.169	0.005
6	**1.847	**0.312	*0.145	**0.186	0.096
9	**1.170	0.076	**0.244	**0.356	.

Table 5.29 (continued)

Exp. No.	$\hat{\beta}_{bb}$	$\hat{\beta}_{tr}$	$\hat{\gamma}$	R^2	Range
1	0.002	0.001	−0.005	0.5127	(0.80-7.26)
2	0.040	0.012	−0.009	0.3929	(0.60-5.53)
3	**0.108	−0.018	−0.013	0.5770	(0.00-4.08)
4	**0.054	−0.022	−0.005	0.5102	(0.90-4.94)
5	**0.054	0.005	−0.001	0.4904	(0.80-4.61)
6	0.041	−0.028	−0.008	0.4856	(0.71-5.70)
9	0.040	0.021	*−0.007	0.5950	(0.70-5.45)

The following conclusions can be drawn from the table:

1. The absolute change of most involved exogenous variables has a highly significant positive effect on the dispersion of forecasts. Note that this even holds for *irrelevant* variables (x in Exp. 1 and 5, z in Exp. 6).

2. The "bangbang" variable is only partly significant, but its influence is positive for all seven experiments.

3. The "trend" variable is neither significant nor has conclusive sign.

4. The dispersion shrinks slightly (but not significantly) during the experiments.

5. The last disturbance has no noticeable influence which is not surprizing since it is not perceived by subjects.

Exp. 7 and 8

For these experiments, seasonal dummies are introduced into the regression as in previous sections. The regression equations estimated are

$$\sigma = \beta_x|\Delta x| + \beta_y|\Delta y| + \beta_z|\Delta z| +$$

$$+\delta_0 D_0 + \delta_1 D_1 + \delta_2 D_2 + \delta_3 D_3 + \beta_{bb} BB + \beta_{tr} TR + \gamma t + \varepsilon \ , \qquad (5.18)$$

$$D_{t,k} = \begin{cases} 1 & \text{if } t \textit{ modulo } 4 = k \\ 0 & \text{else} \end{cases} \quad , \ k = 0, 1, 2, 3$$

for Exp. 7, and

$$\sigma = \beta_y|\Delta y| + \beta_z|\Delta z| +$$

$$+\delta_0 D_0 + \delta_1 D_1 + \delta_2 D_2 \delta_4 D_4 + \delta_4 D_4 + \beta_{bb} BB + \beta_{tr} TR + \gamma t + \varepsilon \ , \ (5.19)$$

$$D_{t,k} = \begin{cases} 1 & \text{if } t \textit{ modulo } 5 = k \\ 0 & \text{else} \end{cases} \quad , \ k = 0, \ldots, 4$$

for Exp. 8. The following table presents the results:

Table 5.30: Regression results for dispersion, Exp. 7 and 8
(*) and (**) mark significance (see Table 5.29 above,
for the dummy variables H_1 is "*Parameter* > 0")

Exp. No.	$\hat{\beta}_x$	$\hat{\beta}_y$	$\hat{\beta}_z$	$\hat{\delta}_0$	$\hat{\delta}_1$	$\hat{\delta}_2$	$\hat{\delta}_3$
7	**0.297	*0.255	**0.327	**3.803	*2.284	**2.162	**2.051
8	·	*0.266	0.141	**6.428	−0.093	**2.378	**3.095

Table 5.30 (continued)

Exp. No.	$\hat{\delta}_4$	$\hat{\beta}_{bb}$	$\hat{\beta}_{tr}$	$\hat{\gamma}$	R^2	Range
7	·	0.056	0.029	0.004	0.9537	(2.22-12.10)
8	**3.465	**0.140	0.037	−0.012	0.9285	(1.11-16.63)

The results on exogenous variables, bang-bang, and trend correspond to the results from Exp. 1-6 and 9. Unfortunately, $\hat{\gamma} > 0$ in Exp. 7, i.e. the dispersion increases slightly over time, in contrast to the results above. Among the dummy variables, D_0 is most significant which means that the dispersion of forecasts dramatically increases in the "crash" periods. This seems plausible. The most amazing result, however, is the high explanation (R^2) in the seasonality experiments. For Exp. 7, the standard deviation of forecasts is even much better explained than average forecasts (see R^2 in regressions in Chapter 3)!

Exp. 10-14

In these experiments, σ cannot be regressed on absolute expected changes since $E\Delta v \equiv 0$ and $|E\Delta w| \equiv 2$, but lagged absolute changes $|\Delta v_{-1}|$ and $|\Delta w_{-1}|$ are included in the regressions. The following equations are estimated:

$$\sigma = \beta_0 + \beta_v|\Delta v_{-1}| + \beta_w|\Delta w_{-1}| + \beta_{bb}BB + \beta_{tr}TR + \gamma t + \varepsilon$$

(for Exp. 10-12)

$$\sigma = \beta_0 + \beta_v|\Delta v_{-1}| + \beta_w|\Delta w_{-1}| + \rho|u_{-1}| + \beta_{bb}BB + \beta_{tr}TR + \gamma t + \varepsilon$$

(for Exp. 13 and 14)

The following table presents the results. (*) and (**) again mark significance of the parameters, where, for the exogenous variables as well as for BB and TR (and for $|u_{-1}|$ in Exp. 13 and 14), H_0 is again tested against H_1 : "*Parameter* > 0".

Table 5.31: Regression results for dispersion, Exp. 10-14

Exp. No.	$\hat{\beta}_0$	$\hat{\beta}_v$	$\hat{\beta}_w$	$\hat{\rho}$
10	**1.117	0.044	−0.029	.
11	**1.403	*0.131	*0.078	.
12	**0.719	0.088	**0.126	.
13	**1.023	0.036	−0.036	−0.062
14	**1.214	**0.176	0.025	−0.082

Table 5.31 (continued)

Exp. No.	$\hat{\beta}_{bb}$	$\hat{\beta}_{tr}$	$\hat{\gamma}$	R^2	Range
10	**0.093	−0.002	−0.001	0.2978	(0.63-2.05)
11	0.031	−0.036	0.001	0.2147	(1.03-2.73)
12	**0.134	*−0.049	0.002	0.3527	(0.77-3.04)
13	**0.156	−0.017	0.001	0.3862	(0.63-2.94)
14	*0.072	0.022	**−0.009	0.3791	(0.49-3.04)

As far as the exogenous variables and the time are concerned, the results are much less conclusive than for the first nine experiments. The influence of bangbang movements, however, remains remarkable, and, again, trends have no noticeable influence.

The explanation is worse than for the first nine experiments, possibly due to the fact that the dispersion is very small in these experiments.

The following conclusions so far can be drawn from the analysis of dispersion:

1. Bangbang movements have a positive influence on dispersion (positive sign of $\hat{\beta}_{bb}$ for all 14 experiments, $\hat{\beta}_{bb}$ significantly positive for 8 out of 14 experiments (at level 5%, for 7 out of 14 experiments even at level 1%)), in spite of the fact that they generally have no significant influence on average forecasts.

2. Although partly relevant for average forecasts, trends have no noticeable influence on dispersion, $\hat{\beta}_{tr}$ is negative for exactly half of the experiments. Replacing short trends $|p_{-1}-p_{-3}|$ by long trends $|p_{-1}-p_{-5}|$ yields similar results.

3. There is no significant decrease in dispersion. However, for 10 out of 14 experiments, $\hat{\gamma}$ is negative.

4. The absolute change of exogenous variables has a positive influence on dispersion.

In order to verify if some decrease in dispersion is present during the first 20 periods (which were not included so far) or over the whole experiment, the same regressions as above were estimated for Periods 1-20 and for all periods. For the first 20 periods, $\hat{\gamma}$ is negative for only 6 experiments, for one of them significantly (5% level). For all periods, however, $\hat{\gamma}$ is negative for 11 out of 14 periods (the proportion 11 out of 14 is significant at the 5% level for a one-sided binomial test of H_0 : *equal frequencies*), and the decrease was significant (5% level) for 7 experiments. Thus, one may conclude that some decrease is present, but it cannot be located within the first 20 periods.

6. Conclusion

This chapter briefly summarizes the experimental results presented in Ch. 3-5.

Aggregate Forecasts: Averages and Medians

The difference between average and median forecasts is small compared to the variation of forecasts. The mean absolute difference is less than one for all experiments. Thus, results obtained for average forecasts hold for medians, too.

Observed average and median forecasts have been compared to realizations and to various prediction concepts such as rational predictions, least-squares-learning (LSL) predictions (for Implemenation 1: all past observations processed, and Implementation 2: only last 15 observations processed), delta predictions, and misspecified predictions (for Exp. 7, 9, and 11). A prediction rule has been postulated ("trend-underestimating predictions") which described aggregate forecasts quite well. The basic criterion for comparison is the mean absolute deviation (*MAD*).

For aggregate forecasts, the following inequalities hold without exceptions:

MAD from rational predictions < mean absolute error
MAD from LSL (Implementation 2) < *MAD* from LSL (Implement. 1)
MAD from delta predictions < *MAD* from rational predictions[1]

Apart from medians in Exp. 1-3, underestimating predictions provide the best description for all experiments. Median forecasts in Exp. 1-3 (full information, no disturbance, no additional influence) are nearly rational.

---

[1] (where delta predictions differ from rational predictions)

Some phenomena closely related to these results have been investigated:

1. Upward Bias

2. Concentration on changes rather than on levels, formalized by "delta models". As a consequence of this behavior, subjects do not perceive past disturbances.

3. Underestimation of changes (highly significant).

4. Misspecified auxiliary models which neglect, for example, autoregressive components and exogenous variables without remarkable variation and without trend.

Learning within the first 20 periods is present for a significant majority of experiments. After the 20th period, however, no noticeable learning is observed. Unlearning at the end of the experiment is not significant in any sense.

As far as the influence of single exogenous variables is concerned, it is difficult to draw *general* conclusions. Here are some observations from this section:

1. Relevance and the sign of influence are assessed correctly for most variables.

2. Corresponding to underestimation of changes, the influence on forecasted changes is absolutely *smaller* than the influence on the change of p in the underlying model.

3. In absence of seasonal fluctuations, highly volatile exogenous variables seem to be overvalued relative to other variables.

4. Corresponding to concentration on changes rather than levels, past disturbances are generally not perceived by subjects.

Some extrapolative behavior has been found in incomplete-information experiments: Subjects replace past changes of involved exogenous variables for unknown actual changes. Apart from this, however, no conclusive results are obtained which support adaption or extrapolation as independent features of forecasts.

As far as psychological factors are concerned, bang-bang movements have no noticeable influence. The influence of past trends depends on the presence of long trend segments and seasonality. Long trend segments support "continuation", seasonality supports "interruption" of past trends. For trend-neutral situations (i.e. neither long trends nor seasonality), "interruption" seems to be prevailing.

Sum Results on Individual Forecasts

This chapter demonstrated that most features of aggregate forecasts found in Chapter 3 hold for a significant majority of subjects:

1. the inequalities for mean absolute deviations from various prediction concepts.

2. the non-rational features "upward bias" and "underestimation of changes". Underestimation of changes is more significant when restricting to periods with absolutely large change of p.

3. Learning behavior, i.e. decreasing absolute deviation from rational predictions.

4. Opposite sign of adaptive and extrapolative component: Negative adaptive behavior corresponds to positive extrapolation, and vice versa.

5. Influence of past trends on forecasts.

Features of Individual Forecasts

The qualitative statements on the sign of influence for each exogenous variable which were given in the questionnaires are broadly matched by actual forecasting behavior found in the regression of forecasted changes on changes of involved exogenous variables. However, quantitative statements often are not matched by regression results: only the stated *relations* were confirmed by the regressions, but the forecasted changes are smaller than those calculated according to quantitative statements.

As far as changing statements are considered, some learning is observed with respect to relevant variables, but not with respect to sunspot variables. Subjects tend to state "no influence" at the beginning and look for positive or negative influence later.

Regressions on changes of involved exogenous variables suggest some categories of typical behavior. Only a minority of subjects approximately follow delta or underestimating delta predictions. Overvaluation of volatile exogenous variables (z in Exp. 1-9) and undervaluation or neglection of relatively stable variables (y in Exp. 1-9, v in Exp. 10-14) often contribute to deviations from delta and underestimating delta predictions.

No relation between categories and certain psychological factors (e.g. adaptive behavior) has been found.

Preference for prominent numbers is significant only for very few subjects, and only in experiments where the p series is highly volatile. However, it is present for a significant majority of subjects after the 20th period. During the first 20 periods, not even a remarkable majority was found. Some correlation between "rounding" and "bad forecasting" has been found.

The time spent per forecasting period shrinks dramatically during the experiment. Some correlation between "long duration" and "good forecasting" was found.

Finally, the dispersion of forecasts is positively influenced by absolute changes of exogenous variables and by bang-bang movements but - in contrast to average forecasts - not by past trends.

Presumably the most general features found in the experiments are:

1. Concentration on changes rather than on levels.

2. Underestimation changes.

3. Overvaluation of volatile variables relative to stable ones.

4. Forecasters fail to predict sharp crashes or rises in seasonal or cyclical movements.

7. Appendix

7.1 Mean Absolute Deviations from Various Prediction Concepts

Legend:

P = Realization

R = Rational Prediction

LSL1 = Least-Squares-Learning Prediction, Implementation 1 (all past observations processed)

LSL2 = Least-Squares-Learning Prediction, Implementation 2 (only last 15 observations processed)

D = Delta Prediction

M = Misspecified Prediction

U = Underestimating Prediction

EXP. 1, MEAN ABSOLUTE DEVIATIONS FROM VARIOUS PREDICTION CONCEPTS
PERIODS 21-END

SUBJ	P = R = LSL = D	U
1	0.000	1.297
2	0.188	1.416
3	0.050	1.341
4	3.538	2.447
5	0.013	1.309
6	0.025	1.272
7	3.125	2.216
8	1.625	1.697
9	2.575	2.503
10	3.138	2.466
11	4.488	4.091
12	2.413	2.141
13	2.925	3.047
14	1.050	1.703
Median	0.538	1.078
Average	1.264	0.924

EXP. 1, MEAN ABSOLUTE DEVIATIONS FROM VARIOUS PREDICTION CONCEPTS
PERIODS 1-END

SUBJ	P = R = LSL = D	U
1	0.370	1.548
2	0.280	1.398
3	0.350	1.463
4	3.440	2.403
5	0.010	1.372
6	0.210	1.368
7	3.280	2.383
8	1.750	1.798
9	2.440	2.313
10	3.260	2.503
11	4.450	3.993
12	2.500	2.213
13	2.850	2.848
14	1.280	1.838
Median	0.675	1.078
Average	1.355	0.926

EXP. 2, MEAN ABSOLUTE DEVIATIONS FROM VARIOUS PREDICTION CONCEPTS
PERIODS 21-END

SUBJ	P = R = D	LSL1	LSL2	U
1	1.338	1.402	1.386	1.679
2	1.400	1.471	1.442	1.041
3	0.263	0.388	0.374	1.053
4	0.588	0.735	0.710	1.222
5	2.838	2.855	2.850	2.059
6	1.825	1.897	1.832	1.997
7	0.513	0.640	0.618	1.122
8	3.563	3.590	3.588	3.328
9	0.563	0.664	0.639	1.066
10	0.313	0.506	0.509	1.116
11	1.163	1.203	1.178	1.116
12	1.350	1.396	1.398	1.359
13	2.538	2.575	2.583	2.284
Median	0.281	0.425	0.404	0.766
Average	0.921	0.936	0.928	0.590

EXP. 2, MEAN ABSOLUTE DEVIATIONS FROM VARIOUS PREDICTION CONCEPTS
PERIODS 1-END

SUBJ	R	LSL1	LSL2	U
1	1.649	1.713	1.696	1.776
2	1.630	1.686	1.662	1.258
3	0.420	0.531	0.513	1.143
4	0.630	0.744	0.722	1.223
5	2.980	2.992	2.982	2.228
6	1.828	1.916	1.868	2.043
7	0.960	1.065	1.047	1.457
8	3.620	3.660	3.656	3.388
9	0.930	1.030	1.005	1.273
10	0.850	1.017	1.015	1.457
11	1.140	1.194	1.172	1.043
12	1.660	1.705	1.700	1.588
13	2.500	2.532	2.541	2.248
Median	0.520	0.637	0.614	0.808
Average	1.052	1.067	1.058	0.668

EXP. 3, MEAN ABSOLUTE DEVIATIONS FROM VARIOUS PREDICTION CONCEPTS
PERIODS 21-END

SUBJ	R	U
1	0.000	0.625
2	3.650	3.142
3	1.288	1.301
4	0.183	0.708
5	1.267	1.500
6	0.000	0.625
7	0.183	0.767
8	0.083	0.675
9	0.900	1.250
10	1.617	1.633
11	0.000	0.625
12	0.033	0.658
Median	0.025	0.633
Average	0.630	0.396

EXP. 3, MEAN ABSOLUTE DEVIATIONS FROM VARIOUS PREDICTION CONCEPTS
PERIODS 1-END

SUBJ	R	U
1	0.112	0.744
2	3.575	3.063
3	1.759	1.655
4	0.363	0.825
5	1.737	1.825
6	0.050	0.663
7	0.300	0.831
8	0.363	0.881
9	1.188	1.425
10	2.163	2.056
11	0.238	0.856
12	0.150	0.756
Median	0.169	0.688
Average	0.788	0.488

EXP. 4, MEAN ABSOLUTE DEVIATIONS FROM VARIOUS PREDICTION CONCEPTS
PERIODS 21-END

SUBJ	P	R	LSL1	LSL2	D	U
1	2.713	2.400	2.498	2.453	2.275	2.103
2	3.050	3.063	3.001	3.033	2.688	2.522
3	3.063	3.050	2.879	2.849	2.800	2.359
4	2.800	2.638	2.579	2.566	2.288	1.866
5	2.488	2.250	2.211	2.165	1.875	2.053
6	3.988	3.725	3.788	3.463	3.550	3.091
7	2.013	1.875	1.755	1.791	1.200	1.509
8	2.113	1.975	1.906	1.849	1.550	1.153
9	2.688	2.575	2.531	2.367	2.150	1.516
10	2.550	2.263	2.238	2.216	2.038	2.053
11	1.975	1.663	1.514	1.647	1.112	1.178
12	2.188	1.900	1.882	1.806	1.525	1.209
Median	1.894	1.731	1.649	1.532	1.244	0.778
Average	1.990	1.785	1.727	1.598	1.329	0.741

EXP. 4, MEAN ABSOLUTE DEVIATIONS FROM VARIOUS PREDICTION CONCEPTS
PERIODS 1-END

SUBJ	P	R	LSL1	LSL2	D	U
1	2.730	2.460	2.556	2.479	2.280	2.058
2	3.080	3.010	2.954	2.897	2.630	2.403
3	3.180	3.210	3.107	2.988	2.910	2.438
4	2.930	2.660	2.666	2.670	2.380	1.947
5	2.670	2.460	2.375	2.252	2.020	2.053
6	3.820	3.570	3.589	3.244	3.250	2.808
7	2.140	2.010	1.893	1.840	1.350	1.543
8	2.390	2.220	2.167	2.035	1.800	1.388
9	2.820	2.770	2.715	2.550	2.290	1.643
10	2.620	2.290	2.264	2.264	2.110	2.108
11	2.210	1.880	1.675	1.687	1.260	1.213
12	2.440	2.170	2.100	1.978	1.690	1.318
Median	2.105	1.915	1.807	1.625	1.365	0.858
Average	2.163	1.949	1.863	1.677	1.424	0.823

EXP. 5, MEAN ABSOLUTE DEVIATIONS FROM VARIOUS PREDICTION CONCEPTS
PERIODS 21-END

SUBJ	P	R	LSL1	LSL2	D	U
1	3.550	3.313	3.349	3.175	3.038	2.256
2	2.425	2.113	1.980	1.975	2.013	1.669
3	2.475	2.313	2.386	2.026	2.038	1.969
4	2.188	1.825	1.850	1.825	1.500	1.244
5	2.188	1.925	1.988	1.870	1.575	1.856
6	2.775	2.413	2.548	2.550	2.488	1.544
7	3.338	3.075	3.063	3.036	2.825	2.181
8	3.380	3.354	3.487	3.538	3.291	2.430
9	2.638	2.400	2.410	2.324	2.100	1.456
10	3.088	2.900	3.036	3.074	2.925	1.819
11	2.950	2.613	2.625	2.603	2.238	1.731
12	3.038	2.924	2.872	2.932	2.899	2.285
13	2.788	2.425	2.454	2.269	2.200	1.881
Median	2.156	1.869	1.874	1.851	1.519	0.813
Average	2.223	1.889	1.895	1.876	1.591	0.734

EXP. 5, MEAN ABSOLUTE DEVIATIONS FROM VARIOUS PREDICTION CONCEPTS
PERIODS 1-END

SUBJ	P	R	LSL1	LSL2	D	U
1	3.720	3.470	3.501	3.389	3.270	2.405
2	2.410	2.120	1.940	1.935	2.000	1.805
3	2.810	2.560	2.597	2.257	2.320	2.195
4	2.420	1.970	1.963	1.879	1.610	1.245
5	2.450	2.080	2.090	1.951	1.660	1.795
6	2.900	2.490	2.549	2.557	2.550	1.575
7	3.360	3.110	3.039	2.924	2.790	2.215
8	3.758	3.636	3.733	3.823	3.667	2.818
9	2.810	2.580	2.545	2.468	2.300	1.525
10	3.560	3.270	3.324	3.351	3.230	2.125
11	3.280	2.970	2.945	2.846	2.570	1.845
12	3.222	2.990	2.959	3.012	3.051	2.409
13	2.920	2.610	2.592	2.402	2.310	1.855
Median	2.335	1.985	1.940	1.905	1.605	0.840
Average	2.417	2.012	1.997	1.968	1.718	0.822

EXP. 6, MEAN ABSOLUTE DEVIATIONS FROM VARIOUS PREDICTION CONCEPTS
PERIODS 21-END

SUBJ	P	R	LSL1	LSL2	D	U
1	3.644	3.136	3.142	3.062	3.068	2.364
2	3.183	2.833	2.825	2.345	2.000	1.833
3	3.350	3.067	2.998	2.694	2.633	1.733
4	2.847	2.508	2.477	2.022	2.458	2.093
5	2.133	1.583	1.684	1.326	1.150	1.750
6	2.867	2.517	2.605	2.392	1.850	2.683
7	3.817	3.400	3.367	3.188	3.300	2.267
8	3.633	3.483	3.624	3.329	2.883	2.933
9	4.083	3.733	3.583	3.671	3.833	3.000
10	4.525	4.200	4.064	4.031	4.300	3.738
11	3.675	3.150	3.079	3.025	3.050	2.163
Median	2.517	2.133	2.133	1.715	1.667	0.800
Average	2.415	2.031	1.974	1.577	1.614	0.663

EXP. 6, MEAN ABSOLUTE DEVIATIONS FROM VARIOUS PREDICTION CONCEPTS
PERIODS 1-END

SUBJ	P	R	LSL1	LSL2	D	U
1	3.705	3.256	3.302	3.237	3.051	2.359
2	3.425	3.100	3.127	2.798	2.350	2.000
3	3.450	3.125	3.117	2.931	2.900	1.963
4	2.835	2.494	2.516	2.178	2.405	1.994
5	2.250	1.775	1.851	1.558	1.350	1.875
6	3.113	2.638	2.699	2.557	2.113	2.650
7	3.738	3.338	3.381	3.290	3.213	2.213
8	3.713	3.588	3.664	3.484	3.013	2.913
9	4.000	3.675	3.604	3.683	3.800	2.888
10	4.517	4.283	4.265	4.213	4.183	3.725
11	3.733	3.433	3.323	3.339	3.033	2.208
Median	2.588	2.213	2.246	1.964	1.763	0.875
Average	2.530	2.186	2.154	1.876	1.741	0.743

EXP. 7, MEAN ABSOLUTE DEVIATIONS FROM VARIOUS PREDICTION CONCEPTS
PERIODS 21-END

SUBJ	P=R=LSL=D	M	U
1	6.888	5.588	5.769
2	7.813	4.263	3.381
3	7.450	5.725	5.169
4	7.300	4.950	4.244
5	4.438	6.188	6.469
6	8.238	4.913	4.419
7	8.300	5.875	6.431
8	7.275	6.025	5.431
9	7.863	5.088	4.606
10	7.100	5.700	4.481
11	7.850	4.625	4.994
12	7.713	4.988	5.006
13	8.588	5.713	4.306
Median	6.175	3.000	2.331
Average	5.711	2.939	2.165

EXP. 7, MEAN ABSOLUTE DEVIATIONS FROM VARIOUS PREDICTION CONCEPTS
PERIODS 1-END

SUBJ	P=R=LSL=D	M	U
1	6.830	5.560	5.640
2	7.780	4.370	3.600
3	7.550	5.580	4.960
4	7.210	5.060	4.560
5	5.240	6.330	6.360
6	8.140	4.870	4.420
7	8.430	6.220	6.640
8	7.260	5.890	5.120
9	8.010	5.280	4.680
10	7.420	5.830	4.580
11	8.240	5.090	5.330
12	7.590	4.980	4.720
13	8.640	5.830	4.410
Median	6.240	3.130	2.350
Average	5.828	3.041	2.155

EXP. 8, MEAN ABSOLUTE DEVIATIONS FROM VARIOUS PREDICTION CONCEPTS
PERIODS 21-END

SUBJ	P=R=LSL=D	U
1	4.363	4.381
2	0.300	4.394
3	4.738	4.719
4	3.550	3.969
5	0.275	4.356
6	4.950	4.106
7	7.800	5.656
8	8.488	6.281
9	5.175	5.019
10	3.888	4.306
11	7.364	6.662
12	5.288	3.956
15	2.638	2.781
16	3.598	2.070

EXP. 8, MEAN ABSOLUTE DEVIATIONS FROM VARIOUS PREDICTION CONCEPTS
PERIODS 1-END

SUBJ	P=R=LSL=D	U
1	5.170	4.590
2	0.590	4.380
3	5.640	5.050
4	4.180	4.210
5	0.340	4.200
6	5.520	4.420
7	7.260	5.530
8	8.470	5.970
9	5.770	5.350
10	4.320	4.290
11	7.082	6.263
12	6.310	4.670
Median	3.170	2.730
Average	3.915	2.096

EXP. 9, MEAN ABSOLUTE DEVIATIONS FROM VARIOUS PREDICTION CONCEPTS
PERIODS 21-END

SUBJ	P=R=D	LSL1	LSL2	M	U
1	3.725	3.731	3.726	2.844	2.991
2	3.650	3.669	3.661	3.456	2.341
3	2.835	2.839	2.839	2.709	2.000
4	3.363	3.387	3.376	3.056	1.909
5	3.013	3.034	3.045	3.056	2.159
6	2.125	2.143	2.128	1.169	1.609
7	2.481	2.456	2.469	2.101	1.582
8	2.788	2.806	2.771	1.769	2.147
9	3.275	3.295	3.289	2.506	1.872
10	1.725	1.716	1.740	1.506	2.166
11	2.838	2.847	2.853	1.756	2.016
12	4.363	4.361	4.378	3.994	3.178
13	2.513	2.524	2.513	1.994	2.091
14	3.025	2.999	2.992	1.931	2.072
Median	2.213	2.220	2.203	1.444	0.922
Average	2.295	2.281	2.264	1.609	0.804

EXP. 9, MEAN ABSOLUTE DEVIATIONS FROM VARIOUS PREDICTION CONCEPTS
PERIODS 1-END

SUBJ	P=R=D	LSL1	LSL2	M	U
1	3.570	3.602	3.599	2.890	2.820
2	3.630	3.673	3.653	3.470	2.310
3	2.848	2.860	2.852	2.702	1.876
4	3.280	3.327	3.317	3.080	2.075
5	2.910	2.955	2.965	3.010	1.990
6	2.220	2.247	2.216	1.390	1.610
7	2.404	2.391	2.394	2.076	1.487
8	2.960	2.998	2.948	2.110	2.360
9	3.210	3.245	3.216	2.670	1.825
10	1.970	1.980	1.977	1.730	2.340
11	2.750	2.763	2.749	1.890	1.990
12	4.100	4.101	4.128	3.890	2.960
13	2.380	2.417	2.384	2.010	2.040
14	3.250	3.268	3.249	2.430	2.305
Median	2.190	2.213	2.176	1.590	0.890
Average	2.246	2.255	2.230	1.734	0.808

EXP.10, MEAN ABSOLUTE DEVIATIONS FROM VARIOUS PREDICTION CONCEPTS
PERIODS 21-END

SUBJ	P	R = D	U
1	2.500	1.667	1.333
2	2.483	1.250	1.450
3	2.400	1.267	0.867
4	2.683	1.517	1.483
5	2.483	1.583	0.883
6	2.517	1.750	1.017
7	2.383	1.183	1.083
8	2.417	1.117	1.417
9	2.119	0.695	1.322
10	2.367	2.000	1.000
11	2.417	1.917	0.983
Median	2.342	1.158	0.708
Average	2.254	1.192	0.560

EXP.10, MEAN ABSOLUTE DEVIATIONS FROM VARIOUS PREDICTION CONCEPTS
PERIODS 1-END

SUBJ	P	R = D	U
1	2.363	1.575	1.350
2	2.338	1.150	1.450
3	2.163	1.100	0.800
4	2.450	1.263	1.313
5	2.288	1.400	0.875
6	2.363	1.550	0.975
7	2.175	1.163	1.063
8	2.225	1.013	1.463
9	2.025	0.772	1.316
10	2.263	1.975	1.000
11	2.388	1.875	0.975
Median	2.119	0.994	0.656
Average	2.075	1.046	0.545

EXP.11, MEAN ABSOLUTE DEVIATIONS FROM VARIOUS PREDICTION CONCEPTS
PERIODS 21-END

SUBJ	P	R = D	M	U
1	2.650	2.650	2.033	1.133
2	2.550	2.617	2.033	1.967
3	2.400	2.067	1.950	1.750
4	2.083	1.917	1.400	1.167
5	2.967	3.000	1.783	1.650
6	1.117	0.050	1.867	1.933
7	2.500	2.200	1.250	1.650
8	2.200	2.167	1.917	1.617
9	2.700	2.600	1.317	1.083
10	2.667	2.667	1.717	1.617
11	2.864	2.847	2.186	2.136
12	1.567	1.333	1.950	1.883
13	2.317	2.150	1.467	1.533
Median	1.933	1.800	1.150	0.817
Average	2.009	1.863	1.108	0.757

EXP.11, MEAN ABSOLUTE DEVIATIONS FROM VARIOUS PREDICTION CONCEPTS
PERIODS 1-END

SUBJ	P	R = D	M	U
1	2.563	2.425	1.850	1.025
2	2.763	2.775	2.125	2.175
3	2.450	2.113	1.788	1.638
4	2.150	1.963	1.288	1.063
5	2.875	2.888	1.663	1.638
6	1.112	0.200	1.800	1.850
7	2.513	2.225	1.200	1.550
8	2.300	2.163	1.763	1.463
9	2.700	2.613	1.388	1.288
10	2.600	2.538	1.538	1.487
11	2.975	2.899	2.215	2.177
12	1.725	1.487	1.862	1.813
13	2.325	2.163	1.413	1.538
Median	1.963	1.800	1.025	0.825
Average	2.025	1.851	1.011	0.755

EXP.12, MEAN ABSOLUTE DEVIATIONS FROM VARIOUS PREDICTION CONCEPTS
PERIODS 21-END

SUBJ	P	R = D	U
1	2.200	1.600	1.217
2	1.917	0.650	0.800
3	2.083	1.550	1.017
4	1.817	1.317	0.667
5	1.833	0.733	0.800
6	2.517	1.417	1.433
7	1.933	1.033	0.967
8	1.950	1.083	1.517
9	2.183	1.283	1.483
10	2.068	1.017	1.458
11	2.417	1.883	1.233
Median	1.800	0.700	0.533
Average	1.834	0.836	0.483

EXP.12, MEAN ABSOLUTE DEVIATIONS FROM VARIOUS PREDICTION CONCEPTS
PERIODS 1-END

SUBJ	P	R = D	U
1	2.488	1.838	1.438
2	1.913	0.638	0.850
3	2.175	1.650	1.088
4	1.975	1.550	0.838
5	1.987	0.863	0.875
6	2.500	1.525	1.362
7	1.963	1.112	1.038
8	2.038	1.213	1.463
9	2.050	1.175	1.450
10	2.165	1.304	1.532
11	2.800	2.300	1.612
Median	1.813	0.813	0.538
Average	1.888	0.971	0.509

EXP.13, MEAN ABSOLUTE DEVIATIONS FROM VARIOUS PREDICTION CONCEPTS
PERIODS 21-END

SUBJ	P	R	D	U
1	2.050	2.017	1.533	0.933
2	2.367	2.033	1.483	1.550
3	2.317	2.317	1.767	1.567
4	2.183	1.750	1.467	2.067
5	2.483	2.217	1.233	1.700
6	2.508	2.254	1.559	1.542
7	2.300	2.233	1.617	1.217
8	2.317	2.050	1.733	0.767
9	1.900	1.633	0.850	1.117
10	2.233	1.933	1.317	1.250
11	2.367	2.133	1.417	1.417
Median	1.958	1.792	0.958	0.908
Average	2.071	1.804	1.095	0.737

EXP.13, MEAN ABSOLUTE DEVIATIONS FROM VARIOUS PREDICTION CONCEPTS
PERIODS 1-END

SUBJ	P	R	D	U
1	2.313	2.113	1.675	1.075
2	2.550	2.275	1.688	1.763
3	2.275	2.225	1.638	1.538
4	2.213	1.813	1.425	2.000
5	2.638	2.388	1.375	1.825
6	2.899	2.582	1.835	1.848
7	2.413	2.213	1.575	1.200
8	2.325	1.925	1.612	0.663
9	2.000	1.700	0.838	1.213
10	2.350	2.000	1.362	1.413
11	2.363	2.063	1.400	1.475
Median	2.094	1.844	0.944	0.981
Average	2.163	1.852	1.097	0.795

EXP.14, MEAN ABSOLUTE DEVIATIONS FROM VARIOUS PREDICTION CONCEPTS
PERIODS 21-END

SUBJ	P	R	D	U
1	2.233	0.617	1.200	0.842
2	2.783	1.400	1.350	1.325
3	2.500	1.350	0.767	0.925
4	2.600	1.317	1.400	1.258
5	2.500	1.183	1.300	1.208
6	2.915	1.864	1.983	1.856
7	2.333	1.117	0.333	0.625
Median	2.292	0.792	0.692	0.600
Average	2.307	0.905	0.845	0.642

EXP.14, MEAN ABSOLUTE DEVIATIONS FROM VARIOUS PREDICTION CONCEPTS
PERIODS 1-END

SUBJ	P	R	D	U
1	2.200	0.813	1.175	0.906
2	2.613	1.575	1.513	1.481
3	2.475	1.413	0.900	1.044
4	2.563	1.375	1.362	1.294
5	2.488	1.325	1.438	1.319
6	2.785	1.949	2.013	1.930
7	2.250	1.088	0.550	0.706
Median	2.269	0.919	0.794	0.750
Average	2.248	1.018	0.916	0.779

7.2 Regression on Single Exogenous Variables

EXP. 1, REGRESSION DF = B0 + B1*DX + B2*DY + B3*DZ + E
PERIODS 21-END

SUBJ	B0	B1	B2	B3	RMSE	RSQU	DW
1	0.000	0.000	1.000	-2.000	0.00	1.0000	1.804
2	-0.165	0.004	1.017	-1.967	0.93	0.9808	2.068
3	-0.051	0.008	1.007	-1.995	0.45	0.9954	2.038
4	-0.472	0.339	0.315	-0.718	2.51	0.5385	2.145
5	0.012	0.004	1.010	-2.001	0.11	0.9997	2.123
6	0.025	0.007	0.985	-1.988	0.22	0.9989	1.031
7	0.521	0.451	0.288	-0.944	1.90	0.7748	1.706
8	-0.204	0.072	0.601	-1.707	2.69	0.8163	1.968
9	0.382	0.039	-0.079	-1.882	1.86	0.9190	1.542
10	0.340	-0.037	0.201	-1.402	2.76	0.7333	2.409
11	0.292	-0.215	-0.256	-1.881	5.01	0.6109	1.292
12	-0.027	0.080	0.290	-1.777	2.61	0.8339	1.595
13	0.844	0.417	0.502	-1.527	4.41	0.5944	1.777
14	0.150	-0.369	0.954	-2.007	1.35	0.9601	1.763
Median	0.200	0.043	0.736	-1.855	0.56	0.9917	2.105
Average	0.118	0.057	0.560	-1.700	0.84	0.9784	1.682

EXP. 2, REGRESSION DF = B0 + B1*DX + B2*DY + B3*DZ + E
PERIODS 21-END

SUBJ	B0	B1	B2	B3	RMSE	RSQU	DW
1	0.334	0.953	0.296	-0.780	2.43	0.7207	2.301
2	-0.134	0.572	0.654	-0.774	1.32	0.8742	2.108
3	0.017	1.007	0.544	-0.998	0.40	0.9929	1.625
4	0.361	0.946	0.570	-0.835	1.94	0.8258	1.945
5	-0.160	0.167	-0.006	-0.501	1.40	0.6155	1.566
6	0.346	0.667	0.552	-0.908	3.02	0.6242	1.776
7	-0.031	0.964	0.477	-0.935	1.10	0.9419	1.845
8	0.618	-0.394	1.497	-0.982	2.29	0.7997	1.598
9	0.038	0.982	0.436	-0.815	1.49	0.8872	1.882
10	-0.112	1.020	0.527	-0.928	1.03	0.9512	2.146
11	-0.056	0.560	0.582	-1.018	1.16	0.9242	2.123
12	0.258	0.656	0.309	-0.960	1.48	0.8728	1.502
13	-0.068	0.374	-0.185	-0.968	2.12	0.7395	1.872
Median	0.019	0.879	0.490	-0.966	0.49	0.9878	2.303
Average	0.109	0.649	0.484	-0.878	0.57	0.9770	1.427

EXP. 3, REGRESSION DF = B0 + B1*DX(-1) +B2*DY(-1) +B3*DZ(-1) + E
PERIODS 21-END

SUBJ	B0	B1	B2	B3	RMSE	RSQU	DW
1	-0.000	-1.000	1.000	0.000	0.00	1.0000	1.239
2	-0.418	-0.053	-0.257	0.249	2.52	0.1237	1.858
3	0.243	-0.645	0.436	-0.037	2.14	0.4452	2.043
4	0.071	-0.895	0.924	-0.014	1.04	0.9043	2.208
5	0.796	-0.739	1.034	-0.065	2.07	0.7060	1.442
6	-0.000	-1.000	1.000	0.000	0.00	1.0000	1.239
7	0.173	-0.995	0.906	0.019	1.07	0.9073	1.949
8	0.076	-1.006	0.975	-0.033	0.53	0.9775	1.137
9	0.514	-0.841	0.626	-0.021	2.08	0.6039	2.240
10	-0.528	-0.283	0.664	0.001	2.03	0.4574	1.890
11	-0.000	-1.000	1.000	0.000	0.00	1.0000	1.239
12	-0.031	-1.014	1.014	0.005	0.26	0.9947	1.136
Median	0.022	-1.003	0.992	-0.014	0.19	0.9970	1.054
Average	0.073	-0.789	0.778	0.009	0.52	0.9655	2.000

EXP. 4, REGRESSION DF = B0 + B1*DX + B2*DY + B3*DZ + R*U(-1) + E
PERIODS 21-END

SUBJ	B0	B1	B2	B3	R	RMSE	RSQU	DW
1	0.501	0.236	0.402	-1.133	-0.044	2.55	0.7037	2.187
2	0.111	0.547	0.845	-0.432	0.019	3.16	0.4846	2.173
3	-0.291	0.598	0.981	-0.370	-0.159	2.30	0.6768	2.103
4	0.589	0.574	0.440	-0.420	0.151	2.55	0.4888	1.684
5	0.080	0.641	0.278	-1.189	-0.221	2.29	0.7989	1.872
6	1.225	0.522	-0.017	-0.357	0.504	3.55	0.2497	1.746
7	0.125	0.989	0.749	-0.829	0.120	1.64	0.8830	1.744
8	0.242	0.675	0.282	-0.697	-0.007	1.39	0.8430	1.892
9	0.378	0.214	0.232	-0.744	0.252	1.47	0.7629	1.887
10	0.096	0.776	0.117	-0.827	-0.142	2.54	0.6827	1.595
11	0.039	0.792	0.578	-0.971	-0.128	1.40	0.9046	1.538
12	0.116	0.871	0.392	-0.614	-0.027	1.43	0.8563	1.845
Median	0.148	0.617	0.426	-0.770	-0.016	0.93	0.9301	1.535
Average	0.268	0.620	0.440	-0.715	0.026	0.87	0.9326	1.346

EXP. 5, REGRESSION DF = B0 + B1*DX + B2*DY + B3*DZ + R*U(-1) + E
PERIODS 21-END

SUBJ	B0	B1	B2	B3	R	RMSE	RSQU	DW
1	0.517	-0.280	0.074	-0.444	0.017	2.45	0.2821	1.869
2	-0.596	0.070	0.732	-0.693	-0.580	2.22	0.6310	1.659
3	0.062	0.158	0.443	-0.853	-0.096	2.28	0.6350	2.095
4	0.520	0.031	0.512	-0.691	-0.103	1.48	0.7410	1.851
5	0.047	0.537	0.645	-0.832	0.086	1.36	0.8742	1.941
6	0.026	-0.043	0.211	-0.386	-0.294	1.79	0.3688	0.952
7	1.001	-0.294	0.546	-0.376	0.239	2.61	0.3340	1.872
8	1.625	-0.118	0.227	-0.082	-0.045	2.24	0.0741	1.420
9	-0.155	-0.003	0.313	-0.786	0.099	1.95	0.6442	1.780
10	0.173	-0.082	-0.076	-0.469	-0.319	1.95	0.4203	2.112
11	0.764	0.135	0.425	-0.430	0.138	2.49	0.3411	2.088
12	0.002	0.345	0.453	-0.263	-0.207	2.68	0.3164	2.124
13	0.165	-0.018	0.161	-0.866	0.046	1.84	0.7044	2.014
Median	0.206	0.066	0.353	-0.595	-0.083	0.86	0.8571	1.784
Average	0.313	0.035	0.360	-0.554	-0.079	0.75	0.8712	1.887

EXP. 6, REGRESSION DF = B0+B1*DX(-1)+B2*DY(-1)+B3*DZ(-1)+R*U(-1)+E
PERIODS 21-END

SUBJ	B0	B1	B2	B3	R	RMSE	RSQU	DW
1	0.947	-0.206	0.343	0.029	0.249	2.86	0.1317	1.886
2	-0.327	-0.645	0.579	0.223	0.595	2.14	0.5859	2.043
3	-0.258	-0.285	0.043	0.104	0.137	1.77	0.1728	2.011
4	0.452	0.063	1.110	-0.158	-0.094	1.95	0.6875	2.239
5	0.382	-0.955	1.055	0.042	-0.286	1.63	0.8319	1.340
6	0.459	-1.704	0.829	-0.196	0.350	1.28	0.9305	2.266
7	0.004	0.166	0.053	0.046	-0.058	2.50	0.0356	1.726
8	-0.199	-0.654	0.838	0.954	0.274	1.61	0.8972	1.034
9	-0.541	0.131	-0.055	-0.200	-0.442	2.84	0.1275	1.937
10	-1.365	-0.283	-0.126	0.026	-0.435	4.06	0.0398	2.389
11	-0.143	-0.221	0.142	-0.388	-0.067	2.37	0.2706	1.904
Median	-0.010	-0.420	0.446	0.076	0.124	1.09	0.6814	2.133
Average	-0.032	-0.420	0.455	0.057	0.039	0.83	0.7873	2.019

EXP. 7, REGRESSION DF = B1*DX + B2*DY + B3*DZ +
+ D0*DUMMY0 + D1*DUMMY1 + D2*DUMMY2 + D3*DUMMY3 + E
PERIODS 21-END

SUBJ	B1	B2	B3	D0	D1
1	-0.075	0.340	-1.520	-3.398	6.640
2	-0.142	-0.114	-0.204	3.921	2.679
3	0.362	0.220	-0.490	-3.638	2.619
4	-0.350	0.892	-1.094	-1.361	1.484
5	-0.542	0.594	-0.872	-12.64	4.903
6	0.127	0.089	-0.148	-1.830	4.954
7	-0.623	1.480	-1.236	1.233	3.560
8	0.515	0.016	0.594	-3.525	3.844
9	0.175	0.775	0.134	0.433	5.356
10	-0.160	-0.501	0.142	-2.263	3.278
11	-0.281	0.840	-0.418	2.893	9.123
12	-0.011	0.894	-0.267	0.784	3.338
13	-0.125	0.322	-0.131	1.566	1.470
Median	-0.017	0.477	-0.391	0.682	4.524
Average	-0.087	0.450	-0.424	-1.089	4.096

SUBJ	D2	D3	RMSE	RSQU	DW
1	2.349	0.081	6.40	0.5018	1.673
2	3.785	3.308	3.34	0.5499	1.727
3	2.551	1.492	6.56	0.2090	2.038
4	0.390	0.010	4.83	0.4247	1.560
5	2.903	4.751	6.46	0.6426	1.790
6	2.125	1.075	5.01	0.2756	1.458
7	2.273	1.164	7.23	0.3805	1.879
8	4.597	3.284	5.51	0.3915	2.167
9	5.211	1.213	5.23	0.4247	1.312
10	3.175	1.947	4.94	0.3021	0.994
11	4.623	3.239	5.35	0.5766	1.280
12	4.792	3.808	6.30	0.3286	1.199
13	1.182	2.891	5.75	0.1297	2.198
Median	3.264	2.491	2.76	0.6303	1.293
Average	3.074	2.174	2.65	0.6250	1.072

EXP. 8, REGRESSION DF = B2*DY + B3*DZ +
+ D0*DUMMY0 + D1*DUMMY1 + ... + D4*DUMMY4 + E
PERIODS 21-END

SUBJ	B2	B3	D0	D1	D2
1	0.306	0.114	-17.62	5.662	4.735
2	1.088	-0.896	-20.04	4.872	5.005
3	0.244	-0.111	-20.52	5.568	5.136
4	0.579	-0.339	-19.78	4.889	2.799
5	1.063	-0.998	-19.99	4.663	5.618
6	1.442	-0.095	-11.43	6.052	3.936
7	0.841	-0.367	-0.721	4.799	2.557
8	0.318	-0.295	-2.293	3.785	1.364
9	-0.033	-0.339	-18.09	3.743	4.625
10	0.821	-0.780	-16.08	4.686	1.750
11	0.249	-0.259	-4.199	5.802	6.962
12	0.853	-0.442	-7.869	5.818	4.437
Median	0.620	-0.343	-16.71	4.750	4.478
Average	0.648	-0.400	-13.22	5.015	4.078

SUBJ	D3	D4	RMSE	RSQU	DW
1	2.583	5.186	3.85	0.8561	1.628
2	4.997	3.883	1.56	0.9819	2.070
3	4.094	2.171	4.85	0.8257	2.113
4	3.121	2.290	3.60	0.8857	1.763
5	4.865	4.701	1.40	0.9859	1.954
6	3.052	2.351	5.22	0.6797	2.412
7	0.370	0.995	6.47	0.2459	1.612
8	1.667	2.041	7.31	0.1353	1.569
9	4.385	4.050	6.74	0.6653	2.092
10	2.150	3.464	4.84	0.7786	1.789
11	-2.407	1.336	8.23	0.2839	2.256
12	3.765	1.538	4.97	0.6049	1.834
Median	3.559	3.230	1.79	0.9625	2.137
Average	2.745	2.845	1.90	0.9418	1.759

EXP. 9, REGRESSION DF = B0 + B1*DX + B2*DY + B3*DZ + E
PERIODS 21-END

SUBJ	B0	B1	B2	B3	RMSE	RSQU	DW
1	0.013	0.131	0.315	-1.167	3.24	0.5910	1.839
2	0.308	0.186	0.199	-0.041	2.43	0.0894	1.406
3	0.728	0.354	0.682	-0.189	2.24	0.4765	1.982
4	0.705	0.150	0.304	-0.263	2.11	0.2504	1.860
5	1.464	0.069	0.374	-0.403	2.34	0.3098	1.475
6	0.156	0.062	0.895	-0.867	1.63	0.8165	1.813
7	-0.148	0.140	0.830	-0.566	1.93	0.6663	1.895
8	0.079	0.049	0.825	-1.003	3.25	0.5635	1.944
9	1.125	0.163	0.475	-0.568	2.68	0.4046	1.662
10	0.148	0.279	1.275	-0.774	1.76	0.8403	1.364
11	0.630	0.470	0.528	-0.842	2.06	0.7306	1.736
12	0.262	0.362	0.349	0.302	3.34	0.2058	1.976
13	0.571	0.281	0.997	-0.778	2.42	0.6843	1.895
14	-0.041	0.637	0.429	-0.793	2.19	0.7138	1.826
Median	0.327	0.276	0.667	-0.634	0.96	0.8849	1.586
Average	0.431	0.237	0.606	-0.569	0.89	0.8882	1.526

EXP. 10, REGRESSION DF = B0 + B1*EDW + B2*DV(-1) + B3*DW(-1) + E
PERIODS 21-END

SUBJ	B0	B1	B2	B3	RMSE	RSQU	DW
1	0.061	0.003	0.312	-0.310	1.30	0.3301	1.913
2	0.772	-0.296	0.122	-0.479	1.36	0.5556	1.289
3	0.062	-0.115	0.347	-0.357	0.78	0.6927	1.558
4	-0.153	-0.021	0.593	-0.699	0.89	0.8260	1.736
5	0.313	-0.026	-0.121	-0.302	1.04	0.3518	1.456
6	-0.055	0.022	0.225	-0.206	0.86	0.3368	1.399
7	0.167	-0.171	0.107	-0.389	1.23	0.4528	1.509
8	0.040	-0.534	0.174	-0.570	1.16	0.7718	1.396
9	-0.043	-1.042	-0.082	-0.008	1.07	0.8046	1.389
10	0.000	0.000	0.000	0.000	0.00	.	.
11	0.256	-0.025	-0.049	-0.033	0.75	0.0409	1.548
Median	0.047	-0.205	0.194	-0.319	0.64	0.7403	1.527
Average	0.128	-0.200	0.148	-0.304	0.40	0.8682	1.235

EXP. 11, REGRESSION DF = B0 + B1*EDW + B2*DV(-1) + B3*DW(-1) + E
PERIODS 21-END

SUBJ	B0	B1	B2	B3	RMSE	RSQU	DW
1	-0.100	-0.048	-0.054	0.069	1.12	0.0187	1.793
2	0.137	0.021	0.269	-0.897	1.87	0.5311	1.200
3	0.196	-0.047	0.435	-0.730	1.74	0.5325	2.329
4	-0.034	-0.197	0.302	-0.364	1.34	0.4686	1.833
5	0.402	-0.079	-0.191	-0.543	1.83	0.3691	1.357
6	-0.015	-0.967	0.992	-0.014	0.22	0.9947	2.741
7	-0.152	-0.501	0.124	-0.628	1.31	0.7360	1.412
8	0.042	0.055	0.473	-0.465	1.72	0.3740	2.248
9	0.140	-0.156	-0.214	-0.581	1.04	0.7019	1.733
10	0.374	-0.140	0.046	-0.418	1.89	0.2615	1.512
11	0.976	-0.279	0.065	0.189	2.13	0.0558	0.767
12	0.113	-0.156	0.926	-0.605	0.92	0.8770	1.840
13	-0.125	-0.475	0.192	-0.359	1.68	0.4887	1.731
Median	0.154	-0.219	0.291	-0.422	0.74	0.7779	1.802
Average	0.153	-0.228	0.258	-0.413	0.54	0.8614	1.565

EXP. 12, REGRESSION DF = B0 + B1*EDW + B2*DV(-1) + B3*DW(-1) + E
PERIODS 21-END

SUBJ	B0	B1	B2	B3	RMSE	RSQU	DW
1	0.287	-0.003	0.265	-0.422	1.51	0.3077	2.168
2	0.271	0.001	0.250	-0.868	0.52	0.9340	2.559
3	0.216	0.060	0.283	-0.288	1.17	0.2776	1.550
4	-0.255	-0.023	0.100	-0.345	0.94	0.4238	2.017
5	0.113	-0.142	-0.072	-0.600	0.91	0.7619	1.941
6	0.344	0.108	0.280	-0.857	1.84	0.4852	2.321
7	-0.129	0.114	0.094	-0.694	1.44	0.4970	2.114
8	-0.280	-0.072	0.038	-1.056	1.33	0.7818	1.450
9	0.472	-0.129	0.151	-0.579	1.87	0.3840	1.031
10	0.217	-0.177	0.169	-0.763	1.59	0.6092	1.847
11	-0.088	0.028	0.276	-0.336	1.38	0.2632	2.005
Median	0.053	0.006	0.178	-0.690	0.49	0.9072	1.844
Average	0.105	-0.020	0.168	-0.620	0.47	0.9008	1.524

EXP. 13, REGRESSION DF = B0+B1*EDW+B2*DV(-1)+B3*DW(-1)+R*U(-1)+E
PERIODS 21-END

SUBJ	B0	B1	B2	B3	R	RMSE	RSQU	DW
1	0.233	-0.067	-0.125	-0.292	0.135	1.13	0.3685	2.023
2	-0.299	-0.127	-0.176	-0.540	0.256	1.58	0.4884	1.919
3	-0.050	0.092	-0.157	-0.491	0.121	1.71	0.3094	1.642
4	-0.100	-0.980	-0.113	-0.095	-0.148	1.92	0.5813	0.909
5	0.045	-0.558	-0.023	-0.204	0.564	1.81	0.4362	1.917
6	-0.146	-0.351	0.069	-0.294	0.480	1.79	0.3361	1.608
7	-0.061	0.028	0.064	-0.457	0.322	1.31	0.3786	1.719
8	-0.131	-0.065	0.003	-0.115	0.131	0.65	0.2513	1.352
9	0.429	-0.374	-0.070	-0.366	-0.087	1.13	0.6489	1.593
10	-0.027	-0.157	-0.028	-0.413	0.061	1.41	0.4193	2.099
11	-0.205	-0.057	-0.208	-0.519	0.450	1.25	0.5824	2.009
Med.	-0.020	-0.229	-0.080	-0.436	0.188	0.78	0.7577	1.646
Aver.	-0.024	-0.238	-0.071	-0.340	0.202	0.64	0.7477	1.416

EXP. 14, REGRESSION DF = B0+B1*EDW+B2*DV(-1)+B3*DW(-1)+R*U(-1)+E
PERIODS 21-END

SUBJ	B0	B1	B2	B3	R	RMSE	RSQU	DW
1	-0.333	0.081	0.050	0.106	-0.822	0.95	0.5989	1.335
2	0.199	-0.009	0.274	0.159	-0.480	1.50	0.2897	1.062
3	0.181	0.065	-0.066	0.094	-0.110	1.06	0.0911	1.628
4	-0.396	0.067	0.488	0.107	-0.586	1.07	0.6220	1.326
5	-0.384	0.055	-0.020	0.077	-0.624	1.48	0.2594	0.921
6	-1.471	0.181	0.439	0.069	-0.860	1.49	0.5208	0.658
7	-0.143	0.086	0.042	-0.019	-0.096	0.63	0.1040	1.720
Med.	-0.246	0.054	0.135	0.027	-0.467	0.66	0.5378	1.710
Aver.	-0.331	0.084	0.171	0.077	-0.504	0.56	0.6868	0.990

8. References

[1] AIGINGER , Karl (1981), "Empirical Evidence on the Rational Expectations Hypothesis Using Reported Expectations", in: Empirica Vol. 1, pp. 25-72.

[2] BECKER, Otwin (1967), Experimentelle Untersuchung der Erwartungsbildung für eine Zeitreihe, in: H. Sauermann (ed.), Beiträge zur experimentellen Wirtschaftsforschung, Tübingen 1967, pp. 226-254.

[3] BECKER, Otwin (1991), Laboratory Researches on Expectation Formation, unpublished manuscript.

[4] BERGMANN, Barbara R. (1988), "An Experiment on the Formation of Expectations", in: Journal of Economic Behavior and Organization vol. 9 (North-Holland), pp. 137-151.

[5] BOLLE, Friedel (1987), "Learning to Make Good Prdictions in Time Series", in:
Tietz, R. et al. (eds.), Bounded Rational Behavior in Experimental Games and Markets, Springer, Heidelberg 1987.

[6] BOLLE, Friedel (1988), "Testing for Rational Expectations in Experimental Predictions", in: MAITAL, Shlomo, Applied Behavioural Economics, Vol. 1, Brighton 1988, pp. 319-334.

[7] BRYAN, Michael F. and William T. GAVIN (1986), "Models of Inflation Expectations Formation: A Comparison of Household and Economist Forecasts", in: Journal of Money, Credit, and Banking, vol. 18 No. 4 (November 1986), pp. 539-544.

[8] BÜNING, Herbert und Götz TRENKLER (1978), Nichtparametrische statistische Methoden, Berlin.

[9] CAGAN, Philip (1956), "The Monetary Dynamics of Hyperinflation", in: Studies in the Quantity Theory of Money, edited by Milton Friedman, pp. 25-117, Chicago (University of Chicago Press).

[10] CARLSON, John A. (1967), "The Stability of an Experimental Market with a Supply-Response Lag", in: The Southern Economic Journal vol. 33, pp. 305-321.

[11] CASKEY, John (1985), "Modeling the Formation of Price Expectations A Bayesian Approach", in: The American Economic Review 75 (Sept. 1985), pp. 768-776.

[12] CHOW, G.C. (1960), "Tests of Equality Between Sets of Coefficients in Two Linear Regressions", in: Econometrica 28 (July 1960), pp. 591-605.

[13] DANIELS, Brian P. and Charles R. PLOTT (1988), "Inflation and Expectations in Experimental Markets", in: R. Tietz, W. Albers, R. Selten (eds.), Bounded Rational Behavior in Experimental Games and Markets, Springer-Verlag, Berlin/ Heidelberg 1988.

[14] FERBER, Robert (1953), "The Railroad Shippers' Forecasts", Urbana (Illinois), Bureau of Economic and Business Research, University of Illinois.

[15] GARNER, Alan C. (1982), "Experimental Evidence on the Rationality of Intuitive Forecasters", in: SMITH, Vernon L., Research in Experimental Economics, vol. 2, Greenwich and London, pp. 113-128.

[16] GRAMLICH, Edward M. (1983), "Models of Inflation Expectations Formation", in: Journal of Money, Credit, and Banking vol. 15 No. 2 (May 1983), pp. 154-173.

[17] KOTTMANN, Thomas (1990), Learning Procedures and Rational Expectations in Linear Models with Forecast Feedback, Diss. Bonn.

[18] LEONARD, Jonathan S. (1982), "Wage Expectations in the Labor Market: Survey Evidence on Rationality", in: The Review of Economics and Statistics 64 (1982), pp. 157-160.

[19] LOVELL, Michael C. (1986), "Tests of the Rational Expectations Hypothesis", in: The American Economic Review 76 (March 1986) pp. 110-124.

[20] MASON, Timothy (1988), Expectation Formation in a Controlled Laboratory Environment, Blomington, Indiana.

[21] METZLER, L.A. (1941), "The Nature and Stability of Inventory Cycles", Review of Economic and Statistics, Vol. 23, pp. 113-129.

[22] MILLS, Edwin S. (1957), "The Theory of Inventory Decisions", Econometrica 25, pp. 222-238.

[23] MUTH, John F. (1961), "Rational Expectations and the Theory of Price Movements", Econometrica, Vol. 29, No.3 (July 1961).

[24] NERLOVE, M. (1958), "Adaptive Expectations and Cobweb Phenomena", Quarterly Journal of Economics, vol. 72 (1958), pp. 227-240.

[25] PESANDO, James E. (1976), "Rational Expectations and Distributed Lag Expectations Proxies", in: Journal of the American Statistical Association March 1976, Volume 71, pp. 37-42.

[26] SCHMALENSEE, Richard (1976), "An Experimental Study of Expectation Formation", in: Econometrica vol. 44, pp. 17-41.

[27] SELTEN, Reinhard (1987), "Equity and Coalition Bargaining in Experimental Three-Person Games", in:
A.E. Ross (ed.), Laboratory Experimentation in Economics, Cambridge University Press.

[28] VISCO, Ignazio (1984), Price Expectations in Rising Inflation, Amsterdam: North-Holland 1984.

[29] WILLIAMS, Arlington W. (1987), "The Formation of Price Forecasts in Experimental Markets", in: Journal of Money, Credit, and Banking vol. 19, pp. 1-18.

Springer-Verlag and the Environment

We at Springer-Verlag firmly believe that an international science publisher has a special obligation to the environment, and our corporate policies consistently reflect this conviction.

We also expect our business partners – paper mills, printers, packaging manufacturers, etc. – to commit themselves to using environmentally friendly materials and production processes.

The paper in this book is made from low- or no-chlorine pulp and is acid free, in conformance with international standards for paper permanency.

Lecture Notes in Economics and Mathematical Systems

For information about Vols. 1–223 please contact your bookseller or Springer-Verlag

Vol. 224: M. Kiy, Ein disaggregiertes Prognosesystem fur die Bundesrepublik Deutschland. XVIII, 276 Seiten. 1984.

Vol. 225: T.R. von Ungern-Sternberg, Zur Analyse von Märkten mit unvollständiger Nachfragerinformaton. IX, 125 Seiten. 1984.

Vol. 226: Selected Topics in Operations Research and Mathematical Economics. Proceedings, 1963. Edited by G. Hammer and D. Pallaschke IX, 478 pages. 1984.

Vol. 227: Risk and Capital. Proceedings, 1983. Edited by G. Bamberg and K. Spremann VII, 306 pages. 1984.

Vol. 228: Nonlinear Models of Fluctuating Growth. Proceedings, 1983. Edited by R.M. Goodwin, M. Krüger and A. Vercelli. XVII, 277 pages. 1984.

Vol. 229: Interactive Decision Analysis. Proceedings, 1983. Edited by M. Grauer and A.P. Wierzbicki. VIII, 269 pages. 1984.

Vol. 230: Macro-Economic Planning with Conflicting Goals. Proceedings, 1982. Edited by M. Despontin, P. Nijkamp and J. Spronk. VI, 297 pages. 1984.

Vol. 231: G.F. Newell, The M/M/8 Service System with Ranked Servers in Heavy Traffic. XI, 126 pages. 1984.

Vol. 232: L. Bauwens, Bayesian Full Information Analysis of Simultaneous Equation Models Using Integration by Monte Carlo. VI, 114 pages. 1984.

Vol. 233: G. Wagenhals, The World Copper Market. XI, 190 pages. 1984.

Vol. 234: B.C. Eaves, A Course in Triangulations for Solving Equations with Deformations. III, 302 pages. 1984.

Vol. 235: Stochastic Models in Reliability Theory Proceedings, 1984. Edited by S. Osaki and Y. Hatoyama. VII, 212 pages. 1984.

Vol. 236: G. Gandolfo, P.C. Padoan, A Disequilibrium Model of Real and Financial Accumulation in an Open Economy. VI, 172 pages. 1984.

Vol. 237: Misspecification Analysis. Proceedings, 1983. Edited by T.K. Dijkstra. V, 129 pages. 1984.

Vol. 238: W. Domschke, A. Drexl, Location and Layout Planning. IV, 134 pages. 1985.

Vol. 239: Microeconomic Models of Housing Markets. Edited by K. Stahl. VII, 197 pages. 1985.

Vol. 240: Contributions to Operations Research. Proceedings, 1984. Edited by K. Neumann and D. Pallaschke. V, 190 pages. 1985.

Vol. 241: U. Wittmann, Das Konzept rationaler Preiserwartungen. XI, 310 Seiten. 1985.

Vol. 242: Decision Making with Multiple Objectives. Proceedings, 1984. Edited by Y.Y. Haimes and V. Chankong. XI, 571 pages. 1985.

Vol. 243: Integer Programming and Related Areas. A Classified Bibliography 1981–1984. Edited by R. von Randow. XX, 386 pages. 1985.

Vol. 244: Advances in Equilibrium Theory. Proceedings, 1984. Edited by C.D. Aliprantis, O. Burkinshaw and N.J. Rothman. II, 235 pages. 1985.

Vol. 245: J.E.M. Wilhelm, Arbitrage Theory. VII, 114 pages. 1985.

Vol. 246: P.W. Otter, Dynamic Feature Space Modelling, Filtering and Self-Tuning Control of Stochastic Systems. XIV, 177 pages.1985.

Vol. 247: Optimization and Discrete Choice in Urban Systems. Proceedings, 1983. Edited by B.G. Hutchinson, P. Nijkamp and M. Batty VI, 371 pages. 1985.

Vol. 248: Pural Rationality and Interactive Decision Processes. Proceedings, 1984. Edited by M. Grauer, M. Thompson and A.P. Wierzbicki. VI, 354 pages. 1985.

Vol. 249: Spatial Price Equilibrium: Advances in Theory, Computation and Application. Proceedings, 1984. Edited by P.T. Harker. VII, 277 pages. 1985.

Vol. 250: M. Roubens, Ph. Vincke, Preference Modelling. VIII, 94 pages. 1985.

Vol. 251: Input-Output Modeling. Proceedings, 1984. Edited by A. Smyshlyaev. VI, 261 pages. 1985.

Vol. 252: A. Birolini, On the Use of Stochastic Processes in Modeling Reliability Problems. VI, 105 pages. 1985.

Vol. 253: C. Withagen, Economic Theory and International Trade in Natural Exhaustible Resources. VI, 172 pages. 1985.

Vol. 254: S. Müller, Arbitrage Pricing of Contingent Claims. VIII, 151 pages. 1985.

Vol. 255: Nondifferentiable Optimization: Motivations and Applications. Proceedings, 1984. Edited by V.F. Demyanov and D. Pallaschke. VI, 350 pages. 1985.

Vol. 256: Convexity and Duality in Optimization. Proceedings, 1984. Edited by J. Ponstein. V, 142 pages. 1985.

Vol. 257: Dynamics of Macrosystems. Proceedings, 1984. Edited by J.-P. Aubin, D. Saari and K. Sigmund. VI, 280 pages. 1985.

Vol. 258: H. Funke, Eine allgemeine Theorie der Polypol- und Oligopolpreisbildung. III, 237 pages. 1985.

Vol. 259: Infinite Programming. Proceedings, 1984. Edited by E.J. Anderson and A.B. Philpott. XIV, 244 pages. 1985.

Vol. 260: H.-J. Kruse, Degeneracy Graphs and the Neighbourhood Problem. VIII, 128 pages. 1986.

Vol. 261: Th.R. Gulledge, Jr., N.K. Womer, The Economics of Made-to-Order Production. VI, 134 pages. 1986.

Vol. 262: H.U. Buhl, A Neo-Classical Theory of Distribution and Wealth. V, 146 pages. 1986.

Vol. 263: M. Schäfer, Resource Extraction and Market Struucture. XI, 154 pages. 1986.

Vol. 264: Models of Economic Dynamics. Proceedings, 1983. Edited by H.F. Sonnenschein. VII, 212 pages. 1986.

Vol. 265: Dynamic Games and Applications in Economics. Edited by T. Basar. IX, 288 pages. 1986.

Vol. 266: Multi-Stage Production Planning and Inventory Control. Edited by S. Axsäter, Ch. Schneeweiss and E. Silver. V, 264 pages.1986.

Vol. 267: R. Bemelmans, The Capacity Aspect of Inventories. IX, 165 pages. 1986.

Vol. 268: V. Firchau, Information Evaluation in Capital Markets. VII, 103 pages. 1986.

Vol. 269: A. Borglin, H. Keiding, Optimality in Infinite Horizon Economies. VI, 180 pages. 1986.

Vol. 270: Technological Change, Employment and Spatial Dynamics. Proceedings, 1985. Edited by P. Nijkamp. VII, 466 pages. 1986.

Vol. 271: C. Hildreth, The Cowles Commission in Chicago, 1939–1955. V, 176 pages. 1986.

Vol. 272: G. Clemenz, Credit Markets with Asymmetric Information. VIII,212 pages. 1986.

Vol. 273: Large-Scale Modelling and Interactive Decision Analysis. Proceedings, 1985. Edited by G. Fandel, M. Grauer, A. Kurzhanski and A.P. Wierzbicki. VII, 363 pages. 1986.

Vol. 274: W.K. Klein Haneveld, Duality in Stochastic Linear and Dynamic Programming. VII, 295 pages. 1986.

Vol. 275: Competition, Instability, and Nonlinear Cycles. Proceedings, 1985. Edited by W. Semmler. XII, 340 pages. 1986.

Vol. 276: M.R. Baye, D.A. Black, Consumer Behavior, Cost of Living Measures, and the Income Tax. VII, 119 pages. 1986.

Vol. 277: Studies in Austrian Capital Theory, Investment and Time. Edited by M. Faber. VI, 317 pages. 1986.

Vol. 278: W.E. Diewert, The Measurement of the Economic Benefits of Infrastructure Services. V, 202 pages. 1986.

Vol. 279: H.-J. Büttler, G. Frei and B. Schips, Estimation of Disequilibrium Modes. VI, 114 pages. 1986.

Vol. 280: H.T. Lau, Combinatorial Heuristic Algorithms with FORTRAN. VII, 126 pages. 1986.

Vol. 281: Ch.-L. Hwang, M.-J. Lin, Group Decision Making under Multiple Criteria. XI, 400 pages. 1987.

Vol. 282: K. Schittkowski, More Test Examples for Nonlinear Programming Codes. V, 261 pages. 1987.

Vol. 283: G. Gabisch, H.-W. Lorenz, Business Cycle Theory. VII, 229 pages. 1987.

Vol. 284: H. Lütkepohl, Forecasting Aggregated Vector ARMA Processes. X, 323 pages. 1987.

Vol. 285: Toward Interactive and Intelligent Decision Support Systems. Volume 1. Proceedings, 1986. Edited by Y. Sawaragi, K. Inoue and H. Nakayama. XII, 445 pages. 1987.

Vol. 286: Toward Interactive and Intelligent Decision Support Systems. Volume 2. Proceedings, 1986. Edited by Y. Sawaragi, K. Inoue and H. Nakayama. XII, 450 pages. 1987.

Vol. 287: Dynamical Systems. Proceedings, 1985. Edited by A.B. Kurzhanski and K. Sigmund. VI, 215 pages. 1987.

Vol. 288: G.D. Rudebusch, The Estimation of Macroeconomic Disequilibrium Models with Regime Classification Information. VII,128 pages. 1987.

Vol. 289: B.R. Meijboom, Planning in Decentralized Firms. X, 168 pages. 1987.

Vol. 290: D.A. Carlson, A. Haurie, Infinite Horizon Optimal Control. XI, 254 pages. 1987.

Vol. 291: N. Takahashi, Design of Adaptive Organizations. VI, 140 pages. 1987.

Vol. 292: I. Tchijov, L. Tomaszewicz (Eds.), Input-Output Modeling. Proceedings, 1985. VI, 195 pages. 1987.

Vol. 293: D. Batten, J. Casti, B. Johansson (Eds.), Economic Evolution and Structural Adjustment. Proceedings, 1985. VI, 382 pages.

Vol. 294: J. Jahn, W. Knabs (Eds.), Recent Advances and Historical Development of Vector Optimization. VII, 405 pages. 1987.

Vol. 295. H. Meister, The Purification Problem for Constrained Games with Incomplete Information. X, 127 pages. 1987.

Vol. 296: A. Börsch-Supan, Econometric Analysis of Discrete Choice. VIII, 211 pages. 1987.

Vol. 297: V. Fedorov, H. Läuter (Eds.), Model-Oriented Data Analysis. Proceedings, 1987. VI, 239 pages. 1988.

Vol. 298: S.H. Chew, Q. Zheng, Integral Global Optimization. VII, 179 pages. 1988.

Vol. 299: K. Marti, Descent Directions and Efficient Solutions in Discretely Distributed Stochastic Programs. XIV, 178 pages. 1988.

Vol. 300: U. Derigs, Programming in Networks and Graphs. XI, 315 pages. 1988.

Vol. 301: J. Kacprzyk, M. Roubens (Eds.), Non-Conventional Preference Relations in Decision Making. VII, 155 pages. 1988.

Vol. 302: H.A. Eiselt, G. Pederzoli (Eds.), Advances in Optimization and Control. Proceedings, 1986. VIII, 372 pages. 1988.

Vol. 303: F.X. Diebold, Empirical Modeling of Exchange Rate Dynamics. VII, 143 pages. 1988.

Vol. 304: A. Kurzhanski, K. Neumann, D. Pallaschke (Eds.), Optimization, Parallel Processing and Applications. Proceedings, 1987. VI, 292 pages. 1988.

Vol. 305: G.-J.C.Th. van Schijndel, Dynamic Firm and Investor Behaviour under Progressive Personal Taxation. X, 215 pages.1988.

Vol. 306: Ch. Klein, A Static Microeconomic Model of Pure Competition. VIII, 139 pages. 1988.

Vol. 307: T.K. Dijkstra (Ed.), On Model Uncertainty and its Statistical Implications. VII, 138 pages. 1988.

Vol. 308: J.R. Daduna, A. Wren (Eds.), Computer-Aided Transit Scheduling. VIII, 339 pages. 1988.

Vol. 309: G. Ricci, K. Velupillai (Eds.), Growth Cycles and Multisectoral Economics: the Goodwin Tradition. III, 126 pages. 1988.

Vol. 310: J. Kacprzyk, M. Fedrizzi (Eds.), Combining Fuzzy Imprecision with Probabilistic Uncertainty in Decision Making. IX, 399 pages. 1988.

Vol. 311: R. Färe, Fundamentals of Production Theory. IX, 163 pages. 1988.

Vol. 312: J. Krishnakumar, Estimation of Simultaneous Equation Models with Error Components Structure. X, 357 pages. 1988.

Vol. 313: W. Jammernegg, Sequential Binary Investment Decisions. VI, 156 pages. 1988.

Vol. 314: R. Tietz, W. Albers, R. Selten (Eds.), Bounded Rational Behavior in Experimental Games and Markets. VI, 368 pages. 1988.

Vol. 315: I. Orishimo, G.J.D. Hewings, P. Nijkamp (Eds), Information Technology: Social and Spatial Perspectives. Proceedings 1986. VI, 268 pages. 1988.

Vol. 316: R.L. Basmann, D.J. Slottje, K. Hayes, J.D. Johnson, D.J. Molina, The Generalized Fechner-Thurstone Direct Utility Function and Some of its Uses. VIII, 159 pages. 1988.

Vol. 317: L. Bianco, A. La Bella (Eds.), Freight Transport Planning and Logistics. Proceedings, 1987. X, 568 pages. 1988.

Vol. 318: T. Doup, Simplicial Algorithms on the Simplotope. VIII, 262 pages. 1988.

Vol. 319: D.T. Luc, Theory of Vector Optimization. VIII, 173 pages. 1989.

Vol. 320: D. van der Wijst, Financial Structure in Small Business. VII, 181 pages. 1989.

Vol. 321: M. Di Matteo, R.M. Goodwin, A. Vercelli (Eds.), Technological and Social Factors in Long Term Fluctuations. Proceedings. IX, 442 pages. 1989.

Vol. 322: T. Kollintzas (Ed.), The Rational Expectations Equilibrium Inventory Model. XI, 269 pages. 1989.

Vol. 323: M.B.M. de Koster, Capacity Oriented Analysis and Design of Production Systems. XII, 245 pages. 1989.

Vol. 324: I.M. Bomze, B.M. Pötscher, Game Theoretical Foundations of Evolutionary Stability. VI, 145 pages. 1989.

Vol. 325: P. Ferri, E. Greenberg, The Labor Market and Business Cycle Theories. X, 183 pages. 1989.

Vol. 326: Ch. Sauer, Alternative Theories of Output, Unemployment, and Inflation in Germany: 1960–1985. XIII, 206 pages. 1989.

Vol. 327: M. Tawada, Production Structure and International Trade. V, 132 pages. 1989.

Vol. 328: W. Güth, B. Kalkofen, Unique Solutions for Strategic Games. VII, 200 pages. 1989.

Vol. 329: G. Tillmann, Equity, Incentives, and Taxation. VI, 132 pages. 1989.

Vol. 330: P.M. Kort, Optimal Dynamic Investment Policies of a Value Maximizing Firm. VII, 185 pages. 1989.

Vol. 331: A. Lewandowski, A.P. Wierzbicki (Eds.), Aspiration Based Decision Support Systems. X, 400 pages. 1989.

Vol. 332: T.R. Gulledge, Jr., L.A. Litteral (Eds.), Cost Analysis Applications of Economics and Operations Research. Proceedings. VII, 422 pages. 1989.

Vol. 333: N. Dellaert, Production to Order. VII, 158 pages. 1989.

Vol. 334: H.-W. Lorenz, Nonlinear Dynamical Economics and Chaotic Motion. XI, 248 pages. 1989.

Vol. 335: A.G. Lockett, G. Islei (Eds.), Improving Decision Making in Organisations. Proceedings. IX, 606 pages. 1989.

Vol. 336: T. Puu, Nonlinear Economic Dynamics. VII, 119 pages. 1989.

Vol. 337: A. Lewandowski, I. Stanchev (Eds.), Methodology and Software for Interactive Decision Support. VIII, 309 pages. 1989.

Vol. 338: J.K. Ho, R.P. Sundarraj, DECOMP: an Implementation of Dantzig-Wolfe Decomposition for Linear Programming. VI, 206 pages.

Vol. 339: J. Terceiro Lomba, Estimation of Dynamic Econometric Models with Errors in Variables. VIII, 116 pages. 1990.

Vol. 340: T. Vasko, R. Ayres, L. Fontvieille (Eds.), Life Cycles and Long Waves. XIV, 293 pages. 1990.

Vol. 341: G.R. Uhlich, Descriptive Theories of Bargaining. IX, 165 pages. 1990.

Vol. 342: K. Okuguchi, F. Szidarovszky, The Theory of Oligopoly with Multi-Product Firms. V, 167 pages. 1990.

Vol. 343: C. Chiarella, The Elements of a Nonlinear Theory of Economic Dynamics. IX, 149 pages. 1990.

Vol. 344: K. Neumann, Stochastic Project Networks. XI, 237 pages. 1990.

Vol. 345: A. Cambini, E. Castagnoli, L. Martein, P Mazzoleni, S. Schaible (Eds.), Generalized Convexity and Fractional Programming with Economic Applications. Proceedings, 1988. VII, 361 pages. 1990.

Vol. 346: R. von Randow (Ed.), Integer Programming and Related Areas. A Classified Bibliography 1984–1987. XIII, 514 pages. 1990.

Vol. 347: D. Ríos Insua, Sensitivity Analysis in Multi-objective Decision Making. XI, 193 pages. 1990.

Vol. 348: H. Störmer, Binary Functions and their Applications. VIII, 151 pages. 1990.

Vol. 349: G.A. Pfann, Dynamic Modelling of Stochastic Demand for Manufacturing Employment. VI, 158 pages. 1990.

Vol. 350: W.-B. Zhang, Economic Dynamics. X, 232 pages. 1990.

Vol. 351: A. Lewandowski, V. Volkovich (Eds.), Multiobjective Problems of Mathematical Programming. Proceedings, 1988. VII, 315 pages. 1991.

Vol. 352: O. van Hilten, Optimal Firm Behaviour in the Context of Technological Progress and a Business Cycle. XII, 229 pages. 1991.

Vol. 353: G. Ricci (Ed.), Decision Processes in Economics. Proceedings, 1989. III, 209 pages 1991.

Vol. 354: M. Ivaldi, A Structural Analysis of Expectation Formation. XII, 230 pages. 1991.

Vol. 355: M. Salomon. Deterministic Lotsizing Models for Production Planning. VII, 158 pages. 1991.

Vol. 356: P. Korhonen, A. Lewandowski, J . Wallenius (Eds.), Multiple Criteria Decision Support. Proceedings, 1989. XII, 393 pages. 1991.

Vol. 357: P. Zörnig, Degeneracy Graphs and Simplex Cycling. XV, 194 pages. 1991.

Vol. 358: P. Knottnerus, Linear Models with Correlated Disturbances. VIII, 196 pages. 1991.

Vol. 359: E. de Jong, Exchange Rate Determination and Optimal Economic Policy Under Various Exchange Rate Regimes. VII, 270 pages. 1991.

Vol. 360: P. Stalder, Regime Translations, Spillovers and Buffer Stocks. VI, 193 pages . 1991.

Vol. 361: C. F. Daganzo, Logistics Systems Analysis. X, 321 pages. 1991.

Vol. 362: F. Gehrels, Essays In Macroeconomics of an Open Economy. VII, 183 pages. 1991.

Vol. 363: C. Puppe, Distorted Probabilities and Choice under Risk. VIII, 100 pages . 1991

Vol. 364: B. Horvath, Are Policy Variables Exogenous? XII, 162 pages. 1991.

Vol. 365: G. A. Heuer, U. Leopold-Wildburger. Balanced Silverman Games on General Discrete Sets. V, 140 pages. 1991.

Vol. 366: J. Gruber (Ed.), Econometric Decision Models. Proceedings, 1989. VIII, 636 pages. 1991.

Vol. 367: M. Grauer, D. B. Pressmar (Eds.), Parallel Computing and Mathematical Optimization. Proceedings. V, 208 pages. 1991.

Vol. 368: M. Fedrizzi, J. Kacprzyk, M. Roubens (Eds.), Interactive Fuzzy Optimization. VII, 216 pages. 1991.

Vol. 369: R. Koblo, The Visible Hand. VIII, 131 pages.1991.

Vol. 370: M. J. Beckmann, M. N. Gopalan, R. Subramanian (Eds.), Stochastic Processes and their Applications. Proceedings, 1990. XLI, 292 pages. 1991.

Vol. 371: A. Schmutzler, Flexibility and Adjustment to Information in Sequential Decision Problems. VIII, 198 pages. 1991.

Vol. 372: J. Esteban, The Social Viability of Money. X, 202 pages. 1991.

Vol. 373: A. Billot, Economic Theory of Fuzzy Equilibria. XIII, 164 pages. 1992.

Vol. 374: G. Pflug, U. Dieter (Eds.), Simulation and Optimization. Proceedings, 1990. X, 162 pages. 1992.

Vol. 375: S.-J. Chen, Ch.-L. Hwang, Fuzzy Multiple Attribute Decision Making. XII, 536 pages. 1992.

Vol. 376: K.-H. Jöckel, G. Rothe, W. Sendler (Eds.), Bootstrapping and Related Techniques. Proceedings, 1990. VIII, 247 pages. 1992.

Vol. 377: A. Villar, Operator Theorems with Applications to Distributive Problems and Equilibrium Models. XVI, 160 pages. 1992.

Vol. 378: W. Krabs, J. Zowe (Eds.), Modern Methods of Optimization. Proceedings, 1990. VIII, 348 pages. 1992.

Vol. 379: K. Marti (Ed.), Stochastic Optimization. Proceedings, 1990. VII, 182 pages. 1992.

Vol. 380: J. Odelstad, Invariance and Structural Dependence. XII, 245 pages. 1992.

Vol. 381: C. Giannini, Topics in Structural VAR Econometrics. XI, 131 pages. 1992.

Vol. 382: W. Oettli, D. Pallaschke (Eds.), Advances in Optimization. Proceedings, 1991. X, 527 pages. 1992.

Vol. 383: J. Vartiainen, Capital Accumulation in a Corporatist Economy. VII, 177 pages. 1992.

Vol. 384: A. Martina, Lectures on the Economic Theory of Taxation. XII, 313 pages. 1992.

Vol. 385: J. Gardeazabal, M. Regúlez, The Monetary Model of Exchange Rates and Cointegration. X, 194 pages. 1992.

Vol. 386: M. Desrochers, J.-M. Rousseau (Eds.), Computer-Aided Transit Scheduling. Proceedings, 1990. XIII, 432 pages. 1992.

Vol. 387: W. Gaertner, M. Klemisch-Ahlert, Social Choice and Bargaining Perspectives on Distributive Justice. VIII, 131 pages. 1992.

Vol. 388: D. Bartmann, M. J. Beckmann, Inventory Control. XV, 252 pages. 1992.

Vol. 389: B. Dutta, D. Mookherjee, T. Parthasarathy, T. Raghavan, D. Ray, S. Tijs (Eds.), Game Theory and Economic Applications. Proceedings, 1990. ??, ?? pages. 1992.

Vol. 390: G. Sorger, Minimum Impatience Theorem for Recursive Economic Models. X, 162 pages. 1992.

Vol. 391: C. Keser, Experimental Duopoly Markets with Demand Inertia. X, 150 pages. 1992.

Vol. 392: K. Frauendorfer, Stochastic Two-Stage Programming. VIII, 228 pages. 1992.

Vol. 393: B. Lucke, Price Stabilization on World Agricultural Markets. XI, 274 pages. 1992.

Vol. 394: Y.-J. Lai, C.-L. Hwang, Fuzzy Mathematical Programming. XIII, 301 pages. 1992.

Vol. 395: G. Haag, U. Mueller, K. G. Troitzsch (Eds.), Economic Evolution and Demographic Change. XVI, 409 pages. 1992.

Vol. 396: R. V. V. Vidal (Ed.), Applied Simulated Annealing. VIII, 358 pages. 1992.

Vol. 397: J. Wessels, A. P. Wierzbicki (Eds.), User-Oriented Methodology and Techniques of Decision Analysis and Support. Proceedings, 1991. XII, 295 pages. 1993.

Vol. 398: J.-P. Urbain, Exogeneity in Error Correction Models. XI, 189 pages. 1993.

Vol. 399: F. Gori, L. Geronazzo, M. Galeotti (Eds.), Nonlinear Dynamics in Economics and Social Sciences. Proceedings, 1991. VIII, 367 pages. 1993.

Vol. 400: H. Tanizaki, Nonlinear Filters. XII, 203 pages. 1993.

Vol. 401: K. Mosler, M. Scarsini, Stochastic Orders and Applications. V, 379 pages. 1993.

Vol. 402: A. van den Elzen, Adjustment Processes for Exchange Economies and Noncooperative Games. VII, 146 pages. 1993.

Vol. 403: G. Brennscheidt, Predictive Behavior. VI, 227 pages. 1993.

GPSR Compliance

The European Union's (EU) General Product Safety Regulation (GPSR) is a set of rules that requires consumer products to be safe and our obligations to ensure this.

If you have any concerns about our products, you can contact us on ProductSafety@springernature.com

In case Publisher is established outside the EU, the EU authorized representative is:

Springer Nature Customer Service Center GmbH
Europaplatz 3
69115 Heidelberg, Germany

Batch number: 10844675

Printed by Printforce, the Netherlands